THE JEWS IN
SOUTH AFRICA

THE JEWS IN SOUTH AFRICA

AN ILLUSTRATED HISTORY

Richard Mendelsohn and Milton Shain

JONATHAN BALL PUBLISHERS
JOHANNESBURG & CAPE TOWN

HALF TITLE PAGE: *Polliacks Music Store, Hanover Street, Distrct Six, 1903.*

TITLE PAGE: *Organisers of the first South African Zionist Bazaar, Johannesburg, 1906.*

Published in 2008 in hard cover by
JONATHAN BALL PUBLISHERS (PTY) LTD
PO Box 33977
Jeppestown
2043

Reprinted 2008

This second updated edition published in
paperback in 2014 by
Jonathan Ball Publishers
A division of Media24 Limited

ISBN 978 1 86842 648 5

Publisher's note:
There are several photographs in the text that are poor quality due to their age. Their importance outweighed their bad quality.

Design and reproduction of text by
Triple M Design & Advertising, Johannesburg
Maps by Jan Booysen
Printed and bound by Craft Print International
Set in 11/14pt Bembo Std

Twitter: www.twitter.com/JonathanBallPub
Facebook: www.facebook.com/JonathanBallPublishers
Blog: http://jonathanball.bookslive.co.za/

CONTENTS

To our parents,
Enid and Leonard Mendelsohn,
&
Abe and Rita Shain.

ACKNOWLEDGEMENTS

This new history of South African Jewry grew out of our long engagement with research and writing on the subject, encouraged by the supportive and stimulating environment provided by the Isaac and Jessie Kaplan Centre for Jewish Studies at the University of Cape Town since its inception in 1980. The Centre provided financial support as has the University Research Committee of the University of Cape Town.

We are very appreciative of the assistance provided by the staff of the University of Cape Town Libraries, specifically Veronica Belling in Jewish Studies, Sandy Shell and Sue Ogterop in African Studies, and Leslie Hart and Janine Dunlop in the Manuscripts and Archives division.

Adrienne Folb has been an indefatigable picture researcher who has unearthed many fresh and long-unseen images. She was assisted in Johannesburg by Naomi and Reuben Musiker who scoured the rich photographic holdings of the South African Jewish Board of Deputies, while David Saks at the Board was always willing to share information.

We thank the following institutions and individuals for the use of photographs from their collections: South African Jewish Board of Deputies; South African Jewish Museum; Isaac and Jessie Kaplan Centre for Jewish Studies and Research, University of Cape Town; Cape Town Holocaust Centre; Office of the Chief Rabbi, United Orthodox Synagogues of South Africa; Sephardi Hebrew Congregation, Cape Town; Cape Town Progressive Jewish Congregation; United Herzlia Schools; King David Schools; Yeshiva College Schools of Johannesburg; Union of Jewish Women; South African Jewish Report; South African Friends of Beth Hatefutsoth; Jacob Gitlin Library; United Hebrew Institutions of

Bloemfontein; Durban United Hebrew Congregation; Telfed; National Library of South Africa, Cape Town Branch; University of Cape Town Libraries; Library of Parliament; Iziko William Fehr Collection; Cape Archives Repository; Free State Provincial Archives Repository; McGregor Museum, Kimberley; Kimberley Public Library; Africana Library, Kimberley; CP Nel Museum, Oudtshoorn; Museum Africa, Johannesburg; Investec; Sammy Marks Museum; Pick 'n Pay; Primedia; Pretoria News; One Up Communications; Michael and Fay Padowich; Estelle Yach; Georgina Jaffee; Lalou Meltzer; Philip Getz; Jowell family; Sidney Mirvish; Len Miller; Leah Chabas; Karel Schoeman; Ali Bacher; Hannah Reeve Sanders; Toni Jade Efune; Colin, Robert and Kerrin Firer; Ivor Shain and Cynthia Maresky.

We would also like to thank the following for their generous assistance: Janine Blumberg; Linda Bester; Myra Osrin; Richard Freedman; Rose Norwich; Geoff Sifrin; Bertha Sherman; Simon Jocum; Micky Glass; Jocelyn Hellig; John Simon; Howard Phillips; Mike Berger; Gwynne Robins; Michelle Sedras; Elisa Metz; Tracy Klass; Diana Henning; Najwa Hendrickse; Melanie Geustyn; Laddy McKechnie; Sunet Swanepoel; Rayda Becker; Sandra Smit; Hilda Boshoff; Kathy Brookes; Mrs K Duminy; Jacqui Rutka; Jessica Jacobson; Cecilia Jacobs; Charles van Onselen; Patricia Hagen; Barbara Beechman; Lettie Ferreira; Melany Rayners; Penguin Books; Kevin Swain; Gary Block; Odette Mendelsohn. The staff of the Scanshop in Cape Town was always obliging and expeditious, while Image World and Bastion Graphics in Johannesburg all provided expert assistance.

The professionalism of the production team at Jonathan Ball – Jeremy Boraine, Francine Blum and Valda Strauss – is hugely appreciated, as is the enthusiasm and encouragement of Jonathan Ball himself. Kevin Shenton's experienced and creative eye greatly enhanced the visual appeal of the book.

Above all, we are grateful for the very careful, critical and constructive reading by Millie Pimstone and Adam Mendelsohn of the full text. Needless to say, the authors take full responsibility for the final outcome.

Richard Mendelsohn and Milton Shain
CAPE TOWN, 2007

INTRODUCTION

Just over 50 years have passed since the publication of the last major general history of South African Jewry. *The Jews in South Africa. A History*, edited by Gustav Saron and Louis Hotz, focused primarily on the founding years of the Jewish community until the eve of the First World War, with an epilogue covering the subsequent decades.

This new history spans the entire Jewish experience in South Africa over the past two centuries, since Sigfried Fraenkel, a ship's surgeon and the first professing Jew to settle in the sub-continent, stepped ashore in August 1807 in Table Bay. Its view is national; it is neither a view from the summit of Table Mountain nor from the top of a Johannesburg mine dump. The South African Jewish saga is located within the broader South African past, as well as within the wider Jewish experience and its intersection with international events.

This fresh survey – drawing on recent scholarship including unpublished research – avoids a 'Whiggish' view that might have sketched a triumphant and inevitable progression of a community from humble origins to present success. Instead, it depicts the fragility of the early foundations, the oscillating fortunes of the community as it matured amidst turbulent currents, both domestic and international, and its latter-day challenges and responses.

It is not a narrow institutional history of a community. Rather it attempts to encompass a broad swathe of Jewish life, from the *bimah* and the boardroom to the bowling green. It avoids a view of an unproblematic, homogeneous and monolithic community, and instead recognises the evolving divisions and tensions along lines of class, ideology and religiosity. At the same time, it acknowledges the centripetal forces at work and the large measure of cohesion the community achieved historically, one of its most striking features.

While the book is wide in scope, it does not intend to provide an exhaustive, encyclopaedic account of the Jewish experience in South Africa. Where individuals appear, they have been included to illustrate broad processes. Accompanying the main text are 'boxes' which explore topics in greater depth.

The history of South African Jewry is divided into four broad periods, each with its defining character. The first of these is the age of the pioneers, the Anglo-German Jews who established a Jewish community in South Africa in the mid-nineteenth century. The second is the age of the Litvaks, the mainly Lithuanian Jewish immigrants who, in the late nineteenth and early twentieth century, invigorated and consolidated Jewish life in South Africa. The third period covers the coming of age in the mid-twentieth century of a South African Jewry – acculturated but not assimilated – after the closing of the gates to Eastern European immigration. The final period, the late twentieth century to the present, is the age of the Jewish South African, well integrated yet more Jewish than ever.

Most general histories of South Africa have effectively ignored the history of Jews in South Africa, despite their consequential and at times contested presence. Hopefully this book will recover the historical experience of this significant minority, albeit one that has never comprised more than 4.5 per cent of the white population and numbers today about 80 000, a contested figure but certainly less than one quarter per cent of the total population.

THE JEWS IN
SOUTH AFRICA

PIONEERS

BEGINNINGS

NO SOUTH AFRICAN JEW TODAY CAN CLAIM ancestral ties to the 17 Jewish males who gathered for prayer in Cape Town at Helmsley Cottage, the home of Benjamin Norden in Helmsley Place, on a spring evening in September 1841, the start of *Yom Kippur*, the Day of Atonement. This *minyan* (religious quorum) was the first occasion, following several earlier 'ineffectual attempts', on which Jews had successfully come together to worship in South Africa. Eight days later, during the Jewish festival of *Sukkoth* (Tabernacles), they founded *Tikvath Israel* (Hope of Israel), subsequently known as the Cape Town Hebrew Congregation, the first organised Jewish community in sub-Saharan Africa.

These pioneers were not the first Jews in southern Africa, let alone in Africa. Jews had ancient connections with North Africa, stretching back to slavery in Pharaonic Egypt. They were among the early explorers who circumnavigated the Cape of Storms, though they and other non-Protestants were denied the right to settle at the Cape during the rule of the Dutch East India Company (1652-1795). Company recruits had to conform to the Reformed religion and attendance at public worship was mandatory. This contrasted with the position of Jews in the possession of the Dutch West India Company in the New World and in Holland

Table Bay, painted by Thomas Baines, 1847.

3

Jews and the sea route to India

Among the Jews associated with Portuguese exploration of the sea route to India were Abraham ben Samuel Zacuto and Fernão Martins. Zacuto had been a distinguished astronomer and astrologist at the University of Salamanca prior to the expulsion of the Jews from Spain in 1492. His astronomical tables, first published in Hebrew and later translated into Latin and Spanish, were widely used by navigators including Christopher Columbus. Following the expulsion from Spain, Zacuto became Astronomer Royal to King John II of Portugal. Before setting out on his epic voyage of discovery in 1497, Vasco da Gama frequently consulted Zacuto who also selected the scientific instruments Da Gama required, some of these specially designed for the explorer by his Jewish mentor. Unlike Zacuto who remained behind in Portugal, Fernão Martins set sail with Da Gama in the *San Gabriel*. Martins, who was in all likelihood a 'New Christian' and who spoke both Hebrew and Arabic, was valued for his interpreting skills. He was probably the first Jew to land on South African soil when, in mid-November 1497, the Da Gama party went ashore at St Helena Bay on the Cape west coast.

Abraham Zacuto.

itself, where there were the beginnings of a more tolerant order. There Jews were reluctantly welcomed for their mercantile contributions in a burgeoning Atlantic economy. Amsterdam, the major entrepôt of the seventeenth-century Atlantic World, provided a measure of religious tolerance unknown in Counter Reformation Western Europe; but, at the time that Van Riebeeck landed at the Cape, Jews still lacked the confidence to challenge the Dutch East India Company's religious restrictions.

Revolutionary events in Europe at the end of the eighteenth century ended this exclusivism. The French revolutionaries' invasion of the Netherlands led to the dilution of the Reformed Church's pre-eminence. At the Cape, Moravian missionaries and Lutherans were allowed to practise freely their variants of Protestantism. Following the first British occupation in 1795, tolerance was extended to Cape Muslims. This tolerance was broadened further under the rule of the Batavian Republic between 1803 and 1806. Flushed with the excitement of Enlightenment tolerance and deism, Governor JW Jannssens and Commissionary-General JA de Mist extended religious tolerance at the Cape in 1804, over the objections of conservative colonists. This new order was maintained by their administrative heirs, the British, who re-occupied the Cape in 1806.

Only a handful of Jews, mainly of English, Dutch and German origin, availed themselves of this new opportunity. Four years after De Mist's proclamation Sigfried Fraenkel was practising medicine in Cape Town. Reputedly the first professing Jew to settle at the Cape, he had followed closely in the footsteps of Benjamin Solomon, a non-practising English Jew who had found his way to Cape Town via St Helena. The majority

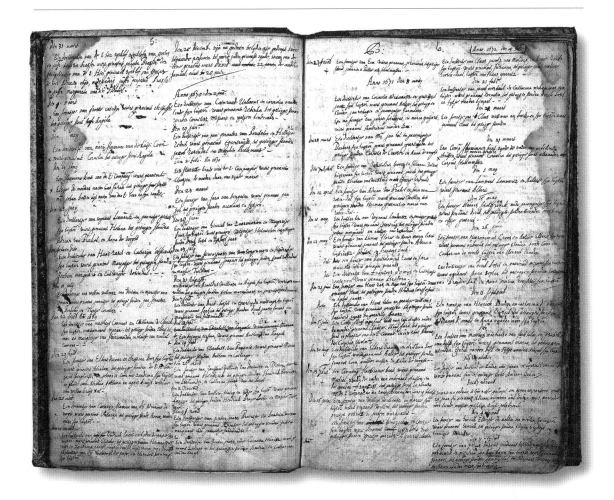

of the early arrivals settled in Cape Town, though some ventured further afield. Benjamin Solomon's cousin, Nathaniel Isaacs, became an intrepid adventurer far beyond the Cape frontier and an associate of the Zulu kings, Shaka and Dingane. A contingent of 18 Jews was among the 1820 settlers who set up home in the remote eastern reaches of the colony. Within a few years most of these Jewish settlers had gravitated towards Grahamstown, the military and trading hub of the Eastern Cape. It was at this remote outpost that Jews took their first collective intiative in South Africa when, in October 1838, five Jews successfully petitioned the Lieutenant-Governor of the Eastern Division of the Cape Colony to grant them a burial site.

One of the most prominent of the Jewish 1820 settlers was

Dutch Reform Church baptismal record of Samuel Jacobson and David Heijlbron: on Christmas Day 1669, 'after confession of faith two adult persons were baptised who were formerly Jews, the one named David being 22 years old and the other Samuel 20 years old.'

5

The Church Ordinance of 1804, granting legal protection to 'all religious associations which for the furtherance of virtue and good conduct respect a Supreme Being.'

ABOVE RIGHT AND BELOW
The 1838 petition for a burial site in Grahamstown, probably 'the oldest Jewish document in South Africa'.

Chicken soup and the Zulus

Nathaniel Isaacs, a young Jewish adventurer and trader, lived among the Zulus in the late 1820s, and recorded his experiences in *Travels and Adventures in Eastern Africa*, first published in London in 1836. The book became a seminal text for the reign of Shaka, the founder of the Zulu kingdom. This flawed and self-serving account, driven by Isaacs's desire to paint a negative portrait of his hosts to encourage colonial expansion, is nevertheless a valuable contemporary source:

Of the Zulus' view of the white visitors, Isaacs wrote:
> … whenever the natives spoke of us it was always with reproach. They called us 'Silguaners', or beasts of the sea, and whenever they pronounced this term, it was accompanied with a gesture of opprobrium that could not be mistaken for kindness …

Of his host:
> We went towards the palace to pay our respects, when Chaka, with a jocose manner, and an artificial smile, said, 'Yabona Tombooser' and told me to point out the part where I was wounded; I complied, when he observed, 'that is a cowardly sign; you must have had your back turned to your enemy; and if you were my man, instead of King George's, I should have you killed.' I was silent, and thanked Heaven for having made me a subject of the King of England, instead of the king of the Zoolas.

On his own occasional role as 'doctor':
> A tall figure, with a head and neck longer than his body, and greatly disfigured by disease, sought relief from the 'Maloonga', or white man … All the old female natives evinced considerable concern at the patient not being able to eat, and, by their supplicating gestures, made strong entreaties for me to administer some relief, with which I complied.
>
> I directed them to make some chicken soup, and give him while I returned home to examine my medicine chest … I sent a dose of salts, with directions to give it to the man … My patient appeared to be recovering, and he himself thought so, when I received the flattering designation of 'Maloonga' doctor. But alas! after all my rubbing, after all my embrocations, liniments, and inward applications – my patient died! and like his forefathers, his corpse was dragged to the side of the distant jungles, where it was left as a bonne bouche for the hyenas.

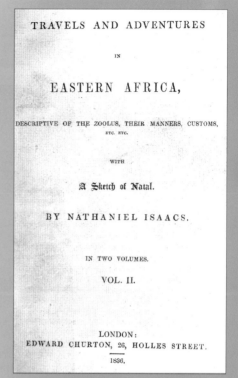

Shaka.

Emissary to King Dingane

In December 1835 Benjamin Norden paid a semi-official visit to the Zulu kingdom on behalf of Sir Benjamin D'Urban, the Governor of the Colony of the Cape of Good Hope. On his return in February 1836 he was interviewed by the *Grahams Town Journal* about his encounter with the Zulu king Dingane:

Mr. Norden who has just returned from Port Natal, has given us some interesting particulars of his voyage, and of his journey from that Port to the residence of the chief Dingaan ... Mr. N. ... was charged with a despatch from His Excellency the Governor. After travelling about 80 or 100 miles, on arriving at the Umtogale River ... he was met by a messenger, and a party of Zoolas, who had been sent by the chief, with directions to await his arrival into his domains. The messenger, in the name of his master, presented our traveller with two cows and some Indian corn for his subsistence on the route; demanding at the same time samples of the goods, which were intended, either as presents to, or for barter with, the Zoola chief, and with which he was charged to return to him with all speed. Having complied with this demand, he resumed his journey, and was agreeably surprised to find at the end of every stage, a party of natives awaiting his arrival with cattle for slaughter. After proceeding for some distance, on arriving at the Congela, he found the messenger ... a second time on his way to meet him, accompanied by men bearing two teeth of ivory, and which he informed our traveller were a letter to him from the chief his master. He further stated to him that his Majesty was impatient at the tardy progress of the wagon, and had commanded that it should be unladen, and the goods conveyed by 200

men, who were to be immediately ordered for the service. The etiquette observed in the Zoola territory not admitting of demur or dispute to the wishes of the chief, the wagon was speedily disencumbered of its load, and Mr. N. soon found himself at the residence of the dreaded and mighty Zoola chief. Here he was detained three days. At first his Majesty appeared to be by no means satisfied, either with the quantity or quality of the articles presented to him, and which consisted of beads, brass-wire, bales of duffle, and, among other things, of an elegant chair, which had been constructed in Grahams Town, especially to suit his Majesty's taste. At length, however, after displaying considerable adroitness in his bargaining, he expressed himself satisfied; and in the course of his negotiations presented Mr. N. with about 5,000 lbs. of ivory, besides eleven oxen for his subsistence on his journey home.

Mr. Norden states that Dingaan seemed much pleased with the contents of the communication to him from the governor, and expressed his willingness to allow traders to enter his territory provided their arrival was reported to him, in order, as he expressed himself, that should any disorders arise he might know who had been the cause of them ...

During Mr. N's stay, the chief ordered for his amusement a dance, and which was performed in the afternoon by a great number of females whose persons were absolutely burthened with a profusion of beads and other trinkets. On quitting the royal residence, a party of three hundred men were ordered to convey the ivory presented by the chief to the limits of his dominions, with positive instructions not to pass beyond the boundary.

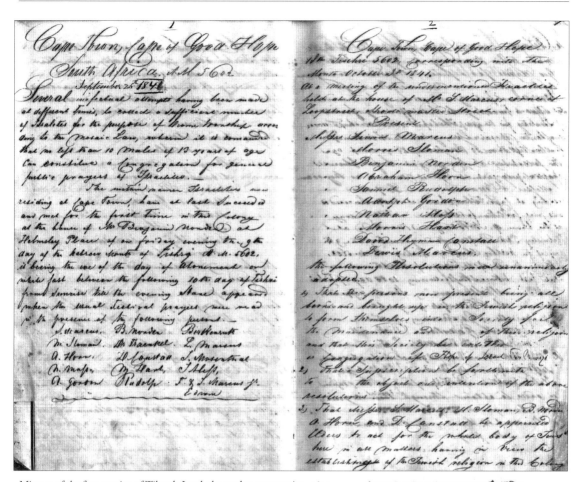

Minutes of the first meeting of Tikvath Israel, the mother congregation, 1841.

the 'cockney' Benjamin Norden who had prospered as a merchant and had served on the Grahamstown municipal board before departing for Cape Town in 1840, a year before he hosted the first *minyan*. The founding fathers of *Tikvath Israel* were in the main middle-aged and had been in the colony for some years. A number were successful merchants. Clearly these were men seeking to recover a sense of community that they had left behind many years earlier. They were part of a broader Anglo-German modernising middle class which subscribed to enlightened norms. In this milieu religion was a domestic concern, and Jews were accorded respect and felt at home.

*Saul Solomon, leading member of the
Cape legislature for 30 years.*

In 1848, seven years after the congregation's formation, Benjamin
Norden welcomed – on behalf of the Jewish community – the triumphant Cape governor, Sir Harry Smith, on his return from a
battle in the interior. The exchange of pleasantries on that occasion
reflected both the Jewish community's good standing and the religiously tolerant and liberal ethos of mid-Victorian Cape society.
All religious denominations, declared the governor, were 'equally
valid' and Jewish interests were 'blended with the people at large,
for whether a man is a Jew or a Christian, he is equally protected by
the law, and I believe equally acceptable in the eyes of God'. Smith's
sentiments succinctly reflected classical nineteenth-century British
liberalism, rooted as it was in respect for the Judaic tradition.

Despite (or perhaps because of) this tolerance, some chose a
path away from Judaism. As elsewhere in the Anglo-Jewish world
assimilationist impulses were powerful. In many cases Jewish iden-

tity was tenuous, especially at a far remove from the centres of Jewish life. The Solomon family of St Helena and later of Cape Town captures this fragility. In such remote outposts it was easy to assimilate informally into the dominant Christian culture without entirely disowning one's roots. Thus Saul Solomon (1817-1892), a pioneering liberal voice in the Cape legislature and an early owner of the *Cape Argus*, was born a Jew according to Jewish law, was belatedly circumcised at the age of five in England, became as an adult a member of the Congregational Church, but retained life-long sentimental ties with his Jewish upbringing. He regularly attended Jewish *Pesach seders* (ritual Passover meals) at one of his many Jewish friends' homes and was a donor to Jewish causes.

The Solomon experience illustrates how fluid and porous boundaries were in the mid-nineteenth century port city of Cape Town. While some Jews clung tenaciously to their religious affiliations, other simply shed these like unwanted old clothes. And yet assimilated Jews who had jettisoned their religion often continued to support Jewish communal efforts, and the community in turn welcomed this support.

The 170 Jews in Cape Town in 1855 as well as the increasing number of Jewish traders in the hinterland thrived in a society that separated Church and state. An act of 1860 that empowered the government to appoint Jews as marriage officers and another act, eight years later, that proscribed any differentiation or penalties on account of religious belief were further indications of tolerance and goodwill. So was the appointment in 1861 of Simeon Jacobs as attorney-general for British Kaffraria, a crown colony alongside the Cape's eastern frontier.

Despite these favourable circumstances the

The first dedicated synagogue, situated in the public gardens, Cape Town.

infant community was at risk. Its first minister, the Reverend Isaac Pulver, had left Cape Town in 1851, after only two years of service, leaving behind a deeply divided and struggling congregation. *Tikvath Israel* remained without a minister till the end of a very troubled decade when the Reverend Joel Rabinowitz arrived in Cape Town from Birmingham. The Polish-born Rabinowitz's arrival coincided with a revival in economic life and a consequent resurgence of communal life, manifest in the building of the first dedicated synagogue on a prime site in Cape Town's public gardens in 1863.

Surviving the first decade

The Cape Town Jewish community barely survived its first decade despite promising beginnings. Among these were the purchase of a burial ground in Albert Road, on the outskirts of the city, in 1842; the celebration of the first Jewish wedding in 1844 between Michael Benjamin of Grahamstown and Amelia Marcus of Cape Town; the first circumcision in 1847, with RJ Joseph circumcising his infant son; the acquisition in 1848 from England of the first *Sefer Torah* (*Torah* scroll); the appointment of the first minister in 1849, the Reverend Isaac Pulver, formerly of Cheltenham; and the consecration of the first synagogue in suitably converted premises close to the public gardens in 1849. Here elaborately crafted rules enforced decorum in a Victorian Anglo-Jewish key: 'A solemn and reverential silence should pervade the Synagogue. A noisy entering, a congregating of individuals, conversation on any subject whatever, [and] the quitting of seats even for saluting the Scroll of the Law' were to be 'most strictly avoided'. Defaulters could be fined 'at the pleasure of the Committee'.

For all these positive initiatives, the community also experienced internecine conflict and even schism. Fractious individuals such as the cantankerous Benjamin Norden who litigated seemingly compulsively against all comers including his fellow congregants, and Simeon Marcus, a would-be schismatic whose habit it was to threaten to abandon the infant community and go his own way when thwarted, almost shipwrecked the frail congregation. The Reverend Pulver rapidly found his new congregation a spiritual desert island, devoid even of a *mikvah* (ritual bath). Resigning after only two years of his ministry, he wrote:

> … my principal reasons for wishing to leave this congregation are, first, that I cannot get Kosher meat; secondly, that I cannot as a Jewish parent bring up my children in a place where so little regard is paid to the principles of our Holy Religion; and thirdly, that notwithstanding nearly two years' trial to live as economically as possible, I could not make my income meet my expenses.

Restricted finances would continue to dog the community after the Reverend Pulver's departure. Pulver's successor, the Reverend Joel Rabinowitz was only appointed at the end of the 1850s.

Albert Road cemetery.

Reverend Isaac Pulver.

The Jews in Cape Town

CAPE TOWN, SEPTEMBER 1857
TO THE EDITOR OF THE *SAC Advertiser* AND *Cape Town Mail*

Sir, – Will you kindly allow me, through the medium of your Journal, to set before the public a few remarks which may not be wholly devoid of interest, especially to the religious portion of your readers.

The Jews of this city, in and of the colony at large, are not a numerous class, nor are they, generally speaking, so wealthy as their co-religionists in most other parts of the world.

With few of the facilities afforded Jews in other civilised countries for the due observation of the rites their laws, custom and religion impose upon them, they at times show how earnestly they cling to the memorials of their far off homes and countries, and to the best of their circumstances celebrate the functions Judaism requires of them around the domestic board, in the friendly circle, and in the Synagogue.

Without Rabbis and other essential persons for keeping our Hebrew fellow-citizens up to the letter of the Jewish ritual, they do the best they can, under the circumstances, to testify that they are the descendants of Abraham, and still follow the Talmud in preference to the unadulterated Word of God, and the blessings held out to them by the Gospel.

With a sincerity of purpose exemplary in the extreme, your town readers might have remarked on Friday the 18th inst., at sunset, most if not all the Jewish places of business closed until sunset the following day. Rosh Hashana, or their civil New Year had commenced, and the Sabbath was celebrated with it. The Jews abstained from business, and with their little ones in some cases congregated in their Synagogue with all due solemnity. Many came in from the country, expressly to unite with their brethren, friends, and families in that festival.

Although they and I differ widely in our tenets it was, nevertheless, to me a sight truly refreshing. I was glad to see that they were not, as too many believe, totally lost to what is so dear to the Jewish heart, the recollections of their forefathers, and the worship of their nation so 'widely scattered and peeled'. But the day of solemn assembly – the day of all in the year nearly if not the most important in the calendar of the Jews, Yom Kippoor, or the Day of Atonement is now …

On Sunday 27th at sunset, this very solemn season commenced, and from an early hour on Monday morning till the evening of the same day was the sacred fast kept, the places of business closed, and the place of worship well resorted to. For that occasion great efforts are made by Jews in the country or at a distance to be for at least that once in a year with their brethren to observe the fast.

… sir, your most obedient servant

The Cape Town residence of Joseph Mosenthal, 1857.

INTO THE HINTERLAND

At the very time that Cape Town Jews were consolidating their communal life, the centre of gravity of the Cape economy was shifting from west to east. Cape wine exports – the backbone of the colonial economy in the first decades after the British occupation – were increasingly overshadowed by the export of wool from the Eastern Cape. Burgeoning demand from the 'dark Satanic mills' of Britain's Industrial Revolution spurred a pastoral revolution in the eastern districts of the colony as woolly-fleeced merino sheep from Spain ousted their fat-tailed Cape cousins.

Among the early importers of these Spanish interlopers was Maximilian Thalwitzer, a German Jew, who brought out experts from Holstein to instruct local farmers in the art of shearing. Thalwitzer, who served as the consul for the Hanseatic cities of Hamburg, Lubeck and Bremen, did much to encourage German interest in Cape wool. However, it was the brothers Adolph and Joseph Mosenthal, German Jews like Thalwitzer, who did most to develop the Cape wool industry. The Mosenthals were instrumental in creating a trading network throughout the wool-producing districts, ensuring the smooth passage of merino wool from farm through trading store and town to the major European markets. Through their trading activities, these merchant capitalists accelerated the transition – for good or ill – from a subsistence to a cash economy.

Beyond the dominant wool industry, Jewish entrepreneurs also

Port Elizabeth staff of Mosenthals.

Adolph Mosenthal (opposite left), pioneer with his brother Joseph (opposite centre) of the Cape wool industry.

Mosenthal bank note issued in 1857, at a time when financing was in its infancy in the Cape Colony.

THE Undersigned having arrived at Algoa Bay, and landed the whole of their

GOODS, EX "SARAH CRISP,"

beg now to inform the public that they have taken the premises belonging to Mr. THORNHILL, and that their goods are now ready for inspection

MOSENTHAL BROTHERS.

MOSENTHAL BROTHERS

ARE now landing

    Superior Marseilla, in quarter casks,
    Pale Brandy, in cases of 1 doz. each,
    Best Jamaica Rum, in cases of 1 doz.
    Liqueurs, assorted
    Real Schedam Gin, in baskets and cases
    Dutch Cheeses, &c. &c.

Port Elizabeth. 15th November, 1842.

Jonas Bergtheil, business pioneer in the colony of Natal.

Aaron de Pass, whose businesses at the Cape included coastal shipping, guano deposits and ship repairing.

played a pioneering role in other attempts to exploit the natural resources of the region. Jonas Bergtheil, yet another enterprising German Jew, did much to develop the new colony of Natal despite his failure to establish a viable local cotton industry. As an answer to a crippling labour scarcity Bergtheil even proposed importing poor Jews from Germany – possibly remnants of the *Betteljuden*, the 'beggar Jews' who desperately roamed the late eighteenth-century German countryside in search of a livelihood. His plan was thwarted by rumours that, on reaching South Africa, these hapless immigrants would be sold as slaves.

Far more successful was the De Pass family whose ancestors had migrated from Holland to Cromwell's England at the very time that other Dutchmen had set their sights on the Cape. The De Pass brothers, Aaron and Elias, appear to have inherited the maritime tradition and com-

The first Torah in South Africa,
brought from London in 1847 by
Aaron de Pass.

mercial initiative of their ancestral home. Besides founding a coastal shipping company and exploiting the fetid guano deposits of the islands off the Cape west coast, the brothers established ship repairing facilities in Table Bay and Simonstown, pioneered cold storage at the Cape, and played a prominent part in Jewish life in Cape Town.

In 1847 Aaron brought the first *Torah* (scroll of the law) to South Africa from London, connect-

ing Cape Town with Sinai, at least in the minds of observant Jews.

Beyond Cape Town such connections were more tenuous. While organised Jewish life followed commerce, it did so only at an interval of years and in a handful of centres. Grahamstown, Graaff-Reinet and Port Elizabeth in the Eastern Cape joined Cape Town as formal Jewish communities in 1843, 1850 and 1857 respectively. For the rest, Jews scattered through the small towns and villages of the Colony and beyond depended on the occasional ministrations of itinerant clerics.

Prior to the 1870s the Reverend Joel Rabinowitz of Cape Town corresponded with and regularly travelled to these isolated pockets of Jewish settlement. His *huisbesoeks* (home visits) provided a spiritual lifeline to those still clinging to Jewish tradition. A sense of the value placed upon these services is vividly illustrated in a letter from a Mr Isaacson, an immigrant obviously ill at ease with English, to Rabinowitz in October 1866:

> My wife having presented me with a son I wish to know whether you are soon coming this way as I want you to yitch [circumcise] him … I am a poor man but I will give twenty pounds but that must include all things. Please let me hear from you dear sir as soon as you can – being very anxious …

Rabinowitz's itinerant services were supplemented in the 1870s by the Reverend Samuel Rapaport of Port Elizabeth. Like his Cape Town counterpart, he would make the lengthy journey by cart from the coast into the interior, even as far as Bloemfontein, for family rites of passages such as the circumcisions of sons and the weddings of daughters.

Rabinowitz and Rapaport were not the only Jews on the road in the early 1870s. Besides the *smouse* (itinerant pedlars) there were also fortune-seekers heading northwards. The discovery in 1867 of a diamond, deep in the interior alongside the Orange River, followed in quick succession by further discoveries nearby at what would become Kimberley, tugged Jews away from their modest rural livelihoods in search of new opportunities. Their departures eroded any prospects

Reverend Joel Rabinowitz, who reinvigorated the struggling Cape Town Hebrew Congregation, following his arrival in South Africa in 1859.

of establishing a viable Jewish life at these remote outposts.

Even the mother congregation in Cape Town felt the gravitational force of this new El Dorado, losing both congregants and subscription revenue. The locals were joined by adventurers from across the seas, similarly seduced by dreams of instant wealth on the diamond fields of Griqualand West. One of these, Louis Cohen, later recalled:

> Rabbis, rebels, rogues and roués from Russia and the Riviera, transports from

Continued on page 25

Isaac Baumann, general merchant and first Jew in Bloemfontein.

The Baumanns of Bloemfontein

Isaac Baumann (1813-1881), an early German Jewish pioneer in the interior, arrived in Bloemfontein in 1849, shortly after the town's founding. He traded first as a jeweller, but later became a prosperous general merchant. On a visit home to Hesse-Cassell he married Caroline Allenburg, a young Jewess 19 years his junior. Baumann subsequently brought out his brothers who joined him in business

The Baumanns, who had eleven children, were thoroughly integrated into the predominantly English-speaking elite of Bloemfontein. Isaac took an active part in civic affairs and served on the boards of the leading local financial institutions. He also had strong ties with the Boer political elite. When his eldest daughter married in 1874, President Brand of the Orange Free State and members of the Volksraad attended the wedding; in the Baumann's honour the day was marked as a public half-holiday.

Isaac Baumann was the first Jew in Bloemfontein. For decades after his arrival the Jewish presence in the Free State capital was not much broader than his extended family. The Baumanns' Jewishness was of a diluted Anglo-German sort. The clan's matriarch Caroline came, according to her daughter Sophie Leviseur, from 'a very liberal Jewish family. We were brought up with great pride of race and taught to be proud of being Jews but that was all the religious teaching we had. Our instruction consisted of half an hour of prayer and a little reading every Sunday morning, for which we were dressed as if we were going to church. We had no church to go to.'

The anglicised German Jewish Baumanns were essentially Free Staters of the Mosaic persuasion. 'No one thought of us as Jews,' Sophie later remembered. She and her siblings 'all grew up to think of themselves as being of just another variety of faith, like Wesleyans or English or Dutch Reformed. She never differentiated between herself and the Christians, nor did others … They considered themselves, and were accepted by others, as full citizens.'

Cohen comes to Kimberley

In 1872, at the age of 18, Louis Cohen arrived in South Africa. Decades later this acerbic observer, deeply marked by the prejudices of his day, recorded his initial impressions of Diamondopolis:

… One afternoon, I caught in the distance my first sight of the Diamond Fields … Many a heart beat faster as the Diamond City of the Plains became less and less indistinct, and those whose everything depended on the success of their expedition, watched this ghost-like series of tents grow whiter and whiter as they outlined clearer and clearer … Nearer and nearer we came.

Canvas shelters were everywhere, and as the coach got into one of the roads leading directly to Du Toit's Pan, the only wooden buildings seen were made of packing cases, though dismal looking iron shanties intermingled with mud-heaps, wells and washing apparatus were on view by the score. However, on we went; the tents got more numerous, less lilywhite, and unwashed diggers popped their heads to see us pass. Naked kaffirs and dogs appeared in plenty …

… It was about three o'clock in the afternoon, and the place was full of people. Niggers and Negresses of different tribes were walking about in the road-

Louis Cohen, mordant observer of early Kimberley.

Early diamond diggings.

way, diggers in woollen shirts and sombrero hats standing without the canteens or drinking inside, and coolies, arrayed in white turbans and linen suits, ringing bells outside the eating houses … Talking to the diggers could be seen quite a number of men – mostly young – dressed in semi-European style. A few, very few, appeared well bred, but most of them postured like pilfering tinkers who had got their best clothes out of pawn. They were, as a rule, smoking large cigars. On driving up the Main Street I noticed the self-same species of gentlemen standing in front of their framed canvas habitations, and when I read on the signs dis-

played outside these tented offices that Abraham, Isaac and Jacob had recovered from their long celestial sleep and gone in for earthly diamond buying, 'at the very highest prices for the European market', I felt a real glow of hope as I inwardly ejaculated, 'Thank the Lord I'm with my own people – and it's not Jerusalem.' But they certainly looked as if they had come from the Sublime East – of London.

Cohen's scurrilous *Reminiscences of Kimberley* resulted in a libel case brought by one of the targets of his barbed pen. Cohen lost and the book was withdrawn.

David Harris, soldier, politician and long-serving chairman of De Beers.

Cockney cousins and carats

Barnet Isaacs, better known as Barney Barnato, and his cousin David Harris were born a week apart, in July 1852, in London where both attended the Spitalfields Jews' Free School. David preceded his cousin to South Africa in 1871. To save the cost of a post cart from Durban to Kimberley he walked the 600 miles, alongside an ox wagon carrying his 'two small portmanteaux'. His initial stabs at diamond digging and dealing were less successful than his first (and only) efforts at the roulette table which funded a brief return visit to London where he dazzled his cousin with his modest suc-

Directors of De Beers 1893, with Cecil John Rhodes (seated, centre), Barney Barnato (seated, third from right) and David Harris (standing, far right).

*Barney Barnato, flamboyant
diamond magnate.*

Cockney cousins and carats continued

cess. Barney followed him to the diamond fields in 1873. A more forceful, flamboyant and daring character, fond of boxing and acting, Barney soon outstripped his more stolid relative. By the 1880s he, with the 'colossus' Cecil John Rhodes, dominated the diamond industry. The great De Beers monopoly was born out of their legendary tussle for control of the industry. The more cautious Harris would later become the long-term chairman of the company.

While Barnato focused on business in Kimberley and on the Witwatersrand where he built a further fortune, Harris established a local reputation as a volunteer soldier, serving with distinction in a series of colonial skirmishes against the 'natives'. Barnato's career ended tragically when, depressed by business difficulties, he jumped overboard off the coast of Madeira on a voyage to England in 1897. David Harris succeeded the 'Great Barnato' as the member for Kimberley in the Cape parliament.

Though Barney on leaving London had reputedly packed his phylacteries and promised his father to *daven* (pray) daily, once on the diamond fields he was barely involved with matters Jewish besides occasional Friday night meals with his cousin David and his German Jewish wife. David and Rosa had married in 1873, reportedly the first Jewish wedding on the diamond fields. (Barnato married a gentile, Fanny Bees of Kimberley, in a registry office in London in 1892.) David Harris maintained a lifelong connection with the Jewish community, defending Jewish interests in parliament and serving as warden and trustee of the Kimberley Synagogue.

Continued from page 18

Tasmania, convicts from Caledonia … and the choicest pickings of the dirtiest street corners in Europe, many of whom were very devout, but nearly all decidedly improper … all came to escape the grinning [sic] poverty which had driven them from their native heaths; or, in many cases, the punishment of their crimes.

When Cohen arrived in 1872, the population of Kimberley had grown to 50 000, many of them black labourers toiling on the claims of some 3 000 individual diggers. Among the newcomers were Jews, mainly from England and Germany, who numbered about 120 by the mid-seventies. Though few in number, they played a significant part in the

rapid evolution of the diamond industry: Jews traded in diamonds, in some cases illicitly; owned and operated mining claims and amalgamated these as part of the consolidation process which characterised the infant industry; and floated diamond-mining companies both locally and in Europe. Among the most successful were the flamboyant East Ender, Barney Barnato, 'silent little' Sammy Marks from Lithuania via Sheffield, his cousin Isaac Lewis, and Hamburg-born 'Little Alfred' Beit, whose parents, like so many German Jews at the time, had converted, at least nominally, to Christianity for reasons of convenience.

Eight years after the discovery of the first diamond, the governor of the Cape Colony, Sir Henry Barkly, laid the foundation stone of Kim-

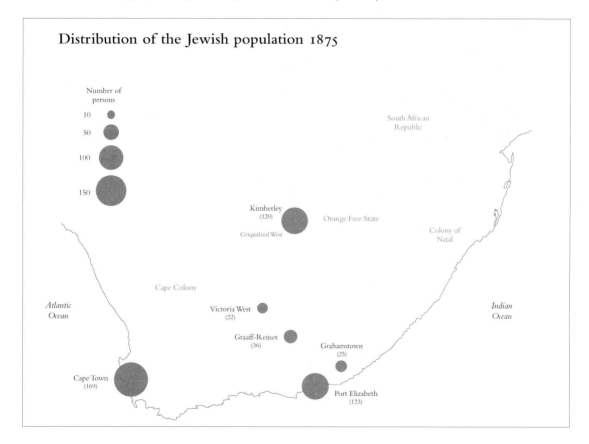

Distribution of the Jewish population 1875

Number of persons

10
50
100
150

South African Republic

Kimberley (120)
Griqualand West
Orange Free State
Colony of Natal

Cape Colony

Atlantic Ocean

Victoria West (22)

Graaff-Reinet (36)

Grahamstown (25)

Indian Ocean

Cape Town (169)

Port Elizabeth (123)

Early Kimberley.

berley's first synagogue. His generous and philo-semitic speech on this occasion captures the generally positive way in which Jews were perceived in mid-Victorian England and its colonies:

> None I am well aware more thoroughly and sincerely participate in the feelings of whole hearted loyalty which is characteristic of the British nation than Her Majesty's subjects of Jewish lineage and faith. I have had opportunities of becoming acquainted with them as a body obedient to the law, ready to take their part on all occasions as good citizens and to cooperate in works of benevolence and mercy. In Griqualand West, especially it has happened, from the first, that some of the most energetic and enterprising members of society have been Jewish.

By the time of Barkly's speech in 1875, Jews comprised a mere fraction of South Africa's white population, itself a small minority of the total population. Besides the 120 in Kimberley (in the crown colony of Griqualand West), the majority still resided in the Cape Colony itself where they made up a paltry 0.23 per cent of the entire white population. Cape Town (169), Port Elizabeth (123), Graaff-Reinet (36), Grahamstown (25), and Victoria West (22) were the only centres in the Colony with significant concentrations of Jews. A handful of Jews resided in the Boer republics of the Transvaal and the Orange Free State and in the colony of Natal, where the first *minyan* was held in Durban in the same year as Barkly spoke in Kimberley.

The great majority were male, and very often single. With the shortage of Jewish women, it was not uncommon to return to the 'old country' to find a spouse. Most South African

Jews were still of Anglo-German origin. They were comfortably bourgeois and acculturated, modelling themselves on the English. Like the Baumanns of Bloemfontein, they were, by and large, well ensconced in colonial and republican society. As Lady Duff Gordon, a visitor to the Cape had noted in 1860, they had 'abandoned the peculiarities of their tradition if not the features of their race'. The Jewish community, in other words, reflected the lifestyle and communal patterns of their 'enlightened' co-religionists in Western Europe. Religion was a private matter and primary allegiance was accorded to the state. The community, moreover, personified the values and norms dearest to nineteenth-century English liberals: loyalty, obedience, civic virtue, charitableness and, above all, enterprise.

Jews flourished in a setting permeated by a tolerant British imperial ethos informed by an assimilationist ideal, at least in so far as the white population was concerned. This tolerance had survived the initial influx of Jewish fortune-seekers following the discovery of diamonds. Indeed, despite the historian James Froude observing among the diggers, 'a hundred or so keen-eyed Jewish merchants ... gathering like eagles over their prey', the image of the Jew in the 1870s remained overwhelmingly favourable.

Their comfortable integration into the wider white community, their small numbers, the gender imbalance, and the assimilatory impulses of a frontier society, all pointed towards the eventual disappearance of this infant Jewish community. But unforeseen events, both near and distant, were in the next decade to transform dramatically the demography and character of South African Jewry.

CHAPTER 2

LITVAKS

ENTER THE GRIENERS

IN MARCH 1881, MEMBERS OF THE PEOPLE'S WILL
Party, a Russian revolutionary group, assassinated Tsar Alexander II on the streets of St Petersburg. Among the plotters was a
young Jewess, Gessia Gelfman. Anti-Jewish rioting broke out six
weeks later in southern Russia and spread across the Ukraine. In
an unstable and fractured society where mass violence was always
latent, Gessia's involvement provided a pretext for these pogroms,
and the pillaging and rape that accompanied them.

Five years later, and half a world away, prospectors on the Witwatersrand, a high-lying region deep in the South African interior, would not have known that their discovery of what was to
become the richest gold reef in the world would offer hope and
opportunity to those seeking an escape from the violence and oppression unleashed by the Tsar's assassination. These two unrelated
events, at opposite ends of the globe, were to change the fate of
South African Jewry.

Gessia Gelfman's involvement can at most be described as a
catalyst for the pogroms and the anti-Jewish measures that followed in the wake of the assassination of Alexander II. The 'May
Laws' of 1882 – a set of harsh restrictions on Jewish rural life – expanded earlier discriminatory policies in what was known as the
Pale of Settlement, the large crescent of territory on the western

Jewish immigrants arriving in Cape Town.

29

Shtetl street scene.

margin of Russia to which Jews had been con-fined by Tsarist decree in the wake of the parti-tion of Poland between Prussia, Russia and Aus-tria at the end of the eighteenth century.

As a result of this partition, Jews had found themselves unwelcome subjects of an antisemitic Russian empire which had previously forbidden them entry. They were the unwanted legacy of Tsarist territorial ambition in Eastern Europe: their new master had accepted their presence very grudgingly, and throughout the nineteenth century had hedged their lives with restrictions great and small.

Despite official attempts at Jewish 'Russifi-cation' through the first half of the nineteenth century, most Jews had maintained their dis-

tinctiveness, rooted in their use of the Yiddish language and their religious tradition. This distinctiveness survived notwithstanding buffeting by currents of secularisation and modernisation through the century. However, while the majority clung to tradition, a minority, the *maskilim*, eagerly identified with the *Haskalah*, the Jewish Enlightenment.

A fivefold population increase during the course of the century – from one million in 1800 to five million in 1900 – coupled with far-reaching social and economic change, resulted in the marginalisation and immiseration of many. Increasingly the economy of the Pale could not absorb the growth in population. 'The Jews live in great congestion, very often several families live in one small room,' wrote a Russian observer of life in the Pale. 'There are tradesmen whose

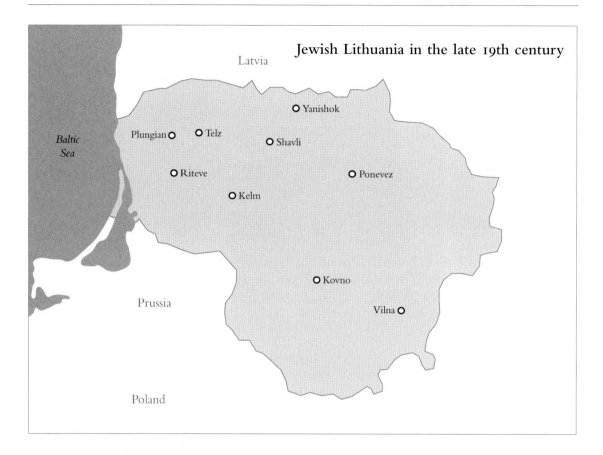

Jewish Lithuania in the late 19th century

Latvia

Baltic Sea

Yanishok

Plungian   Telz   Shavli

Riteve

Kelm

Ponevez

Kovno

Vilna

Prussia

Poland

families fast the whole day till the breadwinner comes home and brings his earnings.'

In such stressful circumstances the pogroms, followed by further restrictions, reinforced a sense of hopelessness and encouraged thoughts of emigration. From the 1880s, what had previously been a trickle became a flood, as Jews sought refuge from an increasingly turbulent world. Although there were relatively few pogroms in Lithuania – the seedbed of South African Jewry – fears of instability and violence contributed in no small measure to a high rate of emigration from that region.

Those emigrant Litvaks (as the Jews of historic Lithuania were known) travelled light in a material though not in a cultural sense. Vilna, once

the capital of Lithuania, had been the home in the eighteenth century of the renowned Gaon of Vilna, the great opponent of Hasidism, a mystical movement guided by charismatic leaders. Following the Gaon's lead, the Jews of the Lithuanian *shtetls* (small towns) had created a distinctive cultural milieu rooted in the cerebral *mitnagdic* (literally oppositional) rather than the pietistic *hasidic* tradition.

The *shtetl* supported a rich and complex infrastructure of cultural, religious and educational institutions. One of these was the *cheder*, the elementary school, where children – the boys of the *shtetl* but not their sisters whose education was a low priority – acquired a basic literacy in Hebrew, the *loshen kodesh*, the holy language of prayer rather than of conversation. After *bar mitzvah*, the traditional coming of age at 13, a privileged few continued to a more advanced form of education provided by the Jewish community, the *yeshiva* or Talmudic academy.

The *shtetl* valued hard work as well as diligence, self-control and sobriety. It prized learning, charity and devotion to family. Beyond the family, the *shtetl* placed a premium on mutual support. *Tsdokeh* (charity) was seen as a prime virtue. These intangibles accompanied the emigrants and would be of inestimable importance in re-establishing a communal life in the new country.

While the *shtetl* esteemed learning, the migrants were generally not the learned. The more professional (few as they were), the more skilled, the more affluent, the more established and the more pious tended to remain at home. Religious luminaries feared and warned against the subversive effects of the New World, the *treyf medina*, the impure and unclean land. Most *yeshiva bochers* (students) would have followed this advice.

Although the United States was the premier destination for these Jewish emigrants, some 40 000 (out of a total of approximately three million) chose South Africa in the three decades before the First World War. The majority of these came from the Kovno province of Lithuania, with certain towns predominating, among them Kovno, Ponevez, Shavli, Riteve, Yanishok and Plungian. Chain migration played a critical role in the migrants' choice of destination. Remittances from those who went first, success stories of 'local boys' who made good, such as Isaac Lewis and Sammy Marks, and reassuring reports in newspapers such as *Ha-Melitz* and *Ha-Tsifirah* about the abundant opportunities in a tolerant

Ha-Melitz, a Hebrew newspaper published in St Petersburg and widely circulated in Lithuania.

environment, all contributed to the attraction and viability of South Africa as a destination.

From the 1890s a further inducement emerged. The Poor Jews' Temporary Shelter in the East End of London, subsidised by the shipping magnate Donald Currie, eased the passage of migrants to South Africa, smoothing their transmigration through England. Currie's steamships of the Castle line in the 1890s – known as the Union-Castle line after its merger with its principal rival in 1900 – carried the overwhelming majority on their onward journey to South Africa, which on the average took over a fortnight.

Travelling in steerage, their needs for kosher food and a space for communal worship were sometimes accommodated by sympathetic ship captains; in other cases observant Jews had to make do with a spare diet of herrings, potatoes and bread. 'Being so religious mad,' Moritz Jacobson later recalled, 'we lived on black bread dipped in sugar water and dried out; you had that with tea and eggs.' Solomon Green, 13 years old when he made the journey, remembered that his family had taken rusks with them. 'We

The Poor Jews' Temporary Shelter

Of the 40 000 Jewish immigrants from Eastern Europe who came to South Africa between 1880 and 1914, some 20 000 passed through the Poor Jews' Temporary Shelter in the East End of London. The Shelter protected transmigrants against the depredations of crooked shipping agents, larcenous porters and grasping lodging-house keepers. In the mid-1890s the Shelter established a mutually beneficial business relationship with the principal shipping lines serving the South African route, Donald Currie's Castle Line and the rival Union Line, which later merged to form the Union-Castle Line.

Migrants bound for South Africa would purchase vouchers in Eastern Europe from agencies linked with the shipping companies, then embark at Hamburg, Bremen or Libau on the Baltic for London. There they were met and safely escorted to the Shelter where they were accommodated and fed for up to 14 days for which the shipping companies paid 1/- and later 2/- per passenger per day. The vouchers were exchanged for ship's tickets in London. Sometimes the journeys to the offices of the shipping companies were fraught, particularly for those escorting the migrants from the Shelter. 'These people whilst being conducted through the city from this institution to your offices,' complained the Shelter to Donald Currie & Co, 'are often molested by boys and roughs and consequently suffer a great deal of annoyance whilst considerable difficulty is often experienced in keeping them together as they have a tendency to disappear suddenly into shops to buy small articles ...' At the end of their brief stay the transmigrants were put on the train to Southampton where an agent of the Shelter saw them on board.

Poor Jews' Temporary Shelter.

LEFT: *Page from the register of the Poor Jews' Temporary Shelter: Frieda Davids was the mother of Helen Suzman, celebrated opponent of apartheid.*

did not eat meat but we ate fish, fried fish with pickles; I loved it, new type of food …'

Disembarking in Cape Town after their journey, the newcomers were often met and assisted by family members or by a *landsman* (compatriot) or, in some instances, by altruistic individuals or representatives of benevolent organisations. One of these, the youthful Bension Hersch, born in Yanishok near Shavli in Lithuania, became a well-known figure at the Cape Town docks in the early 1900s, assisting Yiddish-speakers with basic information about the bewildering immigration procedures and their onward journeys. Hersch was particularly well-equipped for this task: he spoke Hebrew, Yiddish, English, German, Russian and Polish.

Although the overwhelming majority of Jews landed in Cape Town, their destinations varied. While some remained in the city, many others went on to the larger centres in the interior – especially the mushrooming mining metropolis of Johannesburg – or to the other ports. Others chose to disperse into the countryside, either to the *dorps* (small towns) or to isolated locations along the transport routes. Some of the newcomers drew on artisan skills such as tailoring and carpentry brought from the old country; others learned new business skills from their first employers, very often earlier arrivals or kinsmen. Some initially tramped the countryside as *smouse*, selling goods acquired on credit from city wholesalers, while others began their business lives with small loans provided by Jewish mutual aid and philanthropic societies. All bobbed about on the ebb and flow of a volatile but generally burgeoning South African economy. Like other whites, the racial ordering of this economy and the availability of cheap unskilled black labour inclined Jews towards non-manual occupations. Unlike

MARCH 9, 1900
The Jewish World
SOUTHWARD HO!

JEWISH EMIGRANTS' TREATMENT

INTERVIEW WITH SIR DONALD CURRIE

All thoughts and eyes are now turned towards the African Continent. Jews as well as Gentiles are eager for news from the seat of war, for are there not hundreds of soldiers belonging to the Jewish faith who have volunteered to do battle for the land in which every freedom is vouchsafed to them. To the Russian Jew, especially, South Africa is the country which will enable him to better his position and make some provision for the family left behind in the old country.

Having decided upon going, the emigrant next asks himself the question, 'How am I to get there?'

In order to gain complete information upon this point (writes a correspondent of THE JEWISH WORLD), I called at the office of the Castle Line.

By the courtesy of Sir Donald Currie, the head of the firm of Donald Currie & Co., who have been managing the Castle Line, and under whose management the newly amalgamated Union-Castle Line will be, the particulars I sought were given to me.

On the passenger's arrival in London, providing he is travelling further by the Castle Line, he is met at the ship coming from Hamburg, Bremen or Libau, arrangements for that purpose having been made with the Poor Jews' Temporary Shelter, which, also at the expense of the Company, feeds and lodges him until his departure from London, on the day of which he is conducted to the Blackwall Docks.

What mostly concerns the Jewish passenger is the question of kosher food, and the facilities to observe his religious tenets whilst on board. With the view of meeting the religious scruples of their Jewish passengers – Sir Donald Currie and Co.'s steamers carry the bulk of Jews going to the South – arrangements have been made whereby strictly Jewish food, and even separate cooking utensils are supplied, besides setting apart for the Jewish passengers a sepa-

Donald Currie whose ships carried thousands of Jewish immigrants to the Cape.

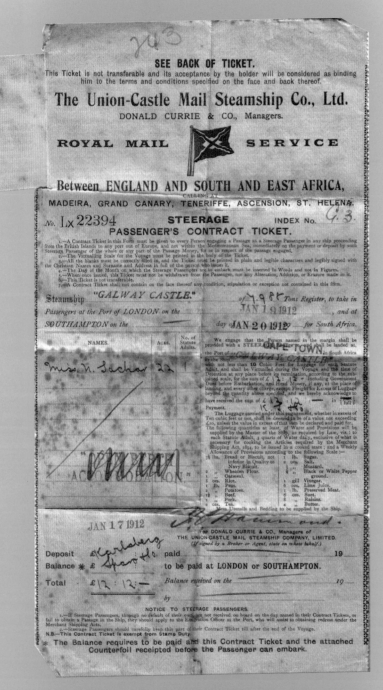

Ship's ticket to South Africa of unaccompanied 22-year-old Jewish woman, 1912.

rate compartment where they can say their prayers. Most of the Jewish passengers travel third saloon.

Every piece of meat is strictly kosher, and is prepared according to the Jewish manner. So anxious are Sir Donald Currie & Co. to study the Jewish passengers that any individual passenger of the Jewish persuasion travelling saloon and second saloon can have everything kosher if he so desires it.

During the High Holydays and festivals special arrangements are made. Thus during Passover weeks matzos and new utensils are provided, and facilities are given to celebrate Seder, and on Rosh Hashana and Yom Kippur prayers can be recited with strictest privacy, and secure from the intrusion of any but members of the Jewish faith.

We have lately heard much of the Russo-Jewish emigrants to South Africa, and considering the very large number passing through the hands of the officials of the Castle Line, their opinion of them is especially interesting at the present moment.

Asked as to the status of these people, the reply was:

'We have all classes of Jews, there are the rich, the middle class, and those who have just sufficient to pay their fare. Our officers on board the ship have never any reason to complain of the conduct of the third saloon passengers, they are well-behaved, and are very grateful for anything that is done for them.'

Arriving in the 'goldene medina'

Writing in 1891 to *Ha-Tsifirah*, a Hebrew-language newspaper published in Warsaw, the journalist, Nechemiah Dov Hoffmann, graphically described the immigrant's experience on landing:

> Tired and weary, exhausted from the hardships of the long and perilous journey across the ocean, the wanderer steps upon the soil of the Cape of Good Hope. His heart churns like the sea, as his feet tread upon the Cape soil. Dizziness overcomes him as he lifts his eyes to the mountains of the Cape Peninsula, which rise to the sky. Looking at these awesome mountains he calls out from the depth of his heart: 'Heavens, from whence cometh my help!' The joyous, tumultuous city of Cape Town, that spreads in her beauty on the slopes of these mountains – her din and the multitudes, that fill her streets, evoke deep wonder and emotion. The newcomer's feelings are further stirred as he remembers that he is far from his homeland, his wife and children and all the things that were near and dear to him. He stands now in the midst of a stormy sea of people with its bellowing, foamy waves of life and struggle for existence ... Thousands of strange people, whose language he knows not and whose ways and manners are foreign to him, pass him by ... His empty pocket, his penury ... these too add sorrow to his grief ... To whom can he turn for aid? Who will spread out the wings of succour over him, and extricate him from his difficulties? Who will take him into his house, advise him, show him whither to turn and what to do? Dispirited and gloomy, he silently walks through the streets of the city to seek out friends or relatives who preceded him to this country. There is no end to his joy and relief when finally he finds such a person ... If his acquaintance is a man of feeling, imbued with love for his fellowman, who has not yet forgotten his own position when he arrived in this country some years before ... he will gladly take the newcomer into his house, will feed and clothe and encourage him, by promising him aid ...

> After the newcomer has rested from his long and arduous journey and regained his strength, his benefactor, for a few pounds sterling, buys some inexpensive wares, teaches him the Hollands names of the merchandise, and the prices, puts his wares in a basket which he loads on the newcomer's back, and sends him away from his house like Noah sending the dove from the Ark ... thus to make the rounds of the farms and sell his wares.

New York or London at this time, the South African Jewish immigrant by and large avoided the gruelling sweatshop experience.

In Cape Town, as in Johannesburg, the newcomers gravitated to inner-city precincts such as District Six or Ferreirastown and Malay Camp. These South African equivalents of New York's Lower East Side, London's East End and Paris's Pletzl, provided ethnic companionship and psychological comfort for the *grieners* (greenhorns). Here they could converse freely in their *mame loshen* (mother tongue), enjoy Yiddish theatre, read the occasional albeit irregular Yiddish newspaper, eat familiar foods, and pray in the less decorous Eastern European mode so alien to their uptown, anglicised and more affluent co-religionists.

Here too they could meet Jews of the opposite sex. While women were initially outnumbered – as in many new immigrant communities – the gender balance gradually equalised. From the start South Africa was seen as a destination of settlement, a new and permanent home where wives and children soon followed in the wake of the male migrant, rather than a transient oppor-

Ferreira's Camp, Johannesburg, 1886.

Bension Hersch, who assisted Jewish immigrants at the dockside in Cape Town.

tunity for enrichment. Besides their vital contribution to the family income, women created the domestic environment essential to Jewish continuity. As elsewhere, they were the guardians of Jewish tradition within the private sphere. The male-dominated public sphere, by contrast, was the site of rapid acculturation.

Jews in Johannesburg and Cape Town straddled the social spectrum. At one extreme, a few played a conspicuous part in the underworld, most flagrantly in the illicit liquor trade on the Witwatersrand during the 1890s. These members of Johannesburg's lumpenproletariat were abusively labelled Peruvians. Some of them, most notoriously the legendary Joe Silver, were involved in the 'white slave trade', the international trafficking in prostitutes, including young 'Russian' Jewish girls.

While a small minority belonged to the demimonde, the great majority anxiously pursued respectability. Secular education was a high

'Vant to puy a vaatch?': the smous

From the early nineteenth century the itinerant trader, the *smous*, became a distinctive feature of the rural landscape. While originally a term associated with all country pedlars, the word *smous* gradually became synonymous with the wandering Jewish trader. The *smous* has been romanticised in South African Jewish memory and characterised, debatably, as a welcome addition to society, appreciated for his services to the isolated and grateful farmer. (The welcome was not always warm, and the *smous* became, for some, a figure of derision.)

The origin of the word *smous* is not certain. The word may be a corruption of the name Moses imported from Holland in the Company period. The corruption arose from the manner in which the Dutch Jews themselves pronounced the name. It has been suggested that the word derives from the German word *Mauschel,* the epithet for the haggling Jewish trader. Further explanations claim that the word is derived from the German *schmuss* (talk, patter) or from the Hebrew *Sh'mu* (tales, news), the reference being to the persuasive eloquence of Jewish traders.

The activities of the *smous* are vividly recalled in the memoirs of a German Jewish country storekeeper in the northern Cape:

> The … smous operated either from a wagon or from an open buggy, loaded to heaven with bales and boxes containing an infinite variety of merchandise. Such a trader would purchase his goods, let us say, in Victoria West or Carnarvon, then proceed towards Van Wyk's Vlei, Kenhardt, Upington, and back via Draghoender and Prieska, touching as many farms as possible. At each farm he unpacked, displayed his wares in front of the homestead – usually on the stoep – did his business, collected his sheep, which travelled with him until he reached his original destination, where he disposed of the live stock and in due course started *de novo*.
>
> I have known traders who were at this game for years, and some made a good living out of it. Their expenses were practically nil, for the farmer, with his proverbial hospitality, entertained

Smous *at rest*.

them free, and they slept in their wagons or under their carts, as the case might be.

These activities were not always appreciated by contemporary observers. Writing to the *Cape Times* in 1900 after a trip to 'Bushmanland', a correspondent complained:

> I noticed on my trip to these parts that the Jewish

traders exercise a great deal of influence and have these squatters in Bushmanland altogether in their power. Not a day passes but there is either a Jew with his cart or wagon coming to the squatters' tent or hut, and making himself at home there for several days, eating their food without paying for it, or doing or giving anything in return, and as they as a rule give unlimited credit and 'tick' to the Dutch and half-caste squatters, they thus have them altogether in their power, and the latter are bound to them, as their stock is nearly if not all mortgaged to the Jewish smous.

The *smous* features prominently if exaggeratedly in South African Jewish myths of origin. In much the same way that modern Australians claim convict descent, many South African Jewish families today proudly claim *smous* ancestry.

Life of the smous

Bitter indeed is the fate of this pedlar or *toeganger* or *smous* as the Afrikaners call him, in the early stages ... For days and weeks he trudges the countryside visiting the farmers, his heavy basket upon his shoulders and the burning rays of the African sun beating down upon him. He will climb high mountains, descend into the valleys and knock upon the door of the Afrikaner to sell his wares. Thus the unfortunate one spends several miserable months, hovering between hope and fear, and curses the day that he decided to come to Africa.

In these months of hardship and turmoil he will, however, acquaint himself with the character of the Boers, learn a little Hollands, and will become accustomed to the ways and customs of the land. He will then begin to feel at ease, for he will meet various people and will be able to describe his bitter fate to them. The Afrikaners, who are by nature humanitarian, will pity the unfortunate pedlar and will buy some of his goods, even if they do not require them, and will pay well. Slowly the sun of success will begin to shine upon him, he will start selling his goods at fair prices and will make a good profit. Then he will buy a small donkey for two or three pounds, and will load it with larger loads of vari-ous wares, leading it by its bridle from farm to farm. As the days pass he will go from strength to strength. After he succeeds in collecting sufficient money he will sell the donkey and acquire a pair of horses or mules and a two-wheeled cart. This he will load with various wares, obtained from the merchants on credit, and will travel further out in the countryside to trade with the farmers. He will barter his wares for goats, sheep, skins and ostrich feathers, and from a pedlar he will soon progress to an ostrich-feather buyer and finally become a storekeeper. Thus he will rise from rung to rung until he becomes a merchant or even a banker. I know some exceedingly wealthy men ... now living in Cape Town, Kimberley, Port Elizabeth, Johannesburg and in smaller towns, who are now regarded as honoured merchants, who arrived here penniless and destitute and became poor struggling pedlars, carrying their wares upon their shoulders. Thanks to their industry and business acumen they have met with great success and are now at the peak of their good fortune.

ND Hoffmann
Ha-Tsifirah, 1891

priority, promising security, independence and upward mobility. A small but highly visible minority rapidly achieved public eminence. Among them were mining magnates like Lionel Phillips and Barney Barnato, and civic notables like Hyman Liberman and Harry Graumann, mayors of Cape Town and Johannesburg respectively. In the latter city in particular, Jews displayed a distinctive confidence, rooted in their pioneering role in the city's creation. Unlike the older port cities, where Jews were latecomers, Jews in Johannesburg were integral to the evolution of the mining town.

This prominence did not always attract favourable notice. For some hostile observers, including JA Hobson of the *Manchester Guardian*, Jews were over-represented among the Randlords and disturbingly ubiquitous. 'The shop fronts and business houses are sufficient to convince one of the large presence of the chosen people. If any doubt remains, a walk outside the [Stock] Exchange ... will dispel it,' wrote Hobson. 'Though figures are so misleading, it is worthwhile to mention that the directory of Johannesburg shows sixty-eight Cohens against twenty-eight Jones and fifty-three Browns.' Hobson's hostile and selective vision was shared by others; by the late 1890s some even referred to Johannesburg as Jewburg.

Jews were also visible in the rural landscape.

Johannesburg in its infancy.

Commissioner Street, Johannesburg.

The Underworld

Early Johannesburg was afflicted with a range of 'social evils', including illicit liquor dealing and prostitution. The extent of the liquor trade in the mushrooming mining town was enormous and a cause of great concern. The Johannesburg Chamber of Mines, recognising the debilitating effects of liquor on its black labour force, claimed that relative to its population, Johannesburg had more licensed houses than any city in the world.

Initially 'foreigners' were singled out as the purveyors of this social evil, but it was not long before such veiled references gave way to specific accusations against Eastern European liquor dealers. A prominent Boer official highlighted the difficulty of 'getting' at the real owners of the liquor dens, arguing that 'the Polish Jews who look after them are the most blackguardly race of men in existence … These Polish Jews have not the slightest sense of decency or modesty in them, and a more depraved race never existed.'

The press followed suit. Eugene Marais's *Land en Volk* specifically identified Jewish canteen-keepers as the chief beneficiaries of the African liquor trade and articles in the *Transvaal Critic* regularly associated 'Peruvian Jews' with the liquor evil. Under enormous pressure from the anti-liquor lobby, Kruger's government prohibited the sale of liquor to blacks from January 1897. Faced with potential ruin, liquor merchants began trading illegally, exploiting unemployed and impoverished Jews in these operations.

The question of Jewish involvement in illicit liquor dealing assumed increasing prominence. 'These people,' reported the *Star*, 'are largely responsible for the sale of the vile decoctions whereby so many natives are driven to the verge of madness, and in which state they commit the hideous crimes daily reported in the columns of the various papers, and many others which are never recorded. Cheap brandy is purchased by the Peruvian in large quantities, and after going through the process known as "doctoring" (a process in which dirty water, cayenne pepper, tobacco and vitriol are freely used), is sold at 5s to 6s per bottle.' According to *Land en Volk*, a major source of illegal sales was the *kaffir eethuis* (African canteen), controlled by Jews.

By 1899 mining interests could no longer tolerate the impact of illicit alcohol on the black labour force and, in a series of sensationalist exposés, the *Transvaal Leader*, a mining-industry mouthpiece, definitively linked the Peruvian Jew with the liquor underworld. Glaring publicity followed the murder of a Mrs Appelbe for allegedly supplying information about the liquor gangs that had carved up the Witwatersrand into criminal fiefdoms. 'How long', ran an editorial in the *Transvaal Leader*, 'is the community to be ridden by these monsters, by these NATHANSONS, the KATZENS, the LEDIKERS and SCHLOSSBERGS and the rest of the off-scourings from a degraded European race whom they employ … There is blood, the blood of an innocent woman, upon the hands of the KANTOR syndicate of Fordsburg.' 'Low class Jews', the newspaper warned, were spoiling the name of 'clean minded and honourable Jews'.

Such accusations generated understandable anxiety among the respectable majority of Jews, and efforts were made by Rabbi JH Hertz and others to counter the hostile portrayals. But this negative labelling was difficult to refute and would survive for many years.

Besides illicit liquor dealings the 'Peruvian' Jew was also associated with the seamier side of Johannesburg's nightlife. It was well known, claimed the *Standard and Diggers' News*, owned by Emanuel Mendelssohn, a Jewish communal leader, that amongst Johannesburg's 'ladies of the night' was 'a large and thriving colony of Americanized Russian women … controlled by an association of macquereaus of pronounced Russian pedigree'. Undoubtedly, Russian Jews – many of them, like Joe Silver, possibly the notorious 'Jack the Ripper', schooled in the London and New York underworlds – made a notable impact on this dimension of the city's life, much to the chagrin of the respectable middle class.

After the Anglo-Boer War, Jewish communal notables, deeply concerned with restoring the public image of the community, joined with the imperial authorities in vetting the returning Jewish refugees to the Witwatersrand. This formed part of ongoing efforts to 'domesticate' and embourgeois the Eastern European newcomers and to eradicate deviant behaviour.

Joe Silver, notorious underworld figure in Johannesburg, Cape Town and Bloemfontein.

The Peruvian

In early Johannesburg the Litvak newcomers formed a conspicuous segment of the mining city's lumpenproletariat. Residing mainly within a three-mile radius of the Market Square, their foreign appearance drew hostile attention. They soon acquired the pejorative label 'Peruvian', a term of obscure origin.

Some argue that it is an acronym for Polish and Russian Union, a Jewish club established in Kimberley in its pioneering days. Others, muddling their geography, argue that the term refers to those immigrants who had first lived in the Argentine (not Peru) under Baron de Hirsch's settlement scheme before coming to South Africa. Another theory is that the term is derived from '*Peruvia*', a mistaken reference to the ancient Latin term for Poland. Yet another theory connects 'Peruvian' with the Yiddish *pruven*, meaning 'trier', a term that was associated with Jewish immigrants struggling to make good.

The first known 'description' of the Peruvian appeared in the *Johannesburg Times* in April 1896:

> To the ordinary members of the public he presents the apparition of a slovenly, unkempt and generally unwashed edition, in various numbers, of the wandering Jew. As a sort of commercial shield, he carries a basket of eggs on his right arm, while holding his money tightly clenched in his sinister hand. He wears no socks. He is a pariah among his own people and among the gentiles. He is only recognized, *en passant,* by the educated part of the Jewish population as a necessary evil ... in tatterdemalion garments, until he has made his pile. Then he transforms like the butterfly; he eschews his garments of many fluttering rags; he dons the everyday, but more romantic, if less dirty raiment of the civilized populace ...

The term 'Peruvian' was originally widely used in South Africa by Jew and non-Jew alike. This distinctively South African term endured among Jews even after the social type had disappeared, being used as a term of opprobrium for uncouth and vulgar fellow Jews.

'Awful Hovels: Peruvian Uncleanliness'

The *Star*, 10 July 1897

Overcrowding, poor sanitation and the associated threat of epidemic disease generated considerable public anxiety in turn-of-the-century Cape Town and Johannesburg. Immigrant Jews – already the targets of xenophobic anti-alienism – were among those identified as likely threats to public health. Hostile reports focused on their living and business habits, especially the preparation of food for sale.

In July 1897 the *Star* reported:

There is an evil in Johannesburg ... which is daily assuming a graver aspect, and one which every citizen among us should aid in representing to the responsible authorities, with a view to its eradication, or at any rate amelioration. There is in our midst a community of some four or five thousand 'Peruvians'. They execrate law and order ... and as for cleanliness, well, that is an unknown quantity among them. The sooner they are sent out of the town the better for all concerned. Failing this, or some other drastic measure being taken, and that soon, the town may be visited with an epidemic which will cost many valuable lives ...

... Hop and ginger beer and fruit vendors etc. herd together in hovels which are sinks of abomination. Here the delectable drinks are manufactured in vessels which are filthy ... Their morning ablutions (when they do indulge) consist of taking a tin pannikin of water outside their hovels, their utilizing their mouths as a means of partially warming the water and then as a means of conveying a continuous stream on their heads. A rub on the face finishes the process ...

In Cape Town in the same year, Wynberg's district surgeon, Dr H Claude Wright, was equally condemnatory of the living conditions of the Jewish immigrants 'who overcrowd and cohabit promiscuously. Amongst them filth and vermin abound, and they have great objection to ventilation, the crevices all being wedged up with rags in many of their rooms. Some of these people are worse than the natives in these matters.'

The influx of Jewish refugees during the Anglo-Boer War only made matters worse. In his *Public Health Report for 1901* Wright stated that 'their houses are filthy in the extreme' and that the children of '80 per cent of that persuasion bathed once a month'. He recommended a 'very rigid supervision' of the dairy products they sold. But only three years later Wright discerned a distinct improvement in the condition of the immigrants, reporting that 'Like Jeshurus of old, they have "waxed fat and kicked", certainly kicked off the trammels of serfdom. I also think they have kicked off the vermin and filth in which they formally lived ...'

Further evidence of the rapid amelioration in the immigrant condition was the declining infant mortality rates among Jews in Cape Town in the years that followed. By 1911 these approximated those of the white population at large, whereas previously they had been even worse than those of Cape Town's impoverished black population.

They were significant agents of the commercial revolution that transformed the South African countryside in the late nineteenth and early twentieth centuries. As they had done for centuries in Eastern Europe, Jews acted as informed and energetic intermediaries between the new markets of the town and the producers, both black and white. Jewish storekeepers and *smouse* bought wool, maize and skins from Boer landowners and from black sharecroppers alike, and then forwarded these to urban markets and wholesalers. In turn, the Jewish country store met the growing needs of these emergent rural consumers.

In addition to their intermediary role between markets and suppliers, Jews also acted on

From The Owl, *13 December 1903*

Joseph & Co., Jansenville.

Hammerschlag store, Kenhardt, 1912.

occasion as primary producers. This is vividly illustrated in the southern Cape town of Oudtshoorn, known to Jews at the time as the 'Jerusalem of Africa' because of its vibrant Jewish life. Here, during the ostrich-feather boom in the decades before the First World War, Jews not only bought and sold feathers but also ran large flocks. The most successful of them, Max Rose, came from Shavli. He had started as a *smous* and eventually became one of the Ostrich Barons. Reminiscent of the Mosenthals in the Eastern Cape, the De Passes on the West Coast and the diamond dealers of Kimberley, Jewish feather merchants helped to connect a local industry to an international market.

Whether trading in feathers in the southern Cape, skins and maize on the Highveld or storekeeping in Cape Town or Johannesburg, Litvak immigrants shared much in common as newcomers striving to integrate into an unfamiliar southern African world. Yet for all this shared social and economic experience, they operated within very different polities. Prior to the turn of the century South Africa was only a geographical expression. If not for broader political developments, a single and unified South African Jewish community might never have emerged. Johannesburg and Cape Town might have remained as far apart as *fin de siècle* Vienna and Warsaw.

OSTRICH FARMING IN SOUTH AFRICA.

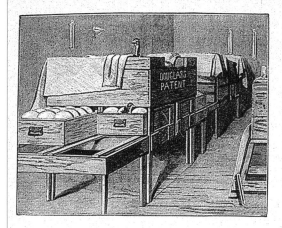

THE INCUBATING ROOM.

A BIRD SITTING.

HELPING OUT A WEAK ONE.

COOLIE WITH YOUNG BIRDS.

FINDING A NEST.

THE FEATHER ROOM.

Interior of St John's Street Synagogue, Oudtshoorn, built by Jews from Kelm. The ark was modelled on that of the main synagogue in their old home town.

Max Rose, Oudtshoorn ostrich baron.

BUILDING A SOUTH AFRICAN COMMUNITY

The British conquest of the Boer Republics in the Anglo-Boer War (1899-1902) effectively prepared the ground for a united South Africa. The subjugated Transvaal and Orange Free State joined the coastal colonies of the Cape and Natal under British rule. In the wake of this great watershed event, all South Africans, including Jews, would share a common destiny.

Prior to the war, Jews in Paul Kruger's South African Republic – unlike their co-religionists under British sovereignty – had faced a range of religious disabilities. The constitution of the Republic bound the Dutch Reformed Church inextricably to the state. Non-Protestants were denied the franchise and debarred from public office. Jewish and Catholic children were effectively excluded from government schools. This policy was not motivated by antisemitic intent but arose out of the Boers' desire to keep control of their country and to guarantee its Calvinist character. The Orange Free State, home to far fewer Jews than the Transvaal, separated church and state though still privileging the Dutch Reformed Church.

By contrast, Jews had enjoyed full rights and substantial participation in public life in the Cape and Natal. The divergent early careers of two Jewish contemporaries illustrate the chasm between the coastal and inland political cultures in so far as Jews were concerned. Both Morris Alexander and Joseph Hertz were born in central Europe and left for South Africa and the United States respectively as young children. Alexander was a star pupil at the prestigious South African College School, a government institution in Cape Town, and graduated from the University of the Cape of Good Hope in 1897 before proceeding to Cambridge to study law. While Alexander fully enjoyed the benefits of a liberal British ethos, albeit racially compromised, the young American-educated Rabbi Hertz, appointed in 1898 to the Witwatersrand Old Hebrew Congregation, fought angrily for the removal of humiliating religious restrictions, though he later acknowledged that these had had little practical impact. Expelled from the Republic soon after the outbreak of the war, Hertz returned after the British had conquered the Transvaal and Free State.

The subjugation of the Republics ended the nascent division of Jews in South Africa and placed them all, south and north, on a common trajectory. Without the war, the coastal and inland communities might have evolved as distinctively as did Canadian and American Jewry, separated by their respective imperial and republican allegiances and experiences, though united by a common Jewish tradition.

The post-war amalgamation of South African Jewry had been foreshadowed in the initiative to establish a South African Zionist Federation (SAZF) in Johannesburg in 1898, a year after the historic first Zionist Congress in Basel, Switzerland. As in *der heim* (the Old Country), most Lithuanian Jews in South Africa (unlike some of their local Anglo-Jewish co-religionists) enthusiastically supported Herzl's vision of a Jewish national renaissance.

Besides engaging with the international Zionist project, the

The Cape Town Jewish Boys and Girls Guild (with Reverend Alfred Bender (rear, third from the right) and the young Morris Alexander (rear, second from the right).

Kruger's Jew

In 1898 President Kruger allowed one of his burghers, Sammy Marks, the extraordinary privilege of private use of the state mint for a day. Marks struck 215 golden 'tickeys' as keepsakes for his relatives and friends, including the president. This remarkable relationship had begun in 1881, 13 years after the young Marks had come to South Africa from Russia via England.

Marks was born in 1844 in Neustadt Sugind, a *shtetl* in Lithuania. The son of a poor itinerant tailor, his education was limited to *cheder*. Before turning 18, he left home for England, possibly to avoid conscription. In Sheffield, Marks turned to peddling. Between trips he lodged with Tobias Guttmann, a cutler who became his mentor. Guttmann suggested he try his luck in South Africa and offered to pay his passage. Prior to departure he presented his young friend with a large case of knives. 'This was my capital,' Marks later recalled.

Marks sailed for Cape Town in 1868 where he hawked Guttmann's knives. He was joined shortly afterwards by a distant cousin, Isaac Lewis, who came from the same *shtetl*. Together they rapidly prospered as pedlars. In 1871 they joined the diamond rush to Kimberley and here they began diamond dealing and investing in claims. Within a decade, Lewis and Marks was considered by the Standard Bank to be 'about the most wealthy firm on the Fields'.

Beyond Kimberley Marks invested in a coalfield on the banks of the Vaal River, the beginnings of the Highveld coal-mining industry. In 1881 Marks visited Pretoria where he met Paul Kruger and discussed with him the possibility of investment in the infant republic. Kruger promised Marks government support for his ventures. The first of these was a distillery outside Pretoria, the first factory in the Transvaal. Marks later established glass and jam factories as well as a brick works.

Nearly all of Marks's businesses depended on government favour. To ensure this he wooed the Boer leaders assiduously with 'soft' loans and gifts large and small.

Marks paid special attention to the president whose goodwill was crucial. Most importantly he helped to secure a property deal that made the president a wealthy man. He also gave Pretoria a large sum for the erection of a statue of Kruger.

Marks was a frequent and very welcome visitor to the president's home. Kruger clearly enjoyed Marks's company – the lively argument, sometimes bordering on the insolent; the crossfire of argument-clinching illustrations from their favourite text, the Bible; and the banter about Marks's supposed religious wrongheadedness:

'Sam, there is one thing I would very much like to do before I die.'

'What is that, President?'

'I would like to make a Christian of you.'

'No, President ... if you could do that you would have to banish me from the country, for a converted Jew is no good.'

Kruger was not always forbearing with Marks. At the height of the political crisis in 1899, Marks 'went down to see the Old Man ... and he refused to discuss anything but politics. When I touched upon business he told me that was all I cared for. I retorted that business was all I could talk about seeing that I was debarred by the laws of the land from taking part in politics. At this he nearly jumped at my throat and said that I ought to know that Jewish disabilities would be removed.'

Besides his personal services for Kruger and other Boer notables, Marks also performed services for the state. Here he emulated both the *Hofjuden* or Court Jews of earlier centuries and Otto von Bismarck's '*Privatjude*', Gerson Bleichröder. Marks served as a broker between the financially inept government and his banker friends in raising state loans. On occasion he even served as an unofficial diplomatic agent for the Boer state.

For all his intimacy with Kruger and the Boer elite, Marks was very much part of the English community who dominated Transvaal commercial life. He married

Sammy Marks, the 'uncrowned king of the Transvaal', and his father who remained in Eastern Europe.

an English Jew, Bertha Guttmann, daughter of his old mentor in Sheffield. His lifestyle at Zwartkoppies, his country estate outside Pretoria, was modelled on the English landed classes whom he admired, and his children were sent to public school in England where he hoped that they would be made over into English gentlemen.

Marks regarded the coming of the Anglo-Boer War as an unmitigated disaster. During the conflict he successfully performed a balancing act between Boer and Brit. Before the occupation of Pretoria he did his duty as a loyal burgher. Once the British arrived, he took the oath of neutrality and served them just as faithfully, yet at the same time kept the friendship of *bittereinder* leaders still in the field. When the Boer generals negotiated peace in 1902, they sent for Marks and discussed with him their course of action. The peace conference at Vereeniging was held on Marks's property where he played an important auxiliary role in strengthening the hands of those in favour of making peace.

After the war Marks was a strong supporter of Milnerism, yet with the resurgence of Afrikanerdom, shifted his support to Louis Botha's party. His reward was to be appointed as a senator in the first Union Parliament and state support in establishing South Africa's first steelworks, an ambition rooted in his early years in Sheffield. Marks died in 1920 at the age of 76.

A Jewish War?

Writing in 1900, JA Hobson, the radical journalist and future theorist of imperialism, made his famous accusation that the Anglo-Boer War was in large part Jewish in origin. Drawing on his experiences as a recent visitor to South Africa, Hobson charged that behind the war's patriotic façade lurked a conspiracy of mining capitalists, mainly Jewish. These, he asserted, sought the overthrow of the Boer republic and its replacement by an administration more supportive of their needs, particularly for a supply of cheap and docile black labour. Hobson's evidence for the Jewish character of this conspiracy was what he took to be the prevalence of Jewish names among the Randlords.

Hobson's views were widely shared in British pro-Boer circles. As the Labour MP, John Burns, proclaimed, 'the British Army, which used to be for all good causes the Sir Galahad of History, has become in Africa the janissary of the Jews … Wherever we examine there is the financial Jew operating, directing, inspiring the agencies that have led to this war.' 'Jewish financiers', and their coded equivalents, 'cosmopolitan capitalists', were stock villains in the Liberal pro-Boer pamphlet campaign against the war.

These oft-repeated charges, which drew on contemporary antisemitic fantasies of the operation in the world of an insidious and overweening Jewish power, were perceived as defamatory by the established Jewish community of Britain and its mouthpiece, the *Jewish Chronicle*. The *Chronicle* rejected the notion of a Jewish capitalist conspiracy manipulating the course of events in South Africa: '… the story of the Transvaal Jews setting the match to the Transvaal powder magazine is an idle and malicious fiction.' It held up to ridicule Hobson's evidence for such a conspiracy, mocking his claim, based on his cataloguing of their Jewish-sounding names, that the Randlords were predominantly Jewish:

> We have always contended that though many of the capitalists of the Rand may, as the joke has it, 'speak in broken accents', it did not follow that they were therefore Jews … many of the capitalists have nothing but a German cognomen to justify the ascription to them of Jewish blood; whilst several of the German financiers who were Jews, have long ago left their people for their people's good, and yielded their immortal souls unto the care of the Roman-Catholic Church.

Furthermore, while the Randlords were not necessarily Jewish, the Jewish Randlords were not necessarily anti-Kruger: '… some of the wealthiest Jewish capitalists like Lewis and Marks … are among Kruger's most determined friends.' Contrary to Hobson's view, noted the *Chronicle*, 'many Jews, chiefly of Continental origin, were so far from soliciting the interference of England that they rallied to President Kruger'.

The *Chronicle* had a surer sense of the diluted Jewishness of the Randlords than Hobson, and of the divisions within their ranks. The complex origins of the Anglo-Boer War cannot be reduced to a capitalist conspiracy, Jewish or otherwise.

Zionist leaders in the Transvaal, headed by Samuel Goldreich, a Prussian-born but English-educated property developer, sought a domestic leadership role. This included representing the Jewish community to the imperial authorities on crucial issues such as the post-war repatriation of refugee Jews to the Transvaal and Jewish immigration, which was increasingly becoming the focus of hostile attention. In this regard the leaders wished to allay imperial concerns about the influx of 'undesirable' Eastern European Jews, stigmatised as 'Peruvians'.

This broader role was challenged by Rabbi Hertz and Max Langermann, an anglicised German Jew. Both had been prominent before the war in Uitlander agitation against Kruger's

Lionel Phillips, Witwatersrand Randlord.

Rabbi Joseph Hertz, vociferous critic of discrimination against Jews in Kruger's republic.

regime. (Langermann had been sentenced to five months' imprisonment for his role in the Jameson Raid, the attempt to overthrow Kruger's republic in the mid-nineties.) Both Hertz and Langermann now advocated the creation of a British-style Jewish representative body, and in 1903 they founded the Jewish Board of Deputies for the Transvaal and Natal that was modelled on its English equivalent.

At the same time, in Cape Town, Morris Alexander and David Goldblatt, a fiery Polish Jewish socialist, challenged the established leadership of Cape Jewry, built around the Anglo-Jewish Cape Town Hebrew Congregation and guided by the urbane, Cambridge-educated Reverend Alfred Philipp Bender. Like their northern counterparts, the 'young Turks' at the Cape were concerned about the pressing issue of Jewish immigration and the growing calls to exclude Eastern European 'undesirables', who for some hostile critics were not quite 'white'.

Matters had reached a crisis point with the passing of the

Jews and the Anglo-Boer War

The outbreak of the Anglo-Boer War in October 1899 precipitated a wholesale exodus, in overcrowded open railway trucks, of the urban Jewish population of the Highveld to the coast, where most would remain till the end of the war in 1902. Exile, uncomfortable and impoverishing for many, was far more prolonged than originally expected; most of the refugees, like the complacent British generals themselves, had anticipated a rapid British victory, and had confidently believed that they would be home on the Highveld by *Chanukah* (Festival of Lights). While most remained in the Cape Colony, particularly in Cape Town, some of the Russian Jewish refugees returned to Britain or to Russia. Those who stayed behind struggled to find employment; many were unemployed for the duration of the war and lived off the charity of others.

Despite the mass exodus, Jewish communal life in the urban centres of the interior continued to function throughout the war but at a much reduced pace. The religious and service institutions remained substantially intact, albeit operated by skeleton staffs. Jewish life in the countryside suffered more substantial damage. Following the British occupation of the Boer republics in 1900, most rural Jews were allowed to remain at their stores after they had taken an oath of neutrality. But once the Boers turned to guerrilla warfare Jews were caught in the middle. Willingly in some cases, unwillingly in others, Jewish storekeepers played an important role in sustaining and encouraging the guerrilla struggle in its initial stages. Their stores effectively became supply depots for the commandos who regularly turned up and took what they needed: boots, clothing, food and fodder for their horses. Faced by these armed men, the hapless storekeepers had little choice.

The Jewish storekeepers were a vital part of an informal economy that sprang up during the guerrilla phase of the war, buying produce from farms whose owners were on commando. This underground economy helped to keep the Boers in the field. Jewish storekeepers became objects of suspicion and, in an atmosphere of paranoia and of denunciation, many fell victim to accusations,

Local Jewish volunteers serving in a colonial Town Guard unit in the Anglo-Boer War.

often malicious, of disloyalty. There were arrests, often repeated, on the basis of reports from informers.

Together with Boer families and black peasants, Jewish storekeepers became the victims of the brutal land clearances conducted by the British forces to deny the commandos any traction in the countryside. Alongside the farm-burning, there was the burning and dynamiting of the elaborate honeycomb of hotels, homes and stores that Jews had established throughout the rural Transvaal and Free State during the 1880s and 1890s. Unlike their Boer and black neighbours Jews, as foreign subjects, were not herded into the concentration camps created by the British throughout the interior of South Africa. Instead, Jews forced off the land made their way

Boer sympathisers, Clara and Sophie Leviseur, visit Alfred Baumann, camp doctor at the Bloemfontein concentration camp.
Dr Baumann, brother of Sophie, fell foul of the camp authorities for excessive prescription of champagne to his patients as a 'stimulant'.

either into the towns of the Free State and Transvaal, or went off to the coast.

The Anglo-Boer War placed few strains on Jewish loyalty. Very little was demanded of Jews during the war and it was possible to sit it out without attracting unfavourable public attention. Neutrality was an acceptable course of action and one the majority of the recently arrived chose. But a not insignificant minority actively supported the Imperial cause. Many joined the town guards, the volunteer forces, raised in mid-war to repel possible Boer attacks on the towns of the Cape Colony. (These never came.) A smaller number supported the republican cause, albeit for varying lengths of time. A handful of Jews rode with the commandos till the 'bitter end'. These included

the 16-year-old Joseph 'Jakkals' Segall, who had arrived in the Orange Free State from Russia a year before the war, and served courageously alongside his friend Wolf Jacobson for the duration.

Other Jews remained loyal only as long as the republican writ ran. The Transvaal mining magnate Sammy Marks was a loyal burgher until Lord Roberts, the conqueror of the Transvaal, arrived at his doorstep, whereupon he, like many non-Jewish Transvalers, willingly accepted the new order. By contrast, the anglicised Baumann-Leviseur clan of Bloemfontein, Free State-born German Jews, clung to their republican loyalties at some personal risk, long after the republican cause had effectively collapsed.

Cape Immigration Restriction Act of 1902 which temporarily obstructed the entry of Yiddish-speaking immigrants into the colony. Differences in approach to dealing with this crisis – Bender's traditional informal, *shtadlan* (intercessor) approach as opposed to Alexander and Goldblatt's formal, institutional inclinations – ultimately led to the upstarts founding the Jewish Board of Deputies for the Cape Colony in 1904, again mimicking the English model.

Both the Transvaal and Natal, and the Cape Boards diligently engaged with the local colonial administrations, playing important roles in the naturalisation of newcomers, in combating antisemitism and in generally safeguarding the interests of Jews. Contact was maintained between the two boards, mirroring the growing broader intercolonial cooperation which finally led to the unification of the four colonies in 1910, a development enthusiastically welcomed by South African Jews.

The institutional separation of Jewish north and south ended soon after the creation of the Union of South Africa. Follow-

ABOVE: *Samuel Goldreich, Zionist leader in early Johannesburg.*

LEFT: *Max Langermann, founder with Rabbi Hertz of the Jewish Board of Deputies for the Transvaal and Natal in 1903.*

OPPOSITE

ABOVE: *David Goldblatt, prominent opponent of the Anglo-Jewish establishment in Cape Town.*

BELOW: *The Reverend Bender performing the opening ceremony of the Cape Jewish Orphanage.*

ing the logic of political union, the two boards merged in 1912 to form the South African Jewish Board of Deputies (hereafter the Board). The time was 'ripe', proclaimed Wolf Ehrlich, who chaired the founding convention in Bloemfontein, 'for a movement to consolidate the forces of Judaism in South Africa, and to create a representative body which can at all times speak with authority…'

The men of Bloemfontein (women were conspicuously absent) reflected the evolution of the community since the start of the Eastern European influx. The executive of the Board, representing all four provinces, were relatively youthful with many in their thirties. All were active in Jewish communal life and some prominent in civic affairs, including the mayoralties of large cities. Most were prominent merchants, some were lawyers, and there was a solitary cleric, the young and gifted Rabbi Moshe Chayim

Hoggenheimer: the making of a myth

The year after the Anglo-Boer War saw the emergence of a popular cartoon character, Hoggenheimer, the quintessential Jewish parvenu. Although DC Boonzaier, the celebrated South African cartoonist, was responsible for this gross representation, Hoggenheimer was not his creation. This distinction belongs to the English playwright, Owen Hall, who created the avuncular millionaire, Max Hoggenheimer, in his musical comedy *The Girl from Kays*. This story of an alluring show dancer who enthralled a South African plutocrat opened at London's Apollo Theatre in 1902, playing for 432 performances before being brought to South Africa.

The loud-mouthed Hoggenheimer became an instant favourite with South African theatre-goers. The English comedian WW Walton delighted audiences with his portrayal of the wealthy Jewish financier of Park Lane. Ten days after *The Girl from Kays* opened at the Good Hope Theatre in Cape Town, Boonzaier published his first Hoggenheimer cartoon in the *South African News*. Subsequently, Hoggenheimer became a regular character in Boonzaier's cartoons. Over the years, Hoggenheimer evolved from generic capitalist to vulgar Semitic caricature, following in the tradition of cartoons that appeared in Europe toward the end of the nineteenth century. Boonzaier himself denied the 'Hebraic' nature of his cartoon creation.

Hoggenheimer manifestly struck a responsive chord. This explains the delight expressed by audiences at Walton's portrayal of the Park Lane millionaire and the enduring popularity of Boonzaier's Hoggenheimer cartoons. The ostensible power of the Randlords and the fallacious association of the Anglo-Boer War with Jewish financiers ensured Hoggenheimer's transition from stage character to popular culture. It is no wonder that, within two years, he became in the words of the Cape politician, John X Merriman, 'a classical character' – one who would endure in South African iconography for much of the twentieth century.

The coming of the scum

Reporting on the workings of the Immigration Act of 1902, Dr AJ Gregory, the Medical Officer of Health for the Cape Colony, pilloried the Jewish newcomers as '... ill-provided, indifferently educated, unable to speak or understand any language but Yiddish, of inferior physique, often dirty in their habits, persons and clothing and most unreliable in their statements.' *The Owl*, a Cape Town weekly, was even more censorious. Anyone, it commented, working in the vicinity of the docks would realise the undesirability of the aliens: 'They are mainly composed of the exiles from Russia, Poland and Germany, the Semitic scum of these countries.'

OPPOSITE

The Grand Parade, Cape Town. Jewish traders on the Parade attracted hostile comment at the turn of the century, an era of heightened anti-alienism.

Saturday by Saturday the "Grand" – Heaven save the word – Parade gets worse. The rotten trash that is put upon the sales there would be a disgrace to Petticoat Lane. Not only this, but the trade is now largely carried out by Polish Jews, who import – no doubt from other Polish Jews in London – the commonest off-scourings of Houndsditch goods. Then these greasy frowzy gentry stand around and sum up things until whoever purchases is sure to be heartlessly swindled....

The fact is Cape Town at the present time is full of those Polish Jew hawkers, who live in dirtier style than Kafirs [sic], and existing on about half a crown a week each, rob the tradesman of his due. They don't pay rent, rates or taxes, yet they are allowed to sell goods just the same as if they kept a store. Respectable Europeans should order these people from their doors. That is the only way to put them down. Let these people do manual work.

The Owl, 23 January 1897.

THE COMING OF THE SCUM

H.Egersdorfer O.C.

Dr. Gregory : "Twenty three per cent of immigrants into the Cape were aliens."
The Owl — "At this rate you'd better print me in Yiddish."

Mirvish of Cape Town. With few exceptions, they were foreign born (mainly in England and Germany) but had spent most of their lives in South Africa, their careers exemplifying immigrant initiative and success. The German-born Wolf Ehrlich, who was elected the first president of the Board, was a prominent merchant and one-time mayor of Bloemfontein. His fellow German Max Langermann, who was elected as vice-president, was a wealthy property developer in Johannesburg, while the Liverpudlian William Sagar was an auctioneer and first Jewish mayor of Kimberley and the 'Brummie' Felix Hollander, a merchant, a freemason (like many others on the Board) and the mayor of Durban. Alongside the businessmen were the lawyers, Morris Alexander and Manfred Nathan, the Cape-born and Johannesburg-based barrister and legal scholar, and the Yiddish journalist and immigrant counsellor Bension Hersch, who

was in his late twenties when elected to the executive.

The executive of the Board represented the public face of South African Jewry in the new Union: anglicised, respectably bourgeois, upwardly mobile, comfortably integrated into the English-dominated cities, and far removed from the world of the Peruvian, a continuing source of shame and embarrassment for the aspirant middle class.

This emergent bourgeoisie – some born in Eastern Europe and anglicised during a sojourn in England – had rapidly entered into and absorbed the standards and values of colonial Edwardian society. Hyman Liberman, mayor of Cape Town from 1904 to 1907, personified this process. Despite a pronounced Polish-Yiddish accent, he enjoyed the genteel lifestyle of his affluent co-religionists in the orderly suburbs of the upper city.

In these pleasant environs much attention was

Felix Hollander.   *William Sagar.*   *Franz Ginsberg.*

ABOVE: *Hyman Liberman.*
OPPOSITE ABOVE: *Hyman Liberman's funeral cortege.*
OPPOSITE BELOW: *Harry Graumann, mayor of Johannesburg, leads a procession on the visit of the Duke and Duchess of Connaught in 1910.*

Mayors and *Machers*

In no country in the world is there a greater cosmopolitan spirit and less religious prejudice. The Jews receive the fullest recognition not only from the government, but from every public body on every possible occasion … I need only mention the remarkable fact that, at the present moment, no fewer than four Jews are mayors of leading South African towns: Mr. H. Liberman, thrice Mayor of Cape Town; Mr. W. Sagar, Mayor of Kimberley; Mr. W. Ehrlich, Mayor of Bloemfontein; … and Mr. F. Ginsberg, Mayor of King William's Town.

Rev AP Bender, interviewed in the
London Jewish Chronicle of 10 May 1907.

Had Reverend Bender been interviewed a few years later he could have added Harry Graumann who, in 1909, became the first Jewish mayor of Johannesburg and Felix Hollander, elected the first Jewish mayor of Durban in 1910. This Jewish civic prominence is striking. At this very time the firebrand Karl Lueger was mayor of Vienna, elected on an antisemitic platform, while New York would have to wait till 1973 before electing its first Jewish mayor.

All these Jewish mayors had immigrated to South Africa as young men. Hollander, Graumann and William Sagar were English-born, Franz (Frank) Ginsberg and

Wolf Ehrlich, German-born, while Hyman Liberman was born in Poland but had spent most of his youth in England. All were successful and respected businessmen and all, barring Graumann and Ginsberg, were prominent in Jewish communal life. Ehrlich was president of the Bloemfontein Hebrew Congregation for 21 years, Sagar of the Griqualand West Hebrew Congregation for 20, Hollander of the Durban Hebrew Congregation for 18 and Liberman warden of the Cape Town Hebrew Congregation for 20 years and a sometime president. Though not as engaged, Graumann was elected president of the Johannesburg Zionist Association in 1905, and even Ginsberg lobbied for Jewish causes as a member of the Cape parliament. Four of the six were to achieve national recognition: Ehrlich, Ginsberg and

Hollander were appointed to the Union Senate, and Graumann was elected to parliament.

Their success in civic politics cannot be attributed simply to ethnic mobilisation and a municipal franchise based on property, though these might have played some part. It also demonstrated a high level of acceptance and respect on the part of the wider society, at least for members of the Anglo-German Jewish elite. At the heart of this lay shared interests and values, including empire loyalism and racial prejudice. Thus, in justifying his decision to exclude the Indian community of Durban from the celebrations for the coronation of King George V, Felix Hollander insisted sanctimoniously that it would 'have the approval and support of the entire white community of the town'.

When Hyman Liberman's funeral cortege wound its way from his home in the Gardens through the streets of Cape Town in June 1923, it was probably one of the longest ever seen in the city. Its passage was watched by large crowds that had gathered to pay homage to a much respected civic leader. The success of Liberman and his fellow notables – immersed simultaneously in Jewish and civic affairs – was ample proof that public recognition of Jews in South Africa did not require 'radical assimilation' as its price.

paid to style and good taste: 'Our hostess,' wrote a social column-
ist in the *South African Jewish Chronicle*, 'wore a very pretty white
matinée jacket tastefully trimmed with pale blue ribbon and a
white accordion-pleated skirt'. Elite Jews in Johannesburg similarly shared in the pleasures of polite society. The well-educated
– some at the Inns of Court in London – were clubmen, habitués
of the Athenaeum, the Rand Club, the New Club and Johannesburg's oddly named Pretoria Club.

Their wives and daughters found new opportunities for self-
expression and began to move beyond the domestic sphere. For
upper-middle-class Jewish women in the larger cities, this was a
new age in which the still powerful constraints imposed upon
them by the Victorian ideal of the 'perfect lady' were slowly
yielding ground to the greater latitude associated with the *fin de
siècle* notion of the 'new woman'. They were 'domestic feminists',

*Children of the South African Jewish
Orphanage, Johannesburg, with
committee members and staff.*

*Committee of the Jewish Ladies'
Communal League, Johannesburg.*

*Helen Ehrlich, one of the founders of
the Women's Enfranchisement League
of the Orange River Colony.*

women who did not necessarily share the views of the militant feminists and suffragists of their time – in fact, often roundly condemned these – but who in their daily lives increasingly practised a tacit feminism of a cautious sort. While domesticity and the household were still emphasised, it became more acceptable for a 'lady' to move beyond the hearth and enter public life, albeit on a limited and 'feminine' basis.

In Johannesburg 'domestic feminists' enlisted in the Jewish Ladies' Communal League, an organisation founded after the Anglo-Boer War to encourage women to play a more active part in Jewish communal life. The League's chief concern was the establishment and management of the first Jewish orphanage in South Africa, later known as the Arcadia Jewish Children's Home. A few women even moved beyond the safe confines of Jewish communal life. In Bloemfontein, Helen Ehrlich, wife of the founding president of the Board, and her sister Sophie Leviseur and their daughters were among the founders of the Women's Enfranchisement League of the Orange River Colony which held its first meeting in the Ehrlich's home in Elizabeth Street in 1909. Sophie went on to chair this provincial organisation, and later served as a vice president of the national Women's Enfranchisement Association, until white women were granted the vote in 1930.

Morris Alexander.

Ruth Schechter.

Ruth Schechter: A Radical Departure

By the early years of the twentieth century Jewish women in South Africa were moving beyond the confines of home but were still bound by the constraints of convention. Occasionally there were radical departures. The most striking instance of this is Ruth Schechter, especially since she came from, and married into, an intensely Jewish home.

Ruth Schechter was the daughter of Solomon Schechter, the great Cambridge scholar of the Cairo Genizah and luminary of the Jewish Theological Seminary in New York who is considered a patriarch of Conservative Judaism. She was 12 when she first met Morris 'Alec' Alexander, then a young law student at Cambridge and frequent guest at her parents' home. The friendship would blossom into a long-range romance after his return to South Africa and her relocation to America. In 1907 Morris travelled to New York to marry the 19-year-old Ruth who returned with him to Cape Town where she settled into the safe and conventional role of the wife of a Jewish communal no-

table, prominent lawyer and politician, and mother of three children.

Rather than remaining within predictable and narrow domestic bounds, Ruth broke out of these and energetically pursued a range of cultural and social interests. Drawing on the intellectual richness of her upbringing, she established a local reputation as a music and literary critic. Her friendships transcended the Jewish middle classes. She became an intimate of the much older Olive Schreiner, the celebrated South African author, who once declared the young Ruth 'the brightest person she knew in South Africa'. Under Schreiner's influence, Schechter campaigned for women's suffrage and identified with progressive causes. Her independence of mind and spirit drew her to some of Cape Town's liveliest intellectuals, including Benjamin Farrington, an ardent Irish Republican and classicist at the University of Cape Town. Defying convention, she divorced Alexander and married Farrington.

Sophie Leviseur and her daughters, campaigners for women's enfranchisement.

Manifestly, the public image projected by these elite Jews, both male and female, only partly reflected the contemporary realities of South African Jewry. For the vast majority of the 46 919 Jews recorded in the first census of the new Union that was conducted in 1911, the year before the creation of the Board, the exclusive club and the ornate drawing room were remote and unimaginable. Most Jews lived modest lives, with many merely eking out a livelihood.

The Jewish population had grown substantially since the Anglo-Boer War. By 1911 it had increased by 23 per cent over the 38 096 Jews recorded in the 1904 censuses of the four colonies. It now comprised 3.68 per cent of the white population and 0.79 per cent of the total population. The proportion of women in the Jewish population was also steadily increasing, growing from 32 per cent in 1904 to 41 per cent in 1911. Most of the new arrivals, who were overwhelmingly Litvaks, were bound for the Witwatersrand where the Jewish population had grown dramatically by 67 per cent; the Cape by contrast had shrunk by 14 per cent as the wartime refugees had returned to the north.

The 1911 census also revealed that there were 44 Jewish 'places

The new Gardens Synagogue, Cape Town, opened in 1905.

of worship' scattered throughout the country of which 21 were in the Cape Province, 17 in the Transvaal, 4 in the Orange Free State and 2 in Natal. These synagogues varied greatly in style, reflecting more accurately than the Board's executive the class and cultural divisions within the community. The elite built edifices, mirroring their aspirations. The synagogue was less a place of regular worship and study than a symbol of the community's social ambitions. Built on an equivalent scale to any Christian place of worship, and with as much care for outward appear-

The Great Synagogue, Wolmarans Street, Johannesburg, modelled on the Santa Sophia Church in Istanbul.

ance, it represented a westernised Jewish community's search for social acceptance in a gentile world. The synagogue was built with half an eye to the community at large; it was a physical demonstration of the solidity and respectability of the Jewish community.

The best examples of the 'edifice complex' in this great age of South African synagogue building were the Byzantine-style Kimberley Synagogue, built in 1902 in Memorial Road and celebrating Jewish sacrifice and imperial patriotism during the Boer War; the grand, Moorish-style Gardens Synagogue designed by John Parker, a leading Cape Town architect, and opened in 1905 by the Governor of the Cape Colony, Sir Walter Hely-Hutchinson; and the Byzantine-style Great Synagogue in Wolmarans Street, Johannesburg, which was built the year after the Board was founded and which was modelled on the Santa Sophia Church in Istanbul. Worship was in the Ashkenazi Anglo-Jewish mode: at Cape Town's Gardens Synagogue, for example, congregants followed the service through the Singer daily prayer book with its English translations opposite the Hebrew text; prayers were recited for the Royal family in English as were the sermons; and wardens wore morning coats, striped trousers and top hats.

These synagogues were clearly very different from the typically modest synagogues of the *shtetl* where form was generally secondary to function: there the *shul* was primarily a place of prayer
and study and relatively little attention was paid to its physical appearance. Their South African equivalents were the *griener shuls*
of Johannesburg, Cape Town and Oudtshoorn. These were more
comfortable and congenial settings for the Yiddish-speaking newcomers than the grand edifices of the elite. Here substance was
considered more important than style; the Orthodox Judaism of
the Anglo-Jewish elite which placed great emphasis on decorum
in worship, seemed lukewarm and constrained to those used to
the more fervent, expressive and uninhibited worship of the Eastern European *shul*, where piety was highly prized and was meas-
ured by the length of time it took to finish praying the *Shmoneh
Esrei* (Silent Prayer).

In the *griener shul* the atmosphere was old-world, the *beth midrash*
serving as a meeting place and house of study. As the son of Rabbi Mirvish of the Beth Hamedrash Hachodosh in Constitution

*The Kimberley Synagogue, built at the
end of the Anglo-Boer War.*

OPPOSITE PAGE
ABOVE: *The Roeland Street 'shul', Cape
Town.*

BELOW: *The 'griener shul', Beth
Hamedrash Hachodosh in District Six,
Cape Town.*

Street in District Six later recalled:

> In the evenings between Minchah and Maariv the synagogue presented a scene of animated activity. The hard struggling Jew, be he shopkeeper, pedlar or alien, would foregather at the conclusion of the day in the Beth Hamedrash and between services he would 'sit' at one of the 'Shiurim' or lectures delivered at long tables with benches all round ... Scores of people, all returning from a hard day's work would sit and listen and concentrate on the intricacies and legalistic complexities of Jewish lore, and would discuss heatedly principles of religion.

Similarly in Ferreirastown, Johannesburg, the Beth Hamedrash was 'the centre of attraction,

District Six: Cape Town's Lower East Side

District Six occupies an iconic place in South African memory as the site of the destruction of a community under apartheid. It is remembered as a dynamic multiracial neighbourhood, situated between Table Bay and the slopes of Devil's Peak, where immigrant Jews and their polyglot neighbours mingled comfortably. In South African Jewish memory, it has become a focus of nostalgia similar to the Lower East Side of New York and the East End of London.

'Fixed in my memory are the noises ... the noise of the vendors hawking their goods at the top of their voices in different accents, the main language being Yiddish interspersed with a sprinkling of newly acquired English words,' recalls Esther Wilkin, a former resident. Cater-

ing to these new immigrants' language and cultural needs were three Jewish booksellers – Beinkinstadt, Melamed and Witten; two Yiddish newspapers – David Goldblatt's *Yiddisher Advocat* and ND Hoffman's *Der Afrikaner*, and a vibrant Yiddish theatre.

In the years immediately after the Anglo-Boer War, *griener* theatre-goers could attend nightly performances, seven days a week, by renowned actors from abroad, at the Winter Gardens in Ayre Street. They could walk to the Oddfellows Hall just outside District Six where Sarah Sylvia (born Serke Goldstein), the grande dame of South African Yiddish theatre, made her stage debut at the age of 12. On Sunday nights they could attend amateur performances at the William Street Theatre where audiences

were spontaneous and vocal, sometimes drowning out the actors. This indecorum, together with the contravention of the Sunday Observance Act, embarrassed the anglicised Jewish elite who supported moves to suppress the Sunday performances and, despite the protestations of the newcomers, these were banned.

Founded in 1903, M Beinkinstadt at 38 Canterbury Street was more than a bookshop. Like the coffee houses of New York and the cities of the Old World, it was a gathering place for the Yiddish-speaking intelligentsia. Regular readings of the Yiddish press were arranged for the less literate, and the bookshop also served as a lending library.

Moshe Beinkinstadt's store was the intellectual hub of a secular Yiddishist culture that coexisted with the more traditional and observant. For the latter the Sabbath retained a spiritual centrality. The son of the famed Rabbi Mirvish of District Six recalls the magical transformation of Jewish hawkers on the eve of the Sabbath:

> … during the week they looked so decrepit, so scraggy, filthy and dirty. Friday, five o'clock they would knock off, go home, have a bath, clean up, not shave, trim their beard a bit, put on their Shabbat outfit and come to Shul. If you saw them during the week and on a Shabbat they were two different people. You wouldn't recognize them. When they came into shul in all their glory, everyone looked like a king. You couldn't tell whether he was a shuster or a shneider or anything like that.

The interior of Beinkinstadt's bookshop. Berl Padowich (seated) was the son-in-law of the founder, Moshe Beinkinstadt, and his successor as proprietor.

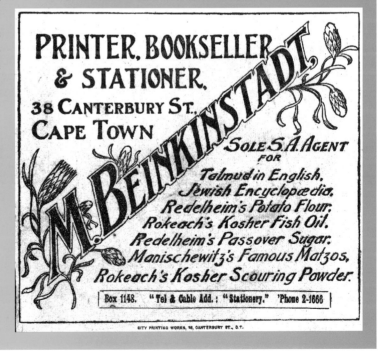

The Cape on District Six

The impression that will prevail in my mind is rows of shabby and unclean shops whose walls and signboards are sprinkled with Yiddish characters, sloping streets crowded with coloured people, Indians, Russians and Poles; narrow lanes where little black and brown babies tumble amidst the discarded rags and the empty canisters flung out of the houses ... I recall the glimpses of indescribable dirt and squalor that I had through open doors and windows ... the group of men that stand around the counters of the tailors and the jewelers holding debates in Yiddish, the lean and ragged little children that rush from miserable and secret lanes into the crowded streets, or crawl out of the doors of the mean houses to stretch their bare brown limbs in the dry gutters, the hard white faces of the wives and the daughters of the hunted Russians, sitting on shabby balconies or lounging against the shop doors.

The Cape, 3 January 1908

Mr Berelowitz in the doorway of his drapery store in Hanover Street, District Six.

a place used by all Yiddish observers. They swarmed like bees around this centre ...,' noted Morris Abrahams, a correspondent of the London *Jewish Chronicle*. 'It was open from early morning till late at night. As soon as a sufficient number were present, prayers were read. When these were finished room was made for a batch of newcomers ... This procedure was repeated an indefinite number of times every day.'

Between the poles of the Eastern European *beth midrash* and the Anglo-Jewish synagogue lay the evolving South African shul, home to

LEFT: *South African Co-operative Bootmakers Union, District Six, Cape Town.*

RIGHT: *Polliacks Music Store, Hanover Street, District Six, 1903.*

the upwardly mobile immigrant and a hybrid of Anglo-Jewish decorum and Eastern European traditionalism. In the Cape Town case, the Roeland Street Synagogue of the New Hebrew Congregation, consecrated in 1902, lay literally at the geographical intersection between 'downtown' and 'uptown' Jewry, spiritually and spatially equidistant between the Gardens Synagogue and the Beth Hamedrash Hachodosh in District Six. Here the young Morris Alexander, decked in mortarboard and academic gown, delivered sermons in English to the immigrant congregants.

The Litvaks brought to South Africa more than their prayer shawls and prayer books. Some of the more secular-minded had imbibed the subversive socialist ideals percolating through the Tsarist Empire, ideas that in 1897 had forged the General Union of Jewish Workers in Lithuania, Poland and Russia. A branch of this organisation, better known as the Bund, was established in Cape Town in 1900. Small groups of Jewish immigrants organised unions and co-operatives among Jewish tailors, cabinet makers, bakers and cigarette makers at the turn of the century. However, these specifically Jewish initiatives were rapidly absorbed into

Jewish education: early beginnings

Formal Jewish education began in South Africa with the establishment in 1868 of classes for 'Hebrew and religious instruction' by the Reverend Joel Rabinowitz of the Cape Town Hebrew Congregation. Kimberley and Port Elizabeth followed suit in the 1870s, and Durban in the early 1880s. The rapid expansion of South African Jewry through the mineral revolution led to the establishment in Cape Town, Barberton and Johannesburg of Jewish 'public' schools.

Hope Mill opened in the Gardens in Cape Town with Mark Cohen brought out from England in 1896 as its first principal. 'The School,' the government inspector reported at the end of Cohen's first year, 'had been removed into commodious premises, in every way suitable … The order and discipline are excellent … The School is in a very efficient state.' Tellingly, the Inspector added that 'the time given to Hebrew is no longer excessive.' Over time the proportion of Jewish pupils at the school would significantly decline as the number of non-Jewish pupils at the school increased.

After faltering beginnings, the Jewish School of Johannesburg opened in 1897 alongside the Park Synagogue in the central city. Here a 'muscular Judaism' was imposed on the children of the Eastern European immigrants. 'Mr Principal Marks has adopted the cult of the Dorians and Greeks based on strength of mind and beauty of body as of vast importance,' noted a reporter from the *Standard and Diggers' News*. 'Mr Carrington … has disciplined these well-set-up little urchins to an extent, I trust, never reached by the doting mollycoddled parent.' After the Anglo-Boer War the school, which had enjoyed no state support in Kruger's Calvinist republic, was ceded to the new British administration. It became the Jewish Government School modelled on its Anglo-Jewish equivalents.

The Miriam Marks School, named after the mother of its principal benefactor, Sammy Marks, opened in Pretoria in 1905. From the start, it admitted non-Jewish children and, on Marks's insistence, continued to do so despite the objections of some members of the community who felt that the presence of these pupils and of gentile teachers diluted the Jewish character of the school.

In essence, all three institutions were schools for Jewish children and not for Jewish education, with the teaching of Hebrew a declining priority. Their chief concern was the anglicisation of their immigrant charges. A more intensive Jewish education was provided by the *Talmud Torahs*, the afternoon schools Jewish children (mainly boys) attended, somewhat reluctantly, after regular schooling. The quality of this education was uneven, and generally of a better standard in the larger centres. The *kolboiniks,* the all-rounders who ministered to *platteland* (country) congregations, were often very indifferent teachers.

While the *Talmud Torahs* flourished, the pioneering 'day schools' waned and ceased to function as Jewish schools. Jewish parents preferred to send their children to non-denominational state schools such as Pretoria High School for Girls, the South African College School in Cape Town and Jeppe High School for Boys in Johannesburg.

ABOVE LEFT: *Consecration of the Miriam Marks' School in Pretoria, built by the philanthropist Sammy Marks and named after his mother.*

ABOVE RIGHT: *Hope Mill Hebrew Public School, Cape Town.*

CENTRE: *The staff of the Jewish Government School, Doornfontein, c1912.*

LEFT: *The opening of the Jewish School in Johannesburg, 1897.*

Mame loshen

*Nehemia Dov Hoffmann, journalist and
pioneer of the Yiddish press in South Africa.*

Although Jewish leaders at the Cape fought tenaciously – and successfully – for the recognition of Yiddish as a European language for the purposes of the (Cape) Immigration Act of 1902, this was not indicative of a communal commitment to perpetuating the use of the language of *der heim*. In fact, the immigrant generation encouraged the rapid acculturation of their offspring with the inevitable loss of a command of the *mame loshen* (mother tongue). Later Hebraists, driven by a Zionist agenda, further undermined the status of Yiddish.

For all that, the language had its literary champions. Nehemia Dov Hoffmann brought the first Hebrew-Yiddish typeface to South Africa in 1889 and one year later established *Der Afrikaner Israelit,* the country's first Yiddish periodical. In 1916 he published his memoirs, *Sefer Hazichroines*, the first Yiddish book to be published in South Africa. The book keenly observes the lives of Boers and blacks, the relationship between Jews and Boers, and includes pen portraits of local Jewish personalities.

The Yiddish press, pioneered by Hoffmann, could not thrive in a community bent on acculturation. Nevertheless there were prolonged bursts of literary creativity, both before and after the Second World War with noted writers such as Jacob Mordechai Sherman, David Fram and Richard Feldman carrying the torch for the embattled Yiddish language. Fram's epic poem about a mythic lost Eden of Lithuania, *Dos Letster Kapitl* (The Last Chapter) published in 1947 in London is regarded as a classic.

existing unions as Jewish workers built solidarity across colour and ethnic lines. But individual Jews would continue to play a leading role in labour struggles for decades to come. For these activists, universalist ideals trumped Jewish particularism, including Zionism to which a majority of South African Jews subscribed.

Among the reasons for the rapid disappearance of specifically Jewish unions was the absence of a substantial Jewish proletariat of the sort found in New York at this time, or in Leeds and Manchester. The South African economy already displayed the character and contours of a racialised capitalism where race and class divisions in-

ABOVE: *Isaiah Israelstam, founder member of the Friends of Russian Liberty, the Socialist Labour Party and the Yiddish-speaking branch of the International Socialist League, founded in 1917.*

RIGHT: *Samuel Rochlin, Secretary of the Young Communist League in 1921. He went on to become a noted archivist at the South African Jewish Board of Deputies.*

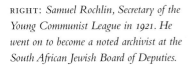

creasingly coincided. As whites in an expanding capitalist economy, Jewish immigrants were well positioned to enter a bourgeoning commercial sector. A comprehensive record of Jewish applications for naturalisation in the Cape Colony between 1904 and 1906 reveals that approximately 33 per cent defined themselves as 'traders and merchants', 11 per cent as 'tailors and outfitters', and 7 per cent each as shoemakers and builders. A further 5 per cent defined themselves as 'clerks and shop assistants', 4 per cent as travellers, 3 per cent for each of feather buyers, butchers, 'cattle dealers and speculators', and 'catering and liquor', and 2 per cent for each of 'watchmaker and jewellers', cabinet makers, bakers and hawkers. Clearly many of these immigrants drew on skills learnt in *der heim* and took advantage of ethnic networks to secure a foothold on the occupational ladder in the new country.

For all the fault lines between anglicised elites and *grieners*, pietists and socialists, workers and employers, Zionists and non-Zionists, the community nonetheless had begun homogenising in a direction set by the elite: collective embourgeoisement, the displacement of Yiddish by English (and, tellingly, not by Afrikaans) as the vernacular, and a comfortable coupling of a Jewish identity, rooted in a respect for tradition, with an emerging sense of a broader (white) South Africanness. This did not demand a discarding of ethnic distinctiveness. In early twentieth-century South Africa, where Afrikaans and English-speakers still saw themselves as separate 'races', there was ample room for Jewish particularism.

SHIRKERS, SUBVERSIVES AND SUCCESSES

Although the process of homogenisation – the merging of Anglo-Jewish and Litvak streams – was well under way by 1914, it was far from complete. As wars often do, the Great War starkly exposed rifts within the community, uncovering the fissures beneath the facade of growing homogeneity. This was apparent in the community's uneven response to the plight of Russian Jews caught up in the Eastern European theatre of war. Jews living in the middle-class suburbs were much less engaged in the communal campaign to raise relief funds than their Russian Jewish brethren in the meaner streets of Johannesburg.

These divisions were even more apparent when it came to the issue of broader loyalties beyond the strictly Jewish. The war generated nationalist passions of great intensity, accompanied by chauvinism and xenophobia of a sort that left minority communities very uncomfortably exposed. The burning issue which brought the question of Jewish loyalty to the fore was that of recruitment. Unlike Britain, South Africa did not resort to conscription but relied instead on volunteering. Jewish responses to the recruiting drives were very mixed. English Jews and anglicised Jews volunteered enthusiastically and in substantial numbers. Less acculturated newcomers from Eastern Europe showed much less eagerness. Britain's alliance with an oppressive, antisemitic Tsarist Russia did nothing to inspire their enthusiasm for the war effort.

This failure to respond to the recruiting appeals cast a spotlight of intense public disapproval on the Jewish community as a whole. Jewish 'shirkers' were denounced from public platforms and in the letter and editorial columns of newspapers, with young Jewish males working in stores along the Rand or holidaying peacefully at Muizenberg being singled out for particularly acerbic comment. This hostile attention at a time of dangerous and potentially violent jingoist passion both alarmed and divided the Jewish community. In 'The Call to the Jew', Lionel Goldsmid, the English-born editor of the *South African Jewish Chronicle*, chastised the Russian Jewish 'shirkers', refusing to accept their excuse that Tsarist Russia had been 'step-motherly' to them:'It is all very well

Isaac Ochberg, founder of the South African Jewish Orphanage in Cape Town, and rescuer of Jewish orphans in post-war Eastern Europe.

Enduring ties: Litvaks and *der heim*

Inevitably *der heim* – the old country – loomed large in Litvak immigrant consciousness. Though at a great physical remove, the new immigrants were deeply concerned about the fate of those they had left behind. Whenever possible money was remitted to assist their communities of origin, Sammy Marks, the industrial magnate, sent funds to his home town of Neustadt Sugind which were disbursed by his father to the needy. On his son's behalf, the old man also gave generous wedding presents to poor couples and funded the building of a *Talmud Torah*. The firm of Lewis and Marks donated close to £1 000 for the rebuilding of the Neustadt Synagogue – a very large sum in local terms given the purchasing power of the pound sterling in a poor Eastern European village.

While few Litvak immigrants could afford such generosity, they nevertheless invested heavily, at least emotionally, in the plight of their co-religionists in the Pale of Settlement. They were outraged at the news of the Kishinev pogrom of 1903 and the antisemitic disturbances that followed, with many making donations, ranging from a shilling to ten guineas, to a nationwide Kishinev Relief Fund. Their indignation and concern were shared by gentile sympathisers like the noted author Olive Schreiner whose message of solidarity, 'A Letter on the Jew', was read at a mass meeting in Cape Town in July 1906.

The First World War generated immense anxiety about the fate of family and friends who had remained behind in *der heim*. South African Jews were acutely aware that the eastern front straddled their home districts in Eastern Europe. Cut off from communication with their kin, all they knew was that their families were caught in the crossfire of a destructive and terrible conflict, and most likely had been forced to flee their homes and reduced to penury. Raising relief funds for these refugees became the principal focus of South African Jewry during the war and money was collected through endless concerts, balls, bazaars, street collections, house-to-house collections, and collections even at *bris milahs* (circumcisions). The amounts raised through the Jewish War Victims' Fund were impressive, especially given the limited resources of what was still very largely a struggling immigrant community. By September 1917, for example, the Western Cape alone had sent what was then the enormous sum of £44 000 to Russia.

The fate of Jewish war orphans – their numbers greatly increased by the post-war wave of pogroms in the Ukraine – particularly exercised the Jewish community. Funds were raised to support them in Eastern European and to aid emigration to Palestine. Most dramatically, Isaac Ochberg, a Ukranian immigrant to Cape Town and a founder of the city's South African Jewish Orphanage, went on a rescue mission to Eastern Europe in 1921. 'My journey is no doubt connected with many difficulties,' he said, 'but I hope with the help of the blessed Almighty I shall be able to overcome everything in my way, and eventually take away the first hundred children from that hell on earth where they are at present, and bring them to this country.' Ochberg returned with 175 orphans who were placed at the Jewish orphanages in Johannesburg and Cape Town.

'Ochberg orphans' brought to South Africa from Eastern Europe in 1921.

for them to argue "If it were not that Russia is an ally I would go." The excuse is that of a man who lacks the courage of his own conviction. Let them say outright "I am afraid ..."'

Other leaders vigorously denied the charges and sought to prove that Jewish volunteering was at least on a par with that of gentiles. Reverend Bender and Morris Alexander wrote jointly to the *Cape Times*, asserting that they 'had ample evidence that the Jews of South Africa, in proportion to their numbers, had come forward as readily, as earnestly, and as fully as any other section of the community for patriotic service in the cause of the Allies. We admitted that there were slackers among the Jews, but not in greater numbers than among other denominations ...'

The Bolshevik Revolution of 1917, greeted in immigrant neighbourhoods in Johannesburg with dancing in the streets, raised further questions about Jewish loyalty.

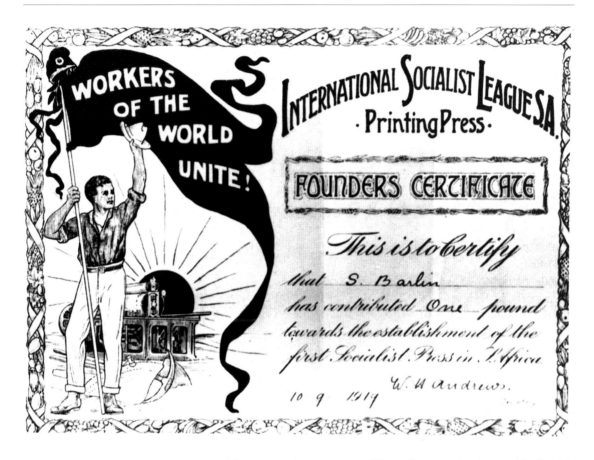

WORKERS OF THE WORLD UNITE!

INTERNATIONAL SOCIALIST LEAGUE S.A.
·Printing Press·

FOUNDERS CERTIFICATE

This is to Certify

that S. Barlin

has contributed One *pound towards the establishment of the first Socialist Press in S. Africa*

W. H Andrews.

10 9 1919

The newcomers were readily and conveniently tarnished with the excesses of the new Russian regime – depicted in South African newspapers as anarchistic and violent – and accused, as in the United States and Britain, of identifying with radical political causes and Bolshevik subversion. These accusations had particular resonance in South Africa because of fears of rising worker consciousness and militancy that were associated with wartime industrialisation and the growth of a restive and increasingly radicalised black proletariat, especially on the Witwatersrand. Despite assurances in 1919 by Bernard Alexander, the chairman of the Executive Council of the Board, that 'every Jew is not a Bolshevist and every Bolshevist is not a Jew', the Rand Revolt three years later was depicted in leading newspapers as a 'Russian-Jewish' conspiracy, an event driven and orchestrated by a small group of Russian-Jewish immigrants. In reality, Jewish participation in this rebellion by white mineworkers against attempts by mine owners to re-

'A remarkable man, a little man with a big heart – a "do-er"'

Perhaps the most remarkable of the Jewish entrepreneurs of the early twentieth century, notable for the innovative nature and impressive range of his activities, the short and stocky New York-born Isadore William Schlesinger (known popularly as IWS) was a pioneer of the South African insurance and entertainment industries. In 1904 he founded the African Life Assurance Society and a decade later laid the foundations of African Consolidated Theatres which was to dominate the entertainment industry for many years. Schlesinger was also one of the trailblazers of film production in South Africa and his African Mirror newsreels became a fixture in South African cinemas for many decades. In addition, he was the founder of a chain of radio stations, the African Broadcasting Company, forerunner of the state-owned South African Broadcasting Company.

Schlesinger displayed extraordinary business versatility, investing in a myriad of enterprises, including property, banking, hotels, amusement parks, advertising and commercial farming, most notably at Zebediela in the northern Transvaal. Here he created the world's largest privately-owned citrus estate, and here he was buried when he died in 1949.

IW Schlesinger, insurance and entertainment entrepreneur.

place them with black workers was minimal.

The tensions surrounding the First World War, the Bolshevik Revolution and the Rand Revolt forcefully reminded Jews of the importance of embracing white South African loyalties enthusiastically and unconditionally, lest they be singled out for unflattering and uncomfortable public attention. For all the conspicuous presence of Jewish immigrants among the radical agitators – including a Yiddish-speaking branch of the International Socialist League, the forerunner of the Communist Party of South Africa – the overwhelming majority of Jews rejected radicalism and identified with the status quo. Most embraced the capitalist order and some contributed significantly to the economy's postwar growth. The Jewish newcomer was the classic *homo economicus*.

In the mid-1920s Jews were not evenly distrib-

uted across the spectrum of economic activities. According to the 1926 census, two thirds of Jewish working males were concentrated in trade and finance, more than three times the proportion among their non-Jewish (white) counterparts. Of the 14 per cent of Jewish women gainfully employed, seven in ten were engaged in commerce, double the proportion among non-Jewish white women. One in ten of these Jewish women was employed in manufacturing, a sector which attracted only 16 per cent of Jewish working males.

A mere 4 per cent of Jews in formal occupations were farmers, though some Jewish traders in the countryside had subsidiary farming interests. Two of the most prominent of these few Jewish farmers were Esrael Lazarus, the 'mealie king', based in the Transvaal maize triangle, and Jacob Ber Lurie, the 'potato king', who farmed

Esrael Lazarus, the 'mealie king'.

Sam Cohen.

in the Orange Free State. Both had arrived in South Africa in 1896 at the age of 18 from Lithuania where Lurie had been a *yeshiva bocher* in Ponevez.

Commercial occupations ranged from the chain-store pioneer through the general dealer to the lowly *kaffireatnik*, the exploited shop assistant in the concession stores and rudimentary dining halls largely catering to black mineworkers. The *kaffireatnik*, often a new immigrant, worked punishing hours, with little free time, for scant reward. 'My dreams are shattered,' lamented Adolph Shapiro. 'I work in a kaffir shop for £5 a month and I am told that I am very lucky.'

Among the retailing innovators were the South African-born (Riversdale, Cape) Gustave Ackerman and the Lithuanian-born Morris Mauerberger, joint founders of the Ackerman's chain, while the London-born Sam Cohen and

Michael Miller.

his partner Michael Miller together established the OK Bazaars retailing empire. Like many other successful immigrants, formal education played little part in their rise to business eminence. Morris Mauerberger had come to Cape Town and started work at the age of 15, while Michael Miller had emigrated at the age of three from Lithuania to England where he left school at 13 before moving to South Africa at 17.

LEFT: *Morris Mauerberger.*
RIGHT: *Gustave Ackerman.*

Most Jews in commerce operated on a more modest scale, though their presence on many high streets was very conspicuous. For example, in Wynberg in the Cape Peninsula, 8 of 16 stores within a single block on the same side of Main Road were Jewish-owned: in succession, an outfitter, a chemist, a shoe store, a tearoom, another outfitter, a watchmaker, a tailor, and a draper. In many towns commerce virtually ground to a halt on the Jewish High Holidays.

Jews in manufacturing had benefited from the disruption of imports during the First World War and continued to benefit from the protectionist policies of the Pact government – a coalition of

the National and Labour parties – during the latter half of the 1920s. Both the emergent furniture and garment industries had a strong Jewish presence as did food processing and milling where the Lithuanian-born Joffe Marks of Premier Milling and the German-born Jacob Frankel were prominent.

In addition to commerce and manufacturing, by the 1920s Jews were entering the professions in significant numbers. The proportion of Jews who were professional men already equalled that of the general white male population, and was rising. Nearly 40 per cent of graduands and diplomates at the University of the Witwatersrand at the end of the 1920s were Jewish. At the University of Cape Town, Jews often made up over 20 per cent of the graduating classes in arts, law, medicine and commerce. Women were under-represented except in arts, music and education. Such was the presence of Jews at the University of Cape Town that all students at the university were jeeringly labelled 'Ikeys', a disparaging moniker with a Jewish ring, by their rivals at the University of Stellenbosch.

Jacob Frankel, whose family milling business later became Tiger Oats under his son Rudy.

TOP: *OK Bazaars first store, Johannesburg, c. 1927.*

91

Joffe Marks, founder of Premier Milling.

This ethnic slur notwithstanding, Jews were comfortably integrated into university life in both Cape Town and Johannesburg where the overwhelming majority studied. Unlike the United States and Eastern Europe, where Jewish students often faced social exclusion or worse, a *numerus clausus*, Jewish students played a full and active role in South Africa. 'The typical university societies are open to all,' commented Arthur Lourie, a Jewish University of Cape Town graduate, 'and though here and there antisemitic feeling on occasion shows its ugly head, on the whole the Jewish student lives, works and plays in harmony with his gentile colleague.' At the merest rumour of the existence of a Jewish quota for a men's residence at the University of Cape Town, the Vice-Chancellor, 'Jock' Beattie, was quick to reassure the Jewish community that 'so long as I and others are here there will be no discrimination against Jews'.

The new university-trained professionals joined an expanding Jewish elite, collectively portrayed in the nearly 900 entries in the 'Who's Who' section of the *South African Jewish Year Book* of 1929, published by the recently founded South African Jewish Historical Society. The first of its kind and the only edition to appear for three decades, the *Year Book* provides a unique window into a community en route to social and cultural homogenisation.

The notables listed in the *Year Book* were overwhelmingly male, many of them youthful and a significant number locally born. Only 29 of those listed were women, and most of these were under 40 and either South African born or reared. Seven were doctors, including Esther Franks, 'the first Jewish Lady Doctor' to qualify at the University of the Witwatersrand. Three were lawyers, including Irene Geffen, the 'first

Sarah Gertrude Millin

Contemporary anxieties about 'race mixing' and 'mongrelisation' are reflected in the writing of Sarah Gertrude Millin, the Lithuanian-born Jewish author who rose to prominence in South Africa during the 1920s. Her 1924 novel, *God's Step-children,* with its central theme of the 'sin' of miscegenation, brought her international acclaim. In the novel a missionary marries a 'Hottentot' girl and fathers two children. As a result, he sinks into squalor and madness, obsessed with the 'sin' of having begotten half-caste children. This 'sin' is then traced through four generations with each generation, although whiter in complexion, frustrated in its desire to enter white society.

Millin's obsession with race reappears elsewhere in her work – her conviction that it was impossible to escape the effects of miscegenation, the original sin of South African society. Her first non-fiction book, *The South Africans,* published in 1926 and extremely well received at home, was an impressionistic account of South Africa's history. It provides numerous examples of Millin's racial attitudes that would later detract from her place in South Africa's literary history.

Only one of her 17 novels, *The Coming of the Lord,* published in 1928, touches on her Jewishness. Reviewing the book, *Time Magazine* noted: 'As perspicacious South African, Mrs Millin reports humorous native idiosyncrasies, pompous white superiorities. As thoughtful Jew, she analyzes the poignant inferiority complex of her race, and the passion for conformity which a Jew despises but cannot resist.'

For all her ambivalence about Jewishness, her South African Jewish contemporaries revelled in her growing fame. Writing on 'The Jew in South African Literature' in the 1929 *Year Book,* SA Rochlin described Millin as 'the greatest inspiration today in literary South Africa, whether it be Jewish or Gentile … She stands, *par excellence*, in a class by herself.' Posterity would not be so kind.

The Rabbinate and the shaping of South African Orthodoxy

By the time of the First World War most Jewish religious functionaries in South Africa were Eastern European in origin, many the products of the *yeshiva* world of Lithuania. Trained at such famous academies as Ponevez, Telz and Slobodka, though in many cases without receiving *smicha* (rabbinical ordination), they found themselves in country towns such as Middelburg and Tulbagh in the Cape, and Ermelo and Kroonstad in the Transvaal. Here they served as *kolboiniks*, rabbinic Jacks-of-all-trades who acted as cantors, *mohelim* (ritual circumcisers), *shochtim* (ritual slaughterers) and *cheder* teachers.

While predominant in numbers, these Eastern Europeans did not determine the direction of South African orthodoxy. Local circumstances, including the distance from larger centres, and economic exigencies played an important part here, eroding the piety of ordinary congregants and modifying religious practice. As important was the leadership role played by the spiritual luminaries of the large centres, in particular the Reverend AP Bender of Cape Town and Rabbis JH Hertz and JL Landau of Johannesburg.

All three were inclined towards a modern style of orthodoxy, combining traditional with secular learn-ing. Lacking a formal *yeshiva* education, the Irish-born Bender, whose father was minister of the Dublin Hebrew Congregation, obtained a first-class degree in Semitic studies at Cambridge. The Slovakian-born Hertz, the son of a prominent Hebraist, completed a PhD at Columbia University concurrent with a rabbinical diploma at the Jewish Theological Seminary in New York. Likewise, Landau, who was born in Galicia in the Austro-Hungarian Empire, received a PhD in Theology at the University of Vienna at the same time as his rabbinical diploma from the *Israelitisch-Theologische Lehranstalt*, a Viennese seminary committed to the *Wissenschaft des Judentums*, the Science of Judaism.

All three were deeply engaged with the wider society and culture beyond the strictly religious. During his interrupted ministry in Johannesburg, between 1898 and 1911, Hertz publicly challenged the Kruger regime and later assisted the Milner administration. Throughout his 42-year ministry in Cape Town, from 1895 to 1937, Bender was, as the famed scholar Solomon Schechter put it after a visit to Cape Town, 'a very good representative of the Jew among the gentiles with whom he is as popular as with members of his con-

Judah Leo Landau.

Alfred Philipp Bender.

JH Hertz, formerly Rabbi of the Witwatersrand Old Hebrew Congregation, Johannesburg, and later Chief Rabbi of the United Hebrew Congregations of the British Empire.

gregation'. Schechter also noted how Bender's 'sermons are celebrated for their apt quotations from the English classics'. (This surely had little appeal to the *grieners* who dismissed him as *der galach*, the priest.) Bender was a part-time professor of Hebrew at the University of Cape Town as was Landau at the University of the Witwatersrand. Landau was also a noted Hebrew poet and playwright, and for most of his nearly four decades in South Africa, from 1903 to 1942, dominated Jewish communal life in Johannesburg.

Bender, Hertz and Landau were all proponents of a modern orthodoxy.

When he later became Chief Rabbi of the British Empire Hertz spoke of 'the golden mean in Judaism', arguing for 'the need of thinking anew and acting anew so as to make orthodoxy a synonym of progress without loss of essential values'. Landau took a similar approach and was willing to innovate, introducing a 'bar-mitzvah for girls' – forerunner of the *batmitzvah*, the female coming of age – and allowing the limited use of English in services.

Bender, Hertz and Landau were obliged to accommodate themselves to a world of waning religiosity, however much they might have lamented this. Landau was particularly scathing about the 'low standards of observance of lay leadership of the synagogues' as well as their congregants. 'All their Judaism,' he wrote in 1905, 'is shrunk within the walls of the synagogue which is empty even on Sabbaths and festivals from one Day of Atonement to the next. For them their synagogue is simply a monument …'

Not much could be expected 'from our local youth with regard to Judaism', Landau ruefully noted during an interview in 1912 with the Yiddish journalist, ND Hoffmann, while on holiday in Muizenberg. 'I am afraid that this generation will be another Tower of Babel … a generation which does not know either their past or their present. The children themselves are not to blame for this – it is their parents who are to blame. The children see that their parents disregard their old traditions – they eat forbidden food; they avoid the synagogue all year round; they desecrate the Sabbath and holy days – and as the parents do, so do the children.'

lady advocate to be admitted in South Africa' and a prominent suffragist. Joan Salomon was an 'Instructress for Speech Defects … the first person to hold such a hospital appointment in [the] Transvaal', while Eugenie Sachs was the 'second Jewess in South Africa to obtain the English qualification as a Chemist and Druggist'. In the arts, Pearl Adler taught dancing in Johannesburg, having qualified in the Russian Imperial Ballet School Method, while Jane Plotz was an 'artist and photographer'. The most prominent of the entries was the author Sarah Gertrude Millin, catapulted to fame by her novel, *God's Stepchildren.*

The male entries in the *Year Book* displayed similar ethnic pride, celebrating success and pioneering efforts. The law took pride of place among the professions, followed closely by medicine and dentistry. The lawyers were increasingly South African trained, joining an older generation, many of whom had qualified in England. The doctors were usually South African born but British trained, often in Edinburgh (or Dublin); medical training in South Africa was only in its infancy and there were longstanding and close links with Scottish higher education. Like medicine, dentistry was a safe route to respectability and status, and a sizeable contingent had studied in England. (The Bloemfontein-born Isidore 'Bok' Bishko, for example, had trained at the Royal Dental Hospital in London.) At this time the other professions were conspicuously undersubscribed. Of the notables listed in the 'Who's Who', few were accountants, teachers, engineers and architects. (Among the latter was the German-born and educated Hermann Kallenbach, a close associate of Mahatma Gandhi during his South African years.)

While many of the notables had a secular

South African Zionism: the early years

Modern Zionism emerged in the late nineteenth century at a time of widespread nationalist stirrings in Europe coupled with an emergent 'Jewish question'. Zionists saw the solution to the latter in a national rebirth rather than in assimilation or socialist revolution. The Zionist ideal gained special traction in Lithuania, and was transported to South Africa by the emigrants. Here, despite challenges, it gained a rapid and relatively easy communal ascendancy, supported by both Lithuanian and English Jews. Beginning in earnest with the *Chovevei Zion* (Lovers of Zion) founded in Johannesburg in 1896, Zionist societies proliferated in town and countryside.

Within a decade there were over sixty of these in South Africa, and in 1905 they met together for the first South African Zionist Conference. Although women were equally enthusiastic and active supporters of the cause, men monopolised the leadership positions. Beyond advocacy, these Zionist societies, with their well-attended meetings, picnics and bazaars, fulfilled a broader function, providing a convivial social milieu for many.

Bnoth Zion, Cape Town, 1903.

Young Israel societies, which proliferated in the 1910s and 1920s, played a similar social role. Easily affordable annual seaside camps, initially at the Strand near Cape Town, provided 'a very fine medium for the cultivation of "Jewishness",' wrote Lewis Pinshaw, a prominent Young Israelite. Ten to fourteen days 'leaves an indelible impression on the camper's mind, which impression is considerably facilitated by a judicious programme of cultural propaganda'.

Unlike their counterparts in Europe and the United States, Zionists in South Africa were not seriously challenged by anti-Zionist ideological rivals. The socialist Bundists and the religious conservatives of the *Agudat Yisrael*, so powerful in Eastern Europe, were never as influential in South Africa. And by the time the Reform movement arrived in South Africa in the 1930s, its initial opposition to

Organisers of the first South African Zionist Bazaar, Johannesburg, 1906.

Zionism had mutated into a greater acceptance of Jewish nationalism. The early disdain for Zionism on the part of some members of the Jewish establishment in England had its echo in Cape Town in the sermonising of Reverend Bender, but this attitude dissipated in the wake of the Balfour Declaration of 1917. In 1897 Bender had belittled the First World Zionist Congress, preaching that 'the sacred purpose of God seeks and finds fulfilment in its own mysterious way without the adventitious aid of conferences and movements and propaganda'. But by the end of the First World War, in the wake of the British promise of a Jewish 'national home', Bender had shifted his stance towards that of his rabbinical colleagues. The other major spiritual leaders of early twentieth-century South African Jewry – Rabbis JH Hertz and JL Landau – had supported Zionism from the start, as had most of the South African rabbinate.

Zionists felt comfortable in South Africa where Jewish nationalism was met with empathy and approval at the highest level. Jan Smuts, for example, subscribed to an ardent 'gentile Zionism', while in the 1920s his political rivals, the Afrikaner Nationalists, publicly aligned their own national struggle with that of the Jews.

Zionism was not seen as incompatible with loyalty to South Africa. Jan H Hofmeyr, a future deputy prime minister, put this succinctly at a public meeting in Johannesburg in 1920: 'One could love one's mother as well as one's father,' he said, affirming the legitimacy of Jewish twin loyalties. In this supportive environment Zionism was to become the civil religion of South African Jewry during the course of the twentieth century.

The first committee of the South African Zionist Federation, Cape Town, 1902.

The first South African Zionist Conference, 1905.

97

'In South Africa I was surrounded by Jews.'
MK Gandhi

Mahatma Gandhi – the famed Indian activist who began his political career in the struggle for Indian civil and political rights in South Africa in the early years of the twentieth century – was befriended by a number of Jewish immigrants.

An English Jew, Henry Polak, became editor of *Indian Opinion* – a mouthpiece of the Indian struggle in South Africa – from 1906 to 1916. Polak and Gandhi were in prison together for participating in the *Satyagraha* or non-violent resistance struggle. The German-educated architect and Tolstoyan, Hermann Kallenbach, was another close associate of Gandhi and a participant in his campaigns. Forsaking material comforts, Kallenbach donated Tolstoy Farm, outside Johannesburg, to Gandhi for the use of the families of *Satyagraha* prisoners. Another English Jew, Louis Walter Ritch, joined Gandhi as an articled clerk, and a Lithuanian-born Jew, Sonia Schlesin, served as his secretary for much of his time in South Africa.

Morris Alexander, the liberal Cape parliamentarian, was also a sympathiser of Gandhi and a supporter of the Indian struggle for justice in South Africa. Enid Alexander, second wife of Morris, records in her biography of her husband how Gandhi, accompanied by Kallenbach (who was related through marriage to Morris), spent his last evening in South Africa in July 1914 at the Alexanders' home:

> During the evening he spoke long and earnestly of his mission for his fellow men, and begged that his small band of supporters should continue to defend their interests. On retiring, Morris offered Gandhi the best bedroom in the house. He refused it and chose instead to sleep on the hard wooden floor of the front *stoep* (verandah). He refused mattress, blankets, pillows, in fact anything that would make for his bodily comfort. He lay down in his robes and slept like a child all through the night.

Hermann Kallenbach, Gandhi and Sonia Schlesin (far right).

higher education, only a handful had a *yeshiva* training. Evidently South African Jewry placed no particular premium on advanced religious learning; South Africa's *balabatim* (communal worthies) were seldom *talmidei chachamim* (Torah scholars). Although many of them were born in the traditional world of Eastern Europe, they had left for South Africa as children.

A large number of the notables were South African born or at least educated in South Africa. Even those arriving in late adolescence from Eastern Europe were able to enter the professions. Jacob Manasewitz, for example, immigrated at the age of 16 and went on to practise law in Witbank. A significant proportion of the notables came from England and were the product of an English education; the imperial connection had ensured a steady stream of Anglo-Jewish migrants alongside the Litvak torrent. With their obvious advantages, these newcomers often achieved positions of prominence in the community. The notables in general were relatively young; a high proportion of them were in their thirties and forties, and a not insignificant number were in their twenties. (The youthful Morris de Saxe, editor of the *Year Book* at the age of 30, typified these.)

Besides the biographical details of prominent individuals, the *Year Book* also contained a detailed and comprehensive listing of the 'chief Jewish Communal Organisations', testimony to the richness and diversity of organised Jewish life by the late 1920s. At the national level there was the South African Jewish Board of Deputies, the representative voice of the community which had 128 affiliates in 1929. There were also the South African Zionist Federation, the umbrella body of the 56 Zionist societies in the Union and its neighbours, and the South African Board

of Jewish Education which had been established in 1928 to coordinate the educational efforts of some 50 Hebrew congregations and *Talmud Torahs* (afternoon Hebrew schools) throughout the country.

All these organisations had their headquarters in Johannesburg. So did the Federation of Synagogues of the Witwatersrand, incorporating 21 constituent synagogues (guided by the powerful and revered Chief Rabbi Judah Leo Landau) and a *Beth Din* (religious court). The United Talmud Torah Schools of Johannesburg provided for the 'Hebrew education' of Jewish children at the Hebrew High School in Wolmarans Street (also known as the Johannesburg Talmud Torah) and at *Talmud Torahs* in areas of dense Jewish settlement such as Yeoville, Berea, Mayfair, Fordsburg and Doornfontein.

In Johannesburg, the numerous *landsmann-schaften* (immigrant fraternal societies) established in the heyday of immigration, such as the Tels Sick Benefit and Benevolent Society and Special Distress Fund, continued to assist their needy 'brethren' with loans and medical attention. Similarly the Witwatersrand Jewish Helping Hand and Burial Society, established in 1888, only two years after the founding of Johannesburg, continued with its dual role as *Chevra Kadisha* (burial society) and principal dispenser of charity. The very lengthy list of Johannesburg organisations did not include the Jewish Workers' Club, founded soon after the *Year Book*'s publication. This organisation, driven by a socialist agenda, was at odds with the bourgeois Jewish mainstream represented by the *Year Book*.

Communal life also flourished beyond Johannesburg, the South African Jewish centre of gravity, with its 25 918 Jews (out of a national total of 71 816) according to the 1926 census.

A time for historical reflection

By the end of the 1920s, Jews in South Africa felt sufficiently rooted in their new home to begin to reflect on their communal past. This new historical sensibility was evidenced in two initiatives at opposite ends of the country: the foundation in Johannesburg in 1927 of the South African Jewish Historical Society and the publication in 1930 of *A History of the Jews in South Africa* by the Cape Town intellectual, Louis Herrman.

These historical projects were informed, at least in part, by anxieties about the place of Jews in South Africa. Like those German Jews who founded the Society for the Culture and Science of the Jews early in the nineteenth century and those English Jews who founded the Jewish Historical Society of England later in the century, their South African counterparts were determined to embed the Jewish community in the wider culture and to ward off those characterising Jews as outsiders.

The communal intellectuals who founded the South African Jewish Historical Society, whose personal histories personify the diverse strands constituting the emergent community, were inspired and led by Chief Rabbi Landau, who held a doctorate from Vienna and who doubled as professor of Hebrew at the University of the Witwatersrand. They defined their task as 'the systematic collection of historical and statistical material concerning South African Jewry' and to this end distributed a questionnaire throughout the country which elicited 'hundreds' of responses. These formed the basis of the *South African Jewish Year Book* published in 1929 – a publication clearly intended to present the public face of the community.

The original editor and lead researcher was Isaac Meyer Goodman, born and educated in Liverpool, who came to South Africa in 1895 at the age of 24. He was awarded the Queen's Medal for Active Service during the Anglo-Boer War and served afterwards on a myriad of public and Jewish organisations. He was the mayor of Springs, a Witwatersrand mining town, during the First World War, and was also the founder and editor of *Ivri Onouchi*, a Hebrew magazine, and the author of the intriguingly titled play, *Sugarman the Shadchan*.

Goodman was replaced as editor by the youthful Morris de Saxe. Educated at Marist Brothers College in Johannesburg, De Saxe served as an officer in the Royal Engineers during the Great War. After the war he obtained a law degree from the University of the Witwatersrand, where he was one of the founders and first president of the Students' Jewish Association. Like many of his young contemporaries, De Saxe served energetically on a wide range of Jewish committees, both religious and secular. Despite his youth, he was an executive member of the Board of Deputies, the honorary secretary of the Witwatersrand Federation of Synagogues and a former executive member of the South African Zionist Federation.

Morris de Saxe.

Isaac Meyer Goodman.

Historian and educationist, Louis Herrman (left), in discussion with David Zuckerman.

While Goodman embodied the Anglo-Jewish presence in the Historical Society (and in the community), and De Saxe the home grown, Abraham ben Jehudah Couzin, born in Poland in 1868, represented the Eastern European.

Couzin typified the cultural hybridity of early twentieth-century South African Jewry and the confluence of its two major immigrant streams. Unlike De Saxe and Goodman, Couzin had a *yeshivah* education in Poland, and then spent 13 years in England before coming to South Africa in 1903. He was an ardent Zionist and also the founder of the Jewish War Victims' Fund in Johannesburg, his 'proudest achievement'. He was also the author of the (no longer extant) *Outlines of the History of the Jews in South Africa*. Couzin was 'greatly interested in Hebrew and Yiddish literary development' and contributed to a range of publications in both Yiddish and English.

Like the *Year Book,* Louis Herrman's *History* portrayed a long-established and resourceful community that had contributed significantly to the society at large. Herrman was born and educated in Southampton where he

qualified as a schoolmaster. He came to Cape Town in 1907 at the age of 24 to take up a position as vice-principal of the Hope Mill Hebrew Public School and, after Hope Mill closed, taught English at Cape Town High School. He obtained an MA (with distinction in Zoology) at the University of Cape Town in 1928 and his doctorate at London University in 1932, for research into the 'Genetic Status of Intelligence in Twins'. Between obtaining these degrees he published *A History of the Jews in South Africa*.

Herrman's *History* began with the Jewish involvement in the Portuguese voyages of discovery and in the Dutch East India Company and took the story up to 1895. It presented a portrait of a Jewish community deeply rooted in the (white) South African past, led by an acculturated Anglo-Jewish establishment situated in Cape Town and committed to the values of Cape Liberalism. Like that of the *Year Book*, this depiction of South African Jewry and its liberal and Anglo-Saxon antecedents, provided an affirmative message to counter hostile critics who questioned the Jewish presence.

Cities such as Cape Town (11 705), Pretoria (2 277), Port Elizabeth (1 502), Bloemfontein (1 415), Kimberley (832) and East London (679), had a plethora of organisations: philanthropic, Zionist, cultural and social. Like Johannesburg, Cape Town had an orphanage, while most cities had Jewish lodges modelled on the Masonic. Durban (2 472) had 'several flourishing institutions' including the Durban Jewish Circle, a social, sports and cultural club founded shortly after the Great War to cater to the needs of young adults, some of whom had returned from service and, being Jewish, were excluded from certain clubs and sporting bodies. Durban also had rival synagogues, the product of a longstanding and 'regrettable division' of the community.

Oudtshoorn (911 Jews), no longer in its Jewish prime, nevertheless had 15 Jewish organisations, including three congregations, four Zionist associations, three charitable organisations, Jewish Boy Scout and Girl Guides troops, and an Amalgamated Board of Shechita overseeing ritual slaughtering. Even the smallest of towns with a Jewish presence had a Hebrew congregation: Maquassi in the western Transvaal had 12 members, Aberdeen in the Eastern Cape 16, and Jagersfontein in the Free State 19. Many also had Zionist societies with memberships roughly comparable, and sometimes even larger in size, than those of the synagogue.

In addition to its communal directory, the 1929 *Year Book* also proudly listed 'Jews occupying Public and Administrative Positions': a judge of the Supreme Court, Leopold Greenberg; an acting judge, Manfred Nathan; six King's Counsels; two senators, Franz Ginsberg and Gustave Hartog; five members of parliament, Eli Buirski (Woodstock), Morris Kentridge (Troyeville), Emile Nathan (Von Brandis), Ernest Oppen-

heimer (Kimberley), Charles (CP) Robinson (Durban Stamford Hill); and five members of the Provincial Councils.

With the exception of Kentridge of the Labour Party, all the members of parliament represented urban constituencies held by the South African Party. This reflected long-standing Jewish political preferences; the party of Louis Botha and Jan Smuts, built upon reconciliation between Boer and Brit, was a more comfortable home than Barry Hertzog's Afrikaner-dominated National Party. Behind this preference lay an abiding loyalty to and respect for British 'fair play' and goodwill dating back to the nineteenth century, a sense of 'fair play' that did not extend to black South Africans.

The pride that Morris de Saxe took in these public figures was equally manifest in his introductory 'Editorial' which extolled the 'pioneering achievements of the early South African Jews', celebrated the revitalising dynamism of 'a generation reared in the *chedorim* [Jewish elementary schools] and *yeshivas* of Eastern Europe' and welcomed the newfound and 'enviable' cohesion of the community. 'From an unwieldy aggregate of individuals, all going their own ways,' observed the editor, 'the community is in process of attaining a unity of thought, purpose and action of which it can be truly proud.' Accounting for this, in his view, was the effective leadership provided by the 'co-ordinating bodies, the common organs of the whole community ...' Moreover he claimed, the 'integrative forces' of Zionism, had further accelerated the 'rapid progress' of South African Jewry 'towards becoming a self-conscious, corporate entity'.

For all its sunny confidence and apparent optimism, the editorial betrayed a certain unease about the attitude of the host society towards the Jewish community. Commenting on the need to record the Jewish experience in South Africa – the raison d'être of the Jewish Historical Society that was responsible for the *Year Book* – De Saxe alerted readers to the threat posed by the misinformation informing gentile attitudes towards Jews in South Africa at the time. Beyond the Jewish community, he contended, 'such information as generally obtains is usually so inaccurate as to be worse than misleading; it frequently becomes a positive source of danger to Jews'.

De Saxe's concerns arose out of increasingly strident calls in the 1920s to curb Jewish immigration from Eastern Europe. Whereas those hostile to the Eastern Europeans in earlier years had stereotyped them as dishonest and subversive, the new discourse was one of 'unassimilability', a questioning of the Jewish potential for integration into South African society. The *Cape Times*, in a particularly xenophobic mood, persistently called for curbs on undesirable immigration from countries where democratic ideals were unknown and 'western concepts of morality are quite unappreciated'.

These ideas, purveyed in English and Afrikaans newspapers across the country, were directly influenced by nativist literature from the United States (which had recently introduced severe immigrations restrictions) as well as by a new domestic segregationist discourse in which race and culture were conflated. Eugenicist-based fears of 'race mixing' and 'mongrelisation' – primarily associated with South African blacks – increasingly informed perceptions of the Eastern European Jew.

Such hostile sentiments underpinned the Quota Act of 1930, which set out effectively to halt Eastern European Jewish immigration by imposing an initial limit of 50 migrants per annum from each of a list of 'quota countries' that included Lithuania, Latvia and Poland. The Act was in part a consequence of the failed courtship of Jewish voters by the ruling National Party, but support for this legislation went well beyond its ranks. 'The Bill will commend itself to most citizens of the Union and has not been introduced a day too soon,' crowed East London's *Daily Dispatch*. For a stunned Jewish community, the Act came as a major blow. It abruptly severed the half-century-old umbilical cord to the Litvak wellspring.

CHAPTER 3

SOUTH AFRICAN JEWS

THE 'JEWISH QUESTION' AND BEYOND, 1930–1948

THE QUOTA ACT OF 1930 USHERED IN A DECADE of profound difficulty and discomfort for South African Jewry. A 'Jewish Question' emerged against a backdrop of economic depression and a burgeoning and exclusivist Afrikaner nationalism that was struggling to capture the political high ground. The Act heralded what the historian Todd Endelman, writing in the European context, terms the transformation of 'private' into 'public' or 'programmatic' antisemitism – the shift from 'expressions of contempt and discrimination outside the realm of public life' to the 'eruption of antisemitism in political life'.

Initially this transformation was evident in the formation of the South African Gentile National Socialist Movement in October 1933. Subsequently known as the Greyshirts, the movement was led by Louis T Weichardt, a hairdresser of German descent. At its peak the Greyshirts had 2 000 members and its success stimulated the mushrooming of similar far-right organisations across the country. Although these assumed Nazi trappings, and although they were inspired by a German *volkisch* discourse, the message they propagated related directly to the South African experience: Jews had fomented the Boer War, incited blacks against

Bowlers at Beaconsfield Club, Johannesburg.

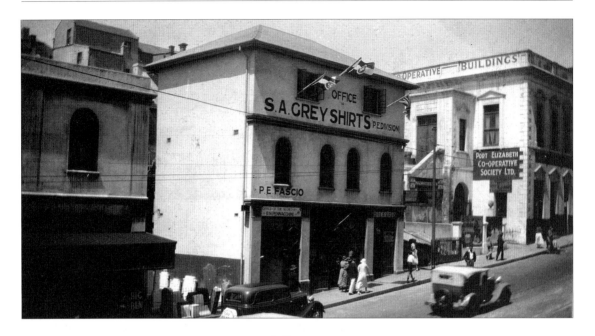

TOP: *The Greyshirt office in Port Elizabeth.*

ABOVE: Die Waarheid/ The Truth, *the*
'official organ' of the Greyshirts.

white civilisation, controlled the press, dominated the economy and exploited Afrikaners. These accusations resonated beyond the ranks of the radical right. For those wrestling with the effects of drought and depression, and fearful of black economic competition, the Jews provided ideal scapegoats.

Anti-Jewish ideas rapidly penetrated the Afrikaner Nationalist mainstream, and were fertilised by a clutch of Afrikaner intellectuals, some of whom had studied in Germany where they had imbibed an affection for the corporate state, an idealist worldview and a sense of exclusivist nationalism. Hostility was exacerbated by the influx, in the wake of Hitler's ascent to power, of Jewish refugees from Germany, a country unaffected by the Quota Act. The groundswell of anti-Jewish feeling prompted demands not only for the ending of Jewish immigration, but also for discriminatory action against recent arrivals.

These calls for the unequal treatment of Jews came from the opposition Purified National

The Transvaler,
*mouthpiece of the Purified
National Party, on the
'Jewish Question',
1 October 1937.*

*Ossewabrandwag leader,
Dr Hans van Rensburg
(centre), flanked by torch-
bearing members during a
rally, 1941.*

The 'Elders of Zion' come to South Africa

Shortly after its formation, Weichardt's Greyshirt movement achieved national notoriety through a sensational trial in Grahamstown, focused on the infamous forgery, the *Protocols of the Elders of Zion*. Already widely disseminated through Europe and the United States, this Tsarist Russian fantasy claimed that in no less than 24 secret meetings, Jews had been plotting the destruction of Christendom and the establishment of world Jewish dominance.

Notwithstanding its exposure as a crude forgery by the London *Times* in 1921, the *Protocols*, suitably adapted to local conditions, were dramatically introduced into South Africa in 1934 when Johannes Strauss von Moltke, the Eastern Province leader of the Greyshirts, claimed

publicly that he had uncovered a sensational Jewish plot revealed in a document allegedly stolen from the Western Road Synagogue in Port Elizabeth. The signature of the 'rabbi' of the synagogue supposedly attested to its authenticity. In the wake of this sensational allegation, *Rapport*, a Greyshirt-supporting newspaper, challenged South African Jewry to 'refute the authenticity of the document to the satisfaction of all non-Jews … If they cannot definitely prove their innocence of this notorious document … there can only be one procedure for our Christian state: the ejectment of Jews from South Africa.' Von Moltke repeated the charge at a huge public meeting in Port Elizabeth, where he appealed to the 'Nordic peoples' to form a self-defence organisation to

Reverend Abraham Levy (second from left) leaving the Supreme Court in Grahamstown after the 'Greyshirt Trial'.

deal with 'such occult, alien organizations as are harboured in the Jewish synagogues'.

The Board of Deputies took up the challenge as it generally did with antisemitic canards throughout these troubled times. Because an individual – the Rev Abraham Levy of the Western Road Synagogue – had been identified, they were legally able to contest the accusation in terms of the law of libel. Taking up the case also provided the Board with an opportunity to bring before a court of law the authenticity of the *Protocols*, palpably the inspiration behind Von Moltke's accusation.

During the 'Greyshirt Trial' in the Supreme Court in Grahamstown it became obvious that Von Moltke's 'stolen' document was inspired by the *Protocols*. Purportedly written by a learned Jew, it was supposedly a copy of lectures delineating Jewish hostility towards Christianity and white South Africa: 'Our Imperialism of Pax Judaica is one for the downfall of western civilization … As we have got control over Russia, so we will also control the Union … Such is the mission of Judah. It is our plan to give South Africa to the natives.'

The trial centred on the authenticity of the document and the motives of the defendants in making it public. After 11 days of hearings, including testimony by Nahum Sokolow, the Zionist leader coincidentally on a visit to South Africa, the court found the documents to be false and the defendants guilty of conspiring to promote the interests of the Greyshirt movement.

Despite the Grahamstown judgement and the Board's subsequent publication of pamphlets combating notions of a Jewish conspiracy, the *Protocols* continued to be quoted and published in South Africa. Manie Maritz, veteran of the Boer War and a leader of the 1914 Rebellion, incorporated substantial portions of the *Protocols* in his autobiography, *My Lewe en Strewe* (My Life and Struggle). On trial in South West Africa (under pressure from the Board of Deputies), Maritz explained that the *Protocols* had opened his eyes to the role of the Jews in the Afrikaners' misfortunes and their nefarious influence on South African history.

Party led by Dr DF Malan following a breakaway from the governing United Party in 1934. They were predicated upon Jewish 'unassimilability' and fears of Jewish power and domination. Malan's party sought to curtail the new immigrants' access to the professions, limit their involvement in certain occupations, and proscribe name changing.

Responding to these pressures and fearful of being outflanked, the ruling United Party introduced the Aliens Act in 1937, designed to restrict Jewish immigration from Germany. In deference to local Jewish opinion, the Act did not mention Jews by name. Instead, immigrants were only to be permitted entry by a selection board, on the grounds of good character and the likelihood of assimilation into the European population.

The Act failed to appease the Purified Nationalists; for them any Jewish immigration was unacceptable. The 'Jewish Question' now became an important plank in their political platform. Malan, under pressure from the far-right Greyshirts, focused increasingly on the Jew as an explanation for the Afrikaners' political misfortunes. The Party's northern mouthpiece, *Die Transvaler* edited by Dr Hendrik Verwoerd, stood at the vanguard of the anti-Jewish agitation, railing on its editorial page against alleged Jewish domination in business and the professions, the unassimilability of Jews, Jewish alienation from the Afrikaners, questionable Jewish commercial morality, and the use of money by Jews to influence government through the English-language press.

The 'Jewish Question' had clearly ceased to be the exclusive concern of fringe groups; it had now become firmly entrenched within mainstream white politics. In the 1938 general election campaign National Party propaganda

The *Stuttgart* incident

The expected arrival in Cape Town in late October 1936 of the German liner, the *Stuttgart*, with 537 German Jewish refugees on board, prompted the best remembered and most dramatic display of Afrikaner anti-Jewish immigrant sentiment of the decade. The ship had been chartered by Jewish organisations in Europe to beat the impending introduction of more restrictive immigration regulations by the South African government: from the beginning of November immigrants would have to make a sizeable cash deposit, clearly an impossibility for refugees from Hitler's clutches.

The *Stuttgart* sailed from Bremerhaven despite the reservations of the South African Jewish leadership, fearful of the potential domestic repercussions of the arrival of a boatload of German Jewish refugees. On the eve of the ship's arrival in Table Bay, the Greyshirts held a protest meeting at the Koffiehuis in Cape Town. A rumour that the *Stuttgart* had already berthed provoked hundreds of those protestors to march prematurely on the docks. By the time the ship actually arrived early the next morning, on a cold and wet Cape winter's day, the crowd had long since dispersed but for a few hardy stragglers who, according to the *South African Jewish Chronicle*, 'gave vent to a few rude cries and some half-hearted raising of their arms, more amusing than alarming'. The Jewish community of Cape Town rallied to help the new arrivals. Their frustrated opponents, including Professor Hendrik Verwoerd of the University of Stellenbosch, continued to rail at public meetings across the country against 'mass' Jewish immigration.

CAPE TIMES, WEDNESDAY, OCTOBER 2

THE STUTTGART ARRIV

The specially chartered German liner Stuttgart arriving with Jewish immigr Town early yesterday morning.

GERMAN JEWS ARRIVE

Stuttgart's Passengers Not Molested

THE intention to hold a demonstration against the landing of German Jewish immigrants from the liner Stuttgart yeste was thwarted by the weather and police precautions, and they not molested.

THUNDER, lightning and torrents of rain completely "washed out" the anti-Semitic demonstration which had been planned as an inhospitable reception to the 550 German Jewish immigrants who arrived from Bremen in the 13,000-ton tourist liner, Stuttgart, at dawn yesterday.

The police, however, had taken every precaution to ensure that the Stuttgart's passengers should disembark unmolested. Barriers, in the form of unused gangways, had been erected during the night at each end of No. 7 Quay, where the vessel was berthed, and large squads of Railway Police and detectives patrolled the vicinity.

outside world may think. Th not want war. Too many o remember the last war. If embarks on another war h find himself faced with a tion."

Other immigrants told st persecution and sudden rem concentration camps.

"A friend of mine," said o grant, "was a Social Demo was not a Jew, a Socialist, o munist, but he had critic Nazis.

"They beat him up with rubber. He was put in a c tion camp but managed to Holland. He is a cripple fo does not know what has

German Jewish refugees disembarking from the Stuttgart *at Cape Town docks, 1936.*

Cape

h

ration

nced

t Meeting

h

ocks

and women of
g many Grey-
to the Docks
night, after
nat the liner
538 German
d entered the
fore she was

at there was
they kicked

warned against the prospect of Jewish domination. The election year also saw the emergence of a new paramilitary authoritarian movement, the *Ossewabrandwag* (OB). Born out of the centenary celebrations of the Great Trek, the *Ossewabrandwag* attacked 'British-Jewish-Masonic' imperialism and capitalism, 'British Jewish' democracy, 'Jewish money-power' and 'Jewish disloyalty'. But it was also the Jew as communist that concerned some detractors. Eric Louw, a leading Nationalist and inveterate antisemite, attacked 'international Jewish communism' together with liberalism, which he saw as a cover for communist ends.

While the accusations were steeped in crude stereotyping and florid fantasy, they nevertheless fed upon an uncomfortable awareness that Jews were succeeding where Afrikaners were failing. While 'poor whites', forced off the farm by drought and debt, struggled desperately to come to terms with life in the alien and inhospitable city, Jews seemed to thrive in these urban settings. Where Afrikaners clustered around the lower rungs of the social ladder, Jews appeared to scale these effortlessly.

This mobility is apparent in a 'statistical survey' conducted by Dr Henry Sonnabend in 1935 of the Jewish population of Johannesburg. Based on a careful sampling of Jews across the social and economic spectrum, from the inner city to the 'fashionable' suburbs of Parktown and Saxonwold, the survey – the first of its kind – portrays a community in rapid transition, adapting relatively easily to modern city life.

Men still outnumbered women, but not by a large margin: 1 054.7 males to 1 000 females. Predictably, the poorer immigrant neighbourhoods had the highest ratio of men to women, significantly higher than in the more affluent

The arrival of the 'Yekkes'

Between Hitler's ascent to power in 1933 and the out-break of the Second World War in 1939, some 6 000 German Jewish refugees entered South Africa, a fraction of the quarter of a million German Jews who fled Nazism. The new arrivals were of all ages, with a preponderance of the young and the middle aged, though a large contingent of 825 'elderly parents', defined as 60 and over, arrived in 1939. Many of the newcomers were well-educated and some had held senior managerial and professional positions prior to the 'Aryanisation' of German society.

German Jewish emigrants were not allowed to take their savings but could send a 'liftvan' of furniture and other possessions to their countries of refuge. These might include Biedermeier furniture, paintings, fur coats and Leica cameras. Helga Bassel, mother of the concert pianist Tessa Uys and satirist Pieter-Dirk Uys, sent her Bluthner grand piano to South Africa in 1936.

Despite the ambivalence of some of its leaders who were fearful of mounting antisemitism, the Jewish community rallied to the aid of the newcomers. A South African Fund for German Jewry was established in 1933. In the years that followed, it assisted the refugees financially, and helped them find accommodation and employment. Leo Raphaely and Max Sonnenberg led the efforts in Cape Town while Bernard Kaumheimer and Joe See-hoff played an important role in Johannesburg where the majority settled. Max Sonnenberg arranged the purchase of Rosecourt in the Gardens in Cape Town as a social and cultural haven for the new-comers. 'Rosecourt was indeed a home from home, where you were made to be aware of the fact that you were becoming part of a caring community,' recalled Miriam Herzfeld.

In Johannesburg the refugees clustered in German 'colonies' in the inner-city suburbs of Doornfontein, Hillbrow, Yeoville

and Berea. One of these was Elfreda Court, an apartment building in Doornfontein where prior to the arrival of the 'liftvan', an 'upturned box covered with oil

Leo Raphaely

Max Sonnenberg.

cloth' might serve as a table in an immigrant's modest apartment. Initially, at least, immigrants typically had to settle for jobs far below their level of qualifications which were usually unrecognised in South Africa. Doctors and lawyers found employment as office and factory workers. The mother of Franz Auerbach (who later became a noted educationalist) had qualified as a dentist in Germany but worked at a sewing machine in a clothing factory in Johannesburg; his father, trained as an electrical engineer, sold polony door-to-door to fellow refugees.

In Johannesburg, the German Jews – jovially known as the *Yekkes* by other Jews – formed a community within a community, at least for a time. They founded their own congregations, *Etz Chayim* in Doornfontein and *Adath Jeschurun* in Yeoville, and their own cultural society, the UKV or *Unabhängige Kulturvereinigung*. They established the Jewish Immigrants' Help to support their fellow immigrants and Our Parents' Home for the elderly. They also pioneered *B'nai B'rith*, the Jewish service organisation, in South Africa.

Beyond their own institutions the German Jews contributed to the broader cultural life of the South African city, enriching the worlds of theatre and of music. After their initial struggle to establish themselves, many went on to pursue successful careers in business and the professions.

suburbs where South African-born Jews predominated. Just under half the Jewish population of Johannesburg was in the 15- to 35-year age group, with a considerably smaller proportion of children than in the (white) 'general population'. Sonnabend attributed this to immigration and a declining birth rate; the average number of children born to Jewish women of childbearing age was just over 2.5 compared to just over 3.5 in the 'general population'. Fertility was higher among poorer immigrant families than among the more affluent: 2.82 in Doornfontein as opposed to 2.25 in Parktown. Irrespective of neighbourhood, Jewish infant mortality rates were substantially lower than among the 'general population', often by as much as a half. Sonnabend ascribed this 'to the extraordinary care of the Jewish mothers for their children. Even in the poorest district the child has all the comforts and all the medical attention it requires.'

Sonnabend's survey suggests that the Jewish community of Johannesburg was at the forefront of the shift to a modern demographic order, characterised by smaller families and low infant mortality rates. Consistent with this shift was the higher age of marriage and increasing divorce rate among Jews.

Sonnabend also surveyed the occupational profile of Johannesburg Jewry. Again this was distinctive. Jewish men, irrespective of neighbourhood, were clustered in 'commerce, finance, insurance': just under 40 per cent of adult males compared to only 18 per cent in the 'general population'. Jews were almost absent from 'mining' which employed nearly 8 per cent of the 'general population', but were over-represented in tailoring and shoemaking, probably a legacy of their immigrant origins.

The survey also confirms the continuing Jewish entry into the professions, at least of men: over 8 per cent of all adult Jewish males, nearly double that of the 'general population'. This ratio was reversed among Jewish women where 2.51 per cent of all adult females were in the professions as opposed to 4.33 per cent among the 'general population'. On the whole Jewish women were less distinctive in occupational choice than Jewish men. As in the case of their gentile counterparts, over 60 per cent were 'housewives'. Just over a quarter of adult Jewish women were in 'gainful occupation' as opposed to just under a quarter of gentile women.

The most striking feature for Sonnabend of Jewish economic

Henry Sonnabend, social researcher of the Jewish
population of Johannesburg, 1935.

activity was the marked preference of Jewish
men for self-employment: no fewer than 44.7
per cent of adult males belonged to the 'independent' class. 'Independence,' Sonnabend wrote,
'remains for the Jew the aim of his economic
endeavour; he dislikes to be in a dependent position, and hopes to improve his financial condition by working on his own. This tendency
is accentuated by the many difficulties encountered by the Jew when seeking employment in
certain branches of the economy.'

These 'difficulties', in areas such as mining and
banking, inclined Jews towards entrepreneurial
initiatives, sometimes with considerable success,
and towards particular sectors of the economy
where there were fewer obstacles, real or perceived, to entry. One of these was clothing and

Rex Trueform, Hanover Street, Cape Town,
and below, its founder Bernard Shub.

fashion where Jewish-founded businesses rose to national prominence during the 1930s. Companies such as Foschini, Truworths, Woolworths, Edgars and Rex Trueform were to become household names in South Africa.

Rex Trueform was founded by the Lithuanian-born partners Bernard Shub, who had arrived from Ponevez at the age of three, and Philip Dibowitz, who had come at eighteen. As a child Dibowitz had weathered the acute dislocations of the First World War and the Russian Revolution, including scavenging among battlefield casualties and traumatic separation from his parents at the age of nine before being reunited with

them years later in Siberia. Forced into tailoring as a young child, he later refined his craft at academies in Riga and Paris, and gained further experience in London's East End before joining an aunt in District Six.

While Dibowitz's odyssey was particularly arduous, many of his peers also rose from modest beginnings. His partner, Bernard Shub, went out to work at the age of 15 as an office boy 'because I felt I had to do something to help my Mother in the care of the family ...' Similarly Sydney Press of the Edgars retailing chain declined a University of Cape Town bursary for fear of burdening his family. Max Sonnenberg,

founder in 1931 of Woolworths which 16 years later established a rewarding business alliance with Marks and Spencer, had come to South Africa from Germany at the age of 14 and had immediately gone to work to earn money to pay for his mother's passage to South Africa.

Other sectors in which Jewish entrepreneurs made their mark in the thirties were in furnish-ing and textiles, where they successfully iden-tified new market opportunities and trends. Phillip Frame, born in Memel in East Prussia in 1904, had learned the textile business in Dres-den before immigrating to South Africa at the age of 20. By the mid-1930s he had established a string of factories catering largely to the emerg-ing black consumer market for blankets, canvas

ABOVE: *Aaron Beare, furniture retailer.*
ABOVE RIGHT: *Phillip Frame, Natal textile magnate.*

OPPOSITE PAGE
Sydney Press, founder of Edgars retailing chain.

shoes and underwear. 'As early as 1930,' wrote Frame, 'it was obvious that the Non-European population of the country was becoming westernised in its habits, manner of clothing and general outlook.' Likewise, the locally-born Aaron Beare of Durban, son of Lithuanian immigrants, transformed a small family furniture business into a thriving concern, built on hire-purchase arrangements which had a special appeal for working-class customers in the wake of the depression.

Jews on the *platteland* were similarly swift to spot business openings. Joe Jowell and an Afrikaner partner took advantage of the sudden termination of the motor service provided by the railways between the railhead at Bitterfontein and Springbok in Namaqualand to set up a transport operation to fill the gap. The makeshift vehicle they drove, a hybrid of a damaged Buick and a Chevrolet truck, was the beginning of a nationwide transport empire.

Joe Jowell's partnership with 'Oom' Jaap du Plessis was a hold-over from an earlier and more harmonious era of Jewish–Afrikaner relations. In the 1930s Jews and Afrikaners were increasingly at odds in the countryside as Nationalist-dominated 'cooperatives' competed fiercely with Jewish businesses. The apostles of *volks-kapitalisme* sought to displace what they saw as the domination of

Joe Jowell of Namaqualand, transport pioneer.

English and Jewish commerce. In the Oudtshoorn district the To-bacco Cooperative successfully diverted trade from Jewish con-cerns; competition sometimes overstepped legal bounds, with unexplained arson attacks on Jewish-owned business premises.

Such hostility entrenched Jewish identification with English-speaking whites. By the mid-1930s Jews overwhelmingly used English as their home language. Of the 90 645 Jews enumerat-ed in the 1936 census, 68 475 spoke English at home while only 1 445 spoke Afrikaans at home. Yiddish was the declared home language of 17 861, indicative of the dwindling legacy of immi-gration.

The novelist Dan Jacobson's recollections of a childhood in Kimberley in the 1930s and early 1940s vividly capture the at-tractions of British culture and empire. 'Those who lived "under the British crown" in those days,' recalls Jacobson, 'could think of themselves as attached to, a part of, a political system that ex-ercised worldwide power and was held in worldwide esteem … the crown, the coinage, the buff envelopes marked "On His Maj-esty's Service", the playing of "God Save the King" at the end of cinema performances … was a source of an enlarged sense of selfhood, even for those who could at best claim to have been stepchildren of the empire.'

With such loyalties, events both at home and in Europe were the source of gathering anxiety. South African Jews were uncomfortably aware that many Afrikaner Nationalists empathised with the Third Reich. Even the *Kristallnacht* outrage of November 1938 was minimised, with details of the antisemitic violence ignored by Nationalist newspapers. It was not for South Africa, argued *Die Burger*, a National Party mouthpiece, to pronounce judgement upon Germany's treatment of its citizens. Germany's expansionist policies were also rationalised away, with Nationalists calling for a policy of neutrality in the event of war.

When Britain and France declared war on Germany on 3 September 1939, Prime Minister Hertzog assumed, mistakenly, that his case for neutrality would be supported, as he was convinced that white South Africans wished to avoid entanglement in yet another European conflagration. But his United Party cabinet was divided and parliament voted narrowly for war. Jan Smuts was asked to form a government and on 6 September 1939 South Africa proclaimed a state of war with Germany.

South African Jewry fully supported Smuts. 'At this critical

Chaplain Ittamar Rom conducting Chanukah service in Italy with South African Jewish soldiers.

Lt SM Bernstein, one of 60 of his extended family on active service during World War Two.

hour when Nazism is destroying the liberties of nations and individuals, and challenging the fundamental ideals of civilisation,' declared the Board of Deputies, it was 'the obligation of every citizen resident in the Union to rally to the defence of the country.' The Jewish community, it pledged, 'will do all in its power to assist the Union and its allies in the fight for victory.'

The call was enthusiastically heeded. Jews played a substantial role in the South African war effort. Unlike the Great War a generation earlier, when recent Russian Jewish immigrants were reluctant to volunteer because of Britain's alliance with a hated Tsarist Russia, the generation of '39 – mainly South African-born – clearly understood their patriotic duty, rallying to a cause

that so directly touched them as Jews. More than 10 per cent of the entire Jewish population – roughly 10 000 men and women – served in the Union Defence Force and other Allied forces. In some families all the youngsters of military age, male and female, joined up. Sixty members of the Bernstein 'clan' of Johannesburg saw active service, a few outside the Union Defence Force.

Of the Jewish volunteers, 357 were killed, 327 were wounded or injured, 143 were mentioned in dispatches, and 94 received various awards for distinguished service. One of South Africa's most decorated bomber pilots, Cecil Margo, flew numerous missions in East Africa, the Western Desert, Crete and Italy. 'On each raid, without exception, Lieutenant-Colonel Margo has displayed outstanding courage, coolness and skill, and has proved himself a leader of very considerable ability,' noted one of his medal citations. Trooper Jeffrey Kark and Corporal Leib Lerer, both 'Desert Rats', won Military Medals for their brave actions in the North African campaign.

On the home front, the Board of Deputies and the Zionist Federation established organisations to raise funds for refugees and the relief of European Jewry. The Jewish War Appeal in particular assisted Jewish victims of the war and South African Jewish soldiers and their dependents. This organisation worked in conjunction with international agencies such as the American Joint Distribution Committee and the South African Red Cross. In the later stages of the war, the Aliens and Refugees Committee raised funds to assist relief operations.

The Board of Deputies also had to contend with a powerful anti-war and antisemitic mood orchestrated by the *Ossewabrandwag* which by 1941 claimed a membership of more than 300 000, including its own violent paramilitary elite, the *Stormjaers*. Their sentiments were shared by an avowedly pro-Nazi party, the *Nuwe Orde*, founded in 1940 by Oswald Pirow, a former United Party defence minister who had met Hitler at the Berghof in Berchtesgaden a fortnight after *Kristallnacht*.

Malan's National Party flirted with the radical right until the middle of the war, when it decisively distanced itself from National Socialism which it rejected as alien to Afrikaner tradition. Nonetheless Afrikaner Nationalists were sceptical of stories of German atrocities, labelling them as unproven accusations or British propaganda. Even an alarming World Jewish Congress report of the appalling plight of European Jewry in June 1942 failed to generate concern, as did Anthony Eden's statement to the British House of Commons in December 1942 that Hitler intended to exterminate the Jews. Such pronouncements did, however, galvanise supporters of the war effort, and a number of mass meetings addressed by non-Jewish leaders and Christian clergy denounced Nazi barbarism. As the Minister of Labour, Walter Madeley, put it, 'The conscience of South Africa has been stirred.'

The enormity of the catastrophe overtaking European Jewry was certainly comprehended by the South African Jewish community. The parliamentarian Morris Kentridge asserted in January 1943 that 'two million Jews [had been] treacherously murdered in the slaughterhouse of Poland' and 'five million more were in hourly peril of the same fate.' With such knowledge South African Jews could hardly divorce themselves from the European calamity. Many hailed from the regions most devastated by Hitler's war machine.

Beginning in 1942, the Board of Deputies co-ordinated official days of mourning for South African Jewry when Jewish businesses closed

Cecil Margo receiving decoration from King George VI (with Group Captain Peter Townsend in attendance).

early and special synagogue services were held. The Board also lobbied the government (unsuccessfully) to permit the entry of more Jewish refugees; Jewish immigration had virtually ceased with the advent of war. But Prime Minister Smuts feared that renewed Jewish immigration would lead to food shortages and pressure on Allied shipping, and further accelerate and widen antisemitism.

Smuts's fears of mounting wartime antisemitism were not unfounded. An opinion survey of politicians, journalists, trade unionists, academics, clergymen and army education officers conducted late in the war by Simon Herman, a Jewish social psychologist at the University of the Witwatersrand, revealed a rising tide of overt

Servicemen relaxing at the Durban Jewish Club during the Second World War.

antisemitism among English-speaking whites. As one interviewee noted: 'Previously you heard occasional anti-Jewish remarks; now it is a tirade.' Jews were accused, both by Afrikaans- and English-speakers of disproportionate economic and professional representation; of seeking 'to control everything'; of being 'loud and ostentatious'; and of shirking military service or of taking 'base jobs in the army'. Moreover, 'most communists are Jews' and 'Jewish communists agitate among natives'. Afrikaans-speaking interviewees felt that Jewish 'friendship for Afrikaners [was] opportunistic' and that they 'took no interest in Afrikaner culture'.

Jews were keenly aware of this hostility. Jewish students surveyed at the University of the Witwatersrand by the same researcher in early 1943 spoke of their exposure from childhood to antisemitic taunts and discrimination. Those from small towns reported that they 'grew up in it' and were inclined to regard it 'as almost something "natural and inevitable"'. All felt an acute discomfort at the activities of the radical right in South Africa and were intensely conscious of events in Europe which they recognised were of far greater import. 'There Jews have actually been persecuted,' a student typically noted. 'Here the antisemites have just been talking about it and have done nothing.'

These hostile sentiments translated into an indifference towards the plight of European Jewry. Even the uncovering of Buchenwald by the American Third Army in 1945 failed to evoke a sympathetic response from opponents of the war, since acknowledging such evidence would have discredited Germany and made the Allied cause acceptable. Instead of acknowledging the horrors of Nazism and the plight of its victims,

BUCKINGHAM PALACE

The Queen and I offer you
our heartfelt sympathy in your
great sorrow.

We pray that your country's
gratitude for a life so nobly
given in its service may bring
you some measure of consolation.

George R.I.

Mr. I. Shain,
P.O. Pienaarsrivier,
Dist. PRETORIA.

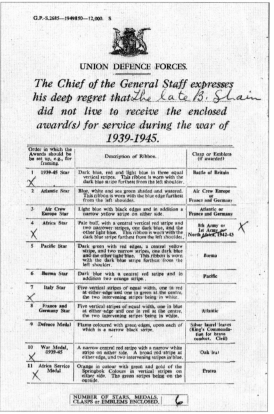

Benny Shain, one of 357 South African Jewish volunteers who fell during the Second World War.

Afrikaner Nationalists concentrated on the sufferings of the German people after the war.

Despite the obvious sympathies in government circles for the primary victims of Nazi aggression, Smuts remained opposed to large-scale Jewish immigration. The South African government considered Palestine to be the preferred solution for displaced Jewish persons. As a result, only 1 512 Jews entered South Africa between 1946 and 1948. Many of these newcomers were Jewish teachers, aged parents of South African citizens, or religious functionaries. It was felt that such persons would not be a strain on the economy and that their entry would satisfy

Leonard Mendelsohn, an officer in the wartime South African Medical Corps, with his proud immigrant parents.

humane imperatives and the particular needs of the Jewish community

For the older generation of South African Jews, the destruction of European Jewry was intensely personalised; the vast majority had their roots in Lithuania where 90 per cent of Jews had been annihilated. At a Day of Mourning observed in all South African synagogues on 14 March 1945, congregants sobbed – and some even fainted – as a mass *kaddish* (mourner's prayer) was recited.

Shortly after the war, in July 1945, the Board of Deputies convened a conference in Johannesburg of the *Landsmannshaften* to mobilise practical support for their surviving European brethren. Food and medical supplies were col-

lected and sent to Europe via the American Joint Distribution Committee (JDC).

In the ensuing months, long lists of survivors with relatives in South Africa were published. With the ongoing publication in the Jewish press of the wrenching accounts of survivors, and the personal testimony of the few who reached South Africa, the horrors and dimensions of the European tragedy became more and more inescapable. In May 1946 a service was held in Johannesburg to commemorate the Warsaw Ghetto Uprising, inspiring the Board of Deputies to explore ways of further assisting Jewish survivors in Europe. A year later the fate of Lithuanian Jewry was movingly recounted for local Jewish audiences by Rabbi Ephraim Oshry, a survivor who toured South Africa, vividly describing the destruction of five Lithuanian communities. By 1947, 38 South African Jews were engaged in relief activity in Europe as part of the JDC staff, while on the home front Jews tried, without success, to influence government immigration policy.

By 1948 the Holocaust had become firmly entrenched in the South African Jewish consciousness. One of its most important short-term effects was to strengthen the already powerful South African Zionist movement. Through the 1930s this had gathered momentum, reinforced by the disturbing combination of domestic and foreign antisemitism that had lent Zionism an immediacy and urgency, and by the growth of Zionist youth movements including *Habonim* and the more leftist *Hashomer Hatzair*, established in South Africa in 1931 and 1936 respectively. By the end of the decade over 21 000 South African Jews were 'shekel holders' (paid-up members of the Zionist movement), only 2 000 less than in Britain with a community three times the size.

Jabotinsky comes to Joburg ... three times

Vladimir Jabotinsky, Zionist Revisionist leader, visiting South Africa.

Vladimir Jabotinsky's Revisionist Zionism – with its un-compromising demand for the creation of a Jewish state on both sides of the Jordan River and its harsh rejection of socialist Zionism – was brought to South Africa by young Eastern European immigrants in the mid-1920s. The Zionist Revisionist Organisation, founded in Johannesburg in 1929, gained momentum as a result of three visits by the founder of the movement in the 1930s.

On his arrival in the autumn of 1930, Jabotinsky defiantly announced that he brought 'not peace but the sword' and that he had come to disrupt the 'blessed state of harmony' within South African Zionism. 'I am afraid that this idyll has now come to an end,' he said. Though his mesmerising oratory attracted mass audiences, he was less successful than he had hoped in raising funds: 'They shouldn't have let me come, knowing that the trip was bound to be a fiasco financially ... I get coldly mad whenever I think of it.'

Despite his disappointment, Jabotinsky's visit had shaken up a hitherto broadly consensual South African Zionism, stimulating internal ideological debate and division. Jabotinsky's better-organised return visit in 1937 deepened these divisions. During his three-and-a-half month visit, Jabotinsky took personal control of the South African Revisionist movement. His fierce tirades against socialist Zionism, at crowded public meetings and in the pages of the newly founded Revisionist newspaper, *The Eleventh Hour* (subsequently the *Jewish Herald*), appealed to many upwardly mobile South African Jews who had fully embraced the free market.

Jabotinsky returned a year later. His apparent success on this visit, including raising a large sum of money for his movement, persuaded him to believe that 'in a year's time all controlling positions will be ours ... South Africa is our main field'. Jabotinsky underestimated local resistance to his programme. There were many within South African Jewry who were repelled by his views. Some even resorted to fisticuffs. The young Rowley Arenstein recalls attempting to attend a Jabotinsky meeting at the Plaza Cinema in Kerk Street Johannesburg: 'We couldn't get in. So we were walking away when we heard a helluva row and we turned around and got the shock of our lives. We found Jews fighting Jews in the middle of Johannesburg. The Jews who were fighting Jews were the Jewish Workers Club, from Doornfontein. Afterwards the police stepped in and there was quiet, and we went up to these Jewish chaps and said, "How can Jews fight Jews?" They said, "Those ... are not Jews, they're fascists ..."'

The birth of the Jewish State

On Sunday 16 May 1948, just two days after David Ben Gurion had declared the birth of the State of Israel, Jews gathered in celebration at the Wolmarans Street Synagogue in Johannesburg. The *South African Jewish Times* reported:

> Long before the service began thousands of people crowded the surrounding street, and outside the synagogue traffic was brought to a virtual standstill. Every available seat was filled in the synagogue; people stood against the walls and in the aisles; and a solemn atmosphere prevailed. A hush fell upon the murmuring crowd as Chief Cantor Alter began the rendering of the Service. His peerless voice swelled to the great hope of Israel, realized after so many centuries; his magnificent rendering of the songs and prayers of dedication brought, to the full, the significance of the occasion ... Throughout the country, thousands sat at wireless sets, listening in to the memorable service, which was broadcast in full by the South African Broadcasting Corporation.
>
> The service began with the singing of *Hatikvah* [the Zionist anthem] by the whole congregation, led by the choir. This was no ordinary singing, but a great rejoicing at the rebirth of Israel. Older members of the congregation wept unrestrainedly, while the youth stood firmly to attention as the strains of the Hebrew National Anthem rang out.

Midnight service at the Old Synagogue, Pretoria, for the birth of the state of Israel.

During the thirties South Africa had become one of the battlegrounds in the struggle between left and right within the international Zionist movement. This engagement was prompted to a large extent by three visits to South Africa by Vladimir Jabotinsky, the Revisionist firebrand. His passionate advocacy of political Zionism – with Jewish statehood as its imperative – resonated powerfully within an increasingly middle-class Jewish community where socialist Zionism had only limited social traction. The Revisionist groundswell, stirred by Jabotinsky's oratory and organisational efforts, gave South African Jewry – a community not noted for Jewish learning or piety – an international visibility it otherwise lacked.

And yet despite Jabotinsky's best efforts, Revisionism did not conquer the community. Many, uncomfortable with factionalism, opposed politicising Zionism in South Africa, while others idealised socialist pioneering in Palestine. A few of these prepared for a pioneer life at *hachsharah* (training) farms near Johannesburg. For the great majority, however, *aliyah* (immigration to the Land of Israel) was not an attrac-

Young Zionists at Balfuria training farm.

Machal

Eight hundred young South African Jews served in Israel's armed forces during the War of Independence as part of *Machal*, the 'Volunteers from Abroad' programme. These numbers were exceeded only by the number of volunteers from the much larger Jewish communities of the United States and Great Britain. This level of enthusiasm and support was indicative of the power of the Zionist idea within South African Jewry.

Most of the volunteers were ex-servicemen who had fought in the Second World War. Those too young to have served were also eager to volunteer and thousands were trained at Koppel Bacher's farm near Krugersdorp and at Wemmershoek outside Cape Town. One of the volunteers, Joe Liebowitz of Johannesburg, an air gunner during the Second World War, became a bomb 'chucker' in the infant Israeli air force. 'I had a strong feeling that we had a moral pact with the slaughtered Six Million of Nazi Europe,' he later recalled. 'This was the first chance to fight back against a world that hadn't cared.' Dr Harry Feldman of Brakpan, a medical officer in the South African forces during the War, felt equally strongly. 'I was never a Zionist in the conventional sense,' he reminisced years later, 'but I was always Jewish, very conscious and proud of my tradition. The idea of a Jewish Land took hold of me.'

South Africa's contribution to Israel's nascent air force and medical corps was particularly striking. Syd Cohen, the bearded 'flying Rabbi of World War II', Boris

South African Machal pilots (from left to right) Boris Senior,
Leslie Shagam, Arnie Ruch, Syd Cohen.

Senior, Rolfe Futerman, Leslie Bloch, Leslie Shagam and Arnold Ruch were among the South African pilots who flew Israel's handful of planes that included, ironically, Messerchmitts they had fought a few years earlier. At David Ben Gurion's personal request, Cecil Margo prepared a plan for the new air force.

Seventy-one South African doctors and nurses served in the medical corps. These included Jack Penn, the renowned plastic surgeon, who performed operations on war casualties under very difficult conditions. Lionel Melzer, who had won a Military Cross and an OBE in the Second World War, played a key role in organising the new medical corps, serving as its deputy commander.

Of the 800 volunteers, about 300 remained and settled in Israel at the end of the war.

Jack Penn.

tive option; South African Zionism at this point was still largely vicarious. Nevertheless, Zionist sentiments were very deeply felt. When Jewish statehood was imminent some years later, and Arab armies stood poised to invade the nascent state, over 800 South African Jews – many of them Second World War ex-servicemen – volunteered to fight.

While the threat posed by local and European fascism had strengthened Zionist commitment for many, a significant number of young Jews were prompted to take an alternative course, opting instead for universalist secular radicalism. Ironically, they sometimes began their journey – usually towards communism – from the Zionist youth movements, especially *Hashomer Hatzair*. The young Joe Slovo, who had arrived in South Africa from Lithuania in 1936 at the age of 10, had been a member of *Habonim* in *der heim*, but joined *Hashomer Hatzair* in Johannesburg before becoming a member of the Communist Party at the age of 16.

The adolescent Slovo was influenced by the socialist rhetoric – often confused and contradictory – that permeated the inner-city dwellings in Johannesburg where his impecunious family lodged. 'My leaning towards left socialist politics was also formed partly by the bizarre and paradoxical embrace of socialism shared by many of the immigrants who filled the boarding houses in which we lived,' writes Slovo in his autobiography. 'I say "bizarre" because they tended to combine a passionate devotion to the Soviet Union with Zionism and the vicious racism towards the majority of the South African population.'

Like many other young Jews, Joe Slovo joined the army during the war and went 'up north'. On their return to South Africa and demobilisation, some of these young volunteers, inspired

The Jewish Workers' Club

The *Yidisher Arbeter Klub* or Jewish Workers' Club (JWC) was founded in 1929 by a group of Johannesburg Jewish craftsmen, shop assistants and manual workers. Apart from its links with various left-wing groups such as the South African Communist Party, the Friends of the Soviet Union, the Left Book Club and Ikaka Laba Sebenzi (the Workers' Shield), the JWC served a valuable social function, providing both a haven for Yiddish-speaking immigrants and a meeting place for like-minded individuals, black and white. Unusual in a deeply segregated society, the JWC's dances, picnics and lectures were racially integrated. Favourite days for the picnics were May Day and, provocatively, *Yom Kippur*. The JWC also ran a Yiddish theatre group and a Yiddish choir which performed at the May Day celebrations. On one occasion it even gave a Yiddish rendition of the 'Red Flag' on national radio.

The cast of Oyfn Grenets, performed by members of the Jewish Workers Club, 1935.

Political education and activism were central activities of the JWC. Members played a conspicuous part in the heady days of public confrontation with the Radical Right in the 1930s. Those injured during the brawls on the Johannesburg City Hall steps were rushed to the nearby rooms of the communist, Dr Max Joffe, rapidly treated, and sent back into 'combat'.

The JWC, so vibrant in the 1930s, dwindled in the 1940s as its members acculturated and ascended the social and economic ladder. There were few new recruits. South African-born English-speaking Jewish radicals did not need or desire the fellowship of a specifically Jewish milieu. Like their more conservative Jewish contemporaries, they had become 'South Africans', albeit of a radical persuasion. In 1948 the JWC's Doornfontein premises burned down and the Club disbanded.

Members of the Jewish Workers Club.

by the fight against fascism, joined the Springbok Legion, a short-lived anti-racist veterans' association, led by Jock Isacowitz, a onetime Zionist socialist, later a communist (and later still a leading member of the anti-apartheid Liberal Party). But the majority of Jews continued to focus on specifically Jewish concerns, despite the surrounding turmoil in post-war South Africa, with Indian passive resistance to expanding segregationism, and exploited African mineworkers striking for living wages.

However, irrespective of their politics and their ideological differences, most Jews were greatly shocked by the defeat of Jan Smuts's United Party in the 1948 general election. The victory of a National Party that had opposed the war effort and that harboured individuals who had previously articulated stridently antisemitic views, was a cause of alarm and concern for the future.

Mike Feldman (left), Joe Slovo (right) and Barney Fehler, Italy, 1944.

National president of ex-servicemen Springbok Legion, Jock Isacowitz (second from left), presents a tribute to Prime Minister Jan Smuts for his wartime services.

For the Workers

I don't think of myself as being Jewish because I just felt that I belong to the world. I am an internationalist.
Ray Alexander

At first I could not understand why Mr Sachs, who was a Jew, fought so hard for the Afrikaner daughters …
I also learnt that Mr Sachs fought not only for garment workers, but for all the workers.
It took a Jew to make me understand that poverty could be wiped out in sunny South Africa …
Hester Cornelius, union organiser

Emil Solomon (Solly) Sachs (1899-1976) and Rachel (Ray) Alexander (1913-2004), both immigrants from Eastern Europe, became iconic figures in the workers' struggle in South Africa in the mid-twentieth century. Sachs grew up in a poor family in Kamaai, a *shtetl* in Lithuania, where he excelled as a student of the *chumash*, the Pentateuch, at *cheder*. He left for South Africa in 1914 to join his father in Johannesburg. Here the family experienced considerable hardship. Sachs's father, a struggling bootmaker, was involved in illicit gold buying and the 'fencing' of stolen boots for which he was sent to jail for nine months. The family lived in Malay Camp, a slum area on the fringe of the Robinson Deep Mine, with Solly and his brother and two sisters sharing a single room.

Ray Alexander came from a more respectable and cultured home. She grew up in Varklian, a small town in Latvia, where her father, a socialist, taught Russian, German and mathematics and also ran a *cheder*. Ray was exposed at an early age to socialist ideas and was a precocious recruit to the Latvian communist underground. She had hoped to study medicine but was sent instead to the ORT technical college in Riga to study dressmaking because her mother feared the virulent antisemitism at the local Latvian university. Afraid that her daughter would be arrested for her political activities, her mother sent her to South Africa at the age of 15 to join her brother and sister in Cape Town. Five days after landing she joined the Communist Party of South Africa.

Sachs's route to socialism and the Communist Party of South Africa was via Malay Camp – where he had firsthand experience of the poverty of its multiracial inhabitants – and through working as a *kaffireatnik*,

Ray Alexander (centre) with officials of the Food and Canning Workers' Union.

an exploited shop assistant in a concesssion store. After interrupted spells as a student at the University of the Witwatersrand and a trip to the Soviet Union, Sachs settled as General Secretary of the Garment Workers' Union where he devoted himself to the interests of its predominantly white Afrikaner women membership, much to the chagrin of Afrikaner nationalists, competing for the loyalty of the same constituency. Alexander was similarly deeply involved in union activity. She became General Secretary of the militant Food and Canning Workers' Union in the Western Cape, a non-racial union serving workers in the fruit-canning and fishing industries.

Solly Sachs (centre) with garment workers.

Inevitably both the 'Jew Communist' Sachs and Alexander were targets of the 'McCarthyism' that followed the National Party's victory in 1948. Sachs was banned under the Suppression of Communism Amendment Act in 1952 and went into exile in Britain the following year. Alexander was repeatedly banned, was forcibly prevented from taking her place as the elected 'Native Representative' in parliament, and eventually went into exile with her husband, the noted academic, Jack Simons, in 1965.

While Sachs and Alexander grew up in intensely Jewish milieus and had childhood experiences of antisemitism, both moved away from ethnic particularism. From an early age, Alexander saw socialist internationalism rather than Zionism as the answer to antisemitism. When as a schoolgirl she was asked by local Zionists to defend the Balfour Declaration in a public debate, she refused the invitation. 'Not all Jews could go to Palestine,' she explained in her autobiography, 'and what would happen to the Palestinians?' Sachs was equally indifferent to matters Jewish, looking to socialism as a universal panacea.

Solly Sachs leads a march of protesting garment workers after receiving 'banning' orders from the government, Johannesburg, 1952.

AT HOME IN APARTHEID
SOUTH AFRICA, 1948–1970

Within two months of Dr Malan's victory, the worst of Jewish fears were allayed. A delegation from the Board of Deputies visited the Prime Minister to discuss Jewish concerns about their place in a Nationalist-ruled South Africa and were assured that the 'Jewish Question' would be laid to rest. As a practical demonstration of the new government's goodwill, Malan permitted South African Jewry to send material aid and manpower to support the fledgling Jewish state's war effort. In May 1949 South Africa officially recognised Israel and four years later Malan became the first head of government to visit the Jewish state. He returned filled with praise and admiration for the achievement of the Jewish people. Two years earlier the National Party in the Transvaal province had lifted its ban on Jewish membership.

The rapprochement between Afrikaner and Jew was indica-

DF Malan with David Ben Gurion, Israel, 1953.

tive of a rapid decline in antisemitism which was already evident in the mid-1940s and which gathered pace in the 1950s. The growing reconciliation was aided by sustained economic growth – driven by a prolonged boom in the international economy – and, more particularly, by the attendant rapid upward mobility for whites. A new Afrikaner bourgeoisie – increasingly well educated, confident and more optimistic than their forebears – began to enjoy the economic fruits of racial exploitation and political power. Like Quebecois nationalists, who had been similarly hostile to Jews as symbols of the modern and the urban, the Afrikaners speedily developed a respect for enterprise and material success. The scaffolding that had underpinned their sense of inferiority was thus removed as they began to experience power and social mobility. A sense of competition with, and fear of, the Jew declined. A post-war consumerist culture meant the erosion of rural values and a new-found respect for the city. No longer was it regarded as an alien and inhospitable place.

Most significantly, however, the impetus of exclusivist Afrikaner nationalism waned. English speakers, including Jews, were necessary for the apartheid project, the National Party's putative solution to South Africa's racial problems. Colour was the essential divide and any lingering views – heard earlier in the century – of the Jew not being 'white' soon disappeared. The National Party wished to put the antisemitic clamour of the 1930s and 1940s behind it. In the apartheid order Jews, as whites, were to have a rightful and welcome place.

While Jews welcomed the disappearance of the 'Jewish Question', their sense of vulnerability persisted and contributed towards a political quiescence as the apartheid project unfolded.

While not endorsing the National Party's systematic and far-reaching imposition of segregation, they by and large restricted dissent to casting their ballots at parliamentary elections for the opposition United Party, with its conservative but less rigid views on race. And although they shared with other middle-class English-speaking whites a distaste for Afrikaner nationalism and its hegemonic agenda, Jews, like their gentile peers, readily accommodated themselves to the new apartheid order and its privileges. As white South Africans, they had been reared in a society where segregation was normative. As was the case with their Jewish counterparts in the American South, they took for granted a racial hierarchy of which they were beneficiaries.

Reflecting and responding to the mood of the community it represented, the Board of Deputies, intensely conscious of Jewish vulnerability, barely questioned in public or openly challenged the prevailing order. But besides its fears, the Board was also beholden to a long-established tradition of restricting its pronouncements to matters Jewish. As far as the Board was concerned, political issues were the domain of the individual conscience and not of the collective. 'Jews participate in South African public life as citizens of South Africa,' it declared, 'and have no collective attitude to the political issues which citizens are called upon to decide.' But for all its public neutrality, behind closed doors its leaders, facing some pressure from within the community, grappled with the moral dilemmas posed by apartheid.

Despite the presence of prominent liberals, notably Ellen Hellmann of the Institute of Race Relations and Arthur Suzman, the Board preferred to deflect ethical conundrums onto the rabbinate, regarded as the custodians of Jewish

Continued on page 142

Constructing a usable past

Between 1930 and 1955 three seminal histories were published, which played a formative role in the self-definition of South African Jewry in the apartheid era: Louis Herrman's *A History of the Jews in South Africa*; Israel Abrahams's *The Birth of a Community;* and *The Jews in South Africa. A History*, edited by Gustav Saron and Louis Hotz. These became standard texts, providing the received version of the South African Jewish past.

The image these books collectively presented was of an industrious, upwardly-mobile, respectable, classless, civic-minded, loyal and uniformly Zionist community, contributing energetically to the commonweal, and generally welcomed by the host society. Written out or minimised were antisemitism, class struggle within the Jewish community, non- and anti-Zionism, the struggle between Yiddishists and Hebraists, and Jewish criminality. A Whiggishness and presentism pervaded these histories, each informed by contemporary needs and by the search for a usable and respectable past.

Herrman, the British-born Cape Town educationalist and intellectual, began his *History* (first published in 1930) as an enquiry into the origins and development of the Cape Town Hebrew Congregation but broadened it into a history of South African Jewry, terminating in the mid-1890s just as the Eastern Europeans had begun to make their mark. The book, which highlighted the long record of Jewish contributions to the broader community, was conceived and written in the 1920s, at the very time that Eastern European Jews were increasingly deemed 'unassimilable' and a threat to the 'Nordic' character of (white) South Africa.

Herrman would have been aware of the demands to curtail the influx of Eastern European Jews. His depiction of South African Jewry and its liberal and Anglo-Saxon antecedents served to counter these. Unsurprisingly, Herrman's history was republished in 1935 by the Board of Deputies. Ostensibly reissued 'in response to a specific demand in South Africa for lower-priced copies of the book,' Jewish communal leaders considered it a weapon in the arsenal of the community's self-defence against burgeoning antisemitism.

Gus Saron, General Secretary of the South African Jewish Board of Deputies and communal historian.

Saron and Hotz's *The Jews in South Africa. A History*, published 20 years later, was similarly informed by the events of the day. While neither of the editors were professional historians, both were deeply immersed in South African Jewish affairs. Saron, a lawyer by training and a one-time lecturer in classics at the University of the Witwatersrand, was the General Secretary of the Board of the Deputies. Hotz was a veteran journalist and experienced social and economic researcher.

The Jews in South Africa was a multi-authored volume, substantial in every sense and much of it based on original research. Contributors were specifically warned that it was 'not intended to be a volume of Jewish apologetics in the sense of highlighting Jewish achievement'. But they were also instructed to present a Jewish community 'which, while preserving and fostering its own culture and way of life was at the same time fully integrated into the life of South Africa, making its due contribution to the progress and development of this country'.

The editors' somewhat contradictory instructions were a product of the context within which the volume was conceived and produced. In the wake of the National Party's advent to power in 1948, Jews were in the process of establishing a *modus vivendi* with a formerly hostile ruling party. Although relations between Jews and Afrikaners had improved, Jews still felt at risk, though significantly less so than in the recent past.

Though the book was not an official publication of the Board of Deputies, the contributors were mainly communal notables – attorneys, educators, journalists and rabbis – all sensitive to potential Jewish vulnerability under National Party rule and all apparently eager to present the Jewish community in the most favourable light. Thus *The Jews in South Africa* focused on the deep-rootedness of the community; its enterprise and contribution; and its supposedly apolitical character. 'Jews as a group, as opposed to individual Jews, have played no part in politics,' explained the editors. 'Whatever political causes individual Jews espoused, they acted as individuals, giving expression to their personal beliefs and convictions, and not as representatives of the Jewish group.'

The editors' disclaimer, which echoed the official mantra of the Board, was a response to mounting accusations that Jews were disproportionately represented in the radical organisations opposing the apartheid order. While noting that a 'few Jews' had 'been among the militant supporters of the campaign for non-European advancement', Saron insisted that 'the majority inclined to moderate, middle-of-the-road policies which avoid the extremes both of the left and of the right'. Significantly, Saron added a last-minute 'postscript', quoting at length generous praise of the Jews by the prime minister, Dr Malan, reported in the *SA Jewish Chronicle* in June 1955. The Jew, explained Malan, had identified 'himself with the country' and had 'become a good national as well as a good Jew … a good South African as well as a true son of Israel'.

This message was largely affirmed in the positive press reviews. *Die Burger*'s response, however, was more ambivalent and a reminder of the underlying tensions and concerns underpinning the book. While praising

Louis Hotz, journalist and social and economic researcher.

the book, it also lamented its 'misleadingly superficial' treatment of the vexed Jewish-Afrikaner relationship during the 1930s and 1940s, and regretted that 'official Jewry' as opposed to the 'Jew in the street' still 'found so little connection with the Afrikaner'.

Published in the same year as Saron and Hotz's history, Chief Rabbi Israel Abrahams's *The Birth of a Community* – which, like Herrman's book, focused on the early years – also included laudatory comments by Dr Malan about South African Jewry. The Jews in South Africa, the prime minister approvingly noted in a preface, had managed to maintain a distinctive 'racial' identity while contributing significantly to the society at large. They could, he argued, serve as a model for a complex 'multiracial country' like South Africa. In turn the author expressed his thanks for 'the deeply significant words of this great Elder Statesman of our country' that he was sure would 'long be remembered as a notable contribution to better race relations, among all sections of the population'.

What is to be done?

The quiescence of the South African Jewish community was the subject of a sharp exchange in November 1957 between Ronald Segal, the youthful editor of *Africa South*, an anti-apartheid quarterly, and Dan Jacobson, a young South African novelist living in London. The exchange was published in *Commentary*, an American journal of opinion.

Ronald Segal

Some time ago … I came across … an article by Dan Jacobson on 'The Jews of South Africa.' When I put the magazine down again, I felt cheated somehow and angry. But it was a good anger, for it forced me to reconsider my moral judgment of the South African Jewish community.

I am, like Mr. Jacobson, a South African Jew. My parents were both communal leaders … My home was in all fundamentals a passionately Jewish one and I was brought up from the beginning to believe that being a Jew entailed unavoidable responsibilities and duties – superficially toward the community and the wider society of which I was a part, basically toward broad principles of justice and generosity. One's first duty was to one's own, but it did not stop there …

South African Jews are forever conscious of injustice, but of the injustice that they alone are made to suffer. They quickly grow furious over the treatment of Israel … Yet they watch with complacency the innumerable daily manifestations of 'apartheid' … How can this one-eyed morality be defended?

… when the Africans of Sophiatown were dispossessed of their homes and their right to own land and property in Johannesburg, when they were driven from their houses in the early morning between lines of armed police, how many leaders of Jewish communal organizations protested? There was not one public statement, not one deputation, no representations to the government were made …

No form of oppression is as intimately an experience of the Jews as the ghetto. Yet no Jewish organization, let alone the bugle of the community, the South African Jewish Board of Deputies, has attacked or even delicately protested against the savage Group Areas Act, which will segregate the races of the country into separate residential pockets at immeasurable sacrifice always to the non-whites …

The invariable excuse for their silence, that Jews as Jews cannot be expected to protest officially against any particular legislation, is ludicrous and, in the context of the community's general pattern of behaviour, hypocritical. Jews as Jews in South Africa have often in the past made representations to the government on immigration laws …

At the time of writing, the Native Laws Amendment bill has passed through the lower house of the South African parliament … it confers … the authority to forbid the attendance of Africans and Europeans at the same religious service. When the terms of the bill were first announced, there was public uproar. Especially were the churches outraged, as they saw in the bill a frontal assault upon religious freedom.

… Only the synagogues have sat on in silence, and to date only one rabbi has protested against the principles of the bill … If ever there was a time when South African Jewry should have cried aloud its protest, it was surely at the introduction of a bill to control the freedom of man to worship as they please. Yet it said nothing …

… I do believe that the Jews have a peculiar heritage and an especial character formed by that heritage. That heritage and that character give them a sharpened sense of the difference between right and wrong, between oppression and liberty, and also a great capacity for sacrifice, yes, even for martyrdom. Unfortunately, that heritage and character also instill in them an enormous fear of authority, a reluctance to fall out with those in power unless it is absolutely necessary to their continued existence as a community. Let us hope that they realize in time just how necessary martyrdom, of the kind of which they have shown themselves so capable in the past, is and will increasingly be. That at the moment they should be on the side of the persecutors and not the persecuted in South Africa, whether by commission or quiet omission, seems to me an abdication of their moral place in history.

Dan Jacobson

I was invited by the editors of *Commentary* to review the recently published *History of the Jews in South Africa* ... In the article I indicated that the Jews of South Africa are not, as Jews, taking a stand against the repressive policies of the South African government toward the non-white citizens of the country: this conclusion Mr. Segal confirms very forcefully indeed ...

... I wish I knew as confidently as Mr. Segal what the Jewish tradition enjoins on Jews in a situation like that prevailing in South Africa today. Mr. Segal is aware that the tradition is a complex thing. He knows that if it seeks justice, it also encourages 'a reluctance to fall out with those in power' ... From such a tradition ... we cannot get a single clear directive to present action ...

Mr. Segal gives details of some of the recent repressive legislation enacted by the South African government, and indignantly denounces the lack of protest from the Jewish community, as a community, against this legislation; he contrasts this with the official pronouncements made by other religious groups in the country. It seems clear to me that the Jewish community has settled into what is admittedly an unheroic posture: it raises its voice when it feels its own immediate interests are threatened ... and for the rest it keeps mum.

... there are very few white people who try to cross the gulf between white and black ... those who do have to make great sacrifices ... while there will always be Jews among these people, these Jews will remain a tiny minority among their co-religionists ... To the minority all honour is due; but to honour the minority does not compel me to regard the majority as altogether despicable, or altogether without dignity ...

'Is the idea that in certain circumstances an entire community should be composed of martyrs really so difficult to entertain?' asks Mr. Segal. It is not merely difficult, it is impossible for me to imagine that any community will ever sacrifice itself for the sake of *another* ... Did any *group* ever sacrifice itself for the sake of the Jews, either in the Middle Ages or later? Did any group sacrifice itself for the Jews of Europe from 1933 onward?

Until the Jews of South Africa as a group are persuaded of an immediate identity of material and spiritual interest between themselves and the non-whites in the country, they are not going to do what Mr. Segal wants them to do.

... as a result of their upbringing in a passionately color-conscious society, South African Jews in general actually *share* all the color prejudices of their fellow whites. When I think in the simplest possible way of my innumerable relatives, friends, and acquaintances in South Africa going about their business and pursuing what they believe to be their interests, in all conscience I can only wonder what people Mr. Segal thinks he is talking about when he issues his appeals for disinterested sacrifices and martyrdoms, and then grows so angry because there is no reply. Is he talking about people at all?

Bold women: challenging the status quo

Like their white gentile peers, middle-class Jewish women in mid-twentieth-century South Africa tended to remain at home rather than pursue careers. When they ventured beyond the home, most devoted their energy to Jewish causes. Few participated in public life which was generally a male preserve. Among the striking exceptions were four Jewish women – Bertha Solomon, Ellen Hellmann, Helen Suzman and Ruth First. Each confronted the South African status quo, albeit in different arenas: Solomon in the legal and parliamentary domain; Hellmann in extraparliamentary research and advocacy; Suzman in parliamentary politics; and First in revolutionary activism.

All four were children of immigrants, all grew up in South Africa, all were university graduates, and all made a major mark on male-dominated terrain. Bertha Solomon (1892-1969) was a pioneering campaigner for women's rights in South Africa. Born in Minsk in White Russia, she came to South Africa as a child of four. Her father, Idel Schwartz, was a noted Hebrew scholar and became a prominent Zionist leader in Cape Town. Solomon attended the Hope Mill Jewish School and the Good Hope Seminary School for Girls before attaining a masters degree in classics at the South African College and a teaching qualification. After marrying and settling in Johannesburg, she qualified as a lawyer and became one of the first female advocates in the country. She was the first woman to present a case before the Appeal Court in Bloemfontein. From the start of her career she was intensely aware of gender inequities in South African law, particularly discrimination against married women. Following her election to parliament in 1938 as a member of the United Party, she fought for years to eliminate these disabilities, culminating in the passage of 'Bertha's Bill', the Matrimonial Affairs Act of 1953.

Ellen Hellmann (1908-1982) was born in Johannesburg to German Jewish immigrant parents. She attended Barnato Park and the Commercial High School before studying social anthropology at the University of the Witwatersrand where she obtained a masters degree for a thesis examining the lives of African slum dwellers.

She was the first woman to obtain a doctorate of philosophy at the University, subsequently published as the *Problems of Urban Bantu Youth*. Hellmann's research inspired a lifelong commitment to fighting racial inequity. She played a leading role in the liberal South African Institute of Race Relations, guiding its highly regarded research activities.

Helen Suzman (1917-) was born in Germiston on the East Rand near Johannesburg and was the daughter of *Litvak* immigrants. Her father, Samuel Gavronsky, was a prosperous businessman. After her schooling at Parktown Convent in Johannesburg, Suzman's university education was interrupted by marriage. After the birth of her children, she returned to the University of the Witwatersrand, completed her degree and became a lecturer in economic history. She entered parliament as a member of the United Party in 1953. Six years later she was part of a liberal breakaway group that founded the Progressive Party. Suzman was its sole representative in parliament for 13 years, energetically championing the disenfranchised, and winning worldwide recognition.

Ruth First (1925-1982) was born in Johannesburg and was the daughter of Julius and Matilda 'Tilly' First, both founder members of the Communist Party of South Africa. Her father Julius, an immigrant from Latvia, was a successful furniture manufacturer. First was educated at Jeppe High School for Girls in Johannesburg and at the University of the Witwatersrand where she combined academic success with political engagement. Subsequently she married Joe Slovo, a fellow communist activist, and became a journalist, working for *The Guardian,* a radical newspaper, where she earned a reputation for her investigative journalism, exposing the abuses of apartheid society. Concurrently, she was involved in political activism and with her husband was one of the Treason Trialists in the late 1950s. In 1963 she was arrested under the draconian '90-day law' and spent 117 days in solitary confinement. She went into exile the following year where she forged a successful academic career. She was killed in Maputo in 1982

Ruth First and her husband, Joe Slovo (centre), with Archbishop Ambrose Reeves during the Treason Trial.

Bertha Solomon.

by a letter bomb sent by agents of the apartheid state.

While Ruth First, as a communist, was dismissive of her ethnic ties (and scornful of those Jews who were publicly quiescent in the face of apartheid though privately opposed), Solomon, Hellmann and Suzman were more attached to theirs. Like her parents Solomon was an ardent Zionist and often visited Israel. Suzman was not active in Jewish causes but supported these, including Israel. Hellmann was actively engaged, serving for a decade on the executive of the Board of Deputies where she hoped to persuade the community to become more engaged with the problems of the society at large.

Ellen Hellmann.

Helen Suzman.

Reform rabbis David Sherman and Moses Cyrus Weiler.

Continued from page 135

values. Few rabbis rose to the challenge. Their general reticence reflected, at least in part, the conservatism and fearfulness of their congregants. When André Ungar, a Reform rabbi in Port Elizabeth and Holocaust survivor, spoke out against the iniquities of apartheid in the mid-fifties, he incurred the wrath of members of his community. As he later ruefully recalled, he faced a 'barrage of telephone calls, personal visits, emergency meetings ... threats, reproofs [and] anonymous letters'. He also earned a stern rebuke from the president of the South African Union of Progressive Judaism, J Heilbron, for criticising 'members of our Government, men with outstanding careers behind them, and men who have been appointed to act as this country's leaders and spokesmen'.

Ungar was denounced in the press by an enraged Jewish correspondent as a 'non-desirable visitor to South Africa' who 'lacks the sense of responsibility and dignity of a responsible leader of a community'. The Board of Deputies distanced itself from Ungar and did not object when the young Hungarian rabbi was forced by the government to leave the country. Even Rabbi Moses Cyrus Weiler, the senior Reform minister in South Africa, who was deeply sensitive to the plight of the black majority, failed to support his outspoken junior colleague.

Speaking out did not always come at a severe personal cost. Ungar's rabbinical colleague in Cape Town, the American-born David Sherman, addressed a mass meeting in the early sixties, protesting the state's assault on civil liberties,

Eastern Province Herald

Oldest newspaper in South Africa.

Registered at G.P.O. as a newspaper.

Vol. 117. No. 291.

PORT ELIZABETH, MONDAY, DECEMBER 10, 1956.

++ PRICE 5d.

MOMENTOUS PARIS TALKS START TODAY

America to forget past discords with Allies

PARIS, Sunday.—(Sapa-Reuter).

MR. JOHN FOSTER DULLES, American Secretary of State, and Mr. Selwyn Lloyd, British Foreign Secretary, arrived in Paris to start what most European diplomats consider one of the most momentous series of discussions within the Western Alliance since World War II.

Immediately he stepped out of the plane bringing him from Washington, Mr. Dulles issued a prepared statement saying America's promise was "to bury past discords in a future of peaceful and fruitful co-operation."

This was understood to indicate Washington's readiness to forget its previous resentment over Anglo-French action in Egypt.

Main item in the diplomatic talks week is a four-day meeting of the Ministerial Council of Nato, but chief interest attaches to direct talks that may take place between America, Britain and France outside the Nato meeting.

In private

Unlike previous Nato gatherings this one will not be presided by an official "Big Three" meeting as Mr. Dulles apparently believes that such a meeting, with French and British troops still in Port Said, would create a wrong impression.

But, he is expected to lose no time in getting into touch separately with the British and French. He is due to lunch with Mr. Selwyn Lloyd, the British Foreign Secretary, tomorrow and is due at the French Foreign Minister, M. Christian Pineau, a few hours later.

The foreign ministers of the 15 nations of the North Atlantic Treaty Organisation will be in Paris to interchange, mainly on defence and finance and defence matters.

— (Sapa-U.P.)

Continued on Page 2

West must share its burdens

WASHINGTON, Sunday.

THE shock over Suez will serve as a catalyst to produce a wholesale re-examination of Western policies and responsibilities, and a more careful sharing of burdens, said the Washington Post in an editorial today.

"Bold and radical solutions are needed to put Western Europe really on its feet again.

"There was a great deal that the European countries themselves could do to remove internal trade barriers, to join in a common market, to develop an atomic energy pool and to promote political association. But there are also some essential tasks for the United States to perform," said the editorial.

— (Sapa-U.P.)

ILLICIT LIQUOR GANG SMASHED

From Our Correspondent

JOHANNESBURG, Sunday.

A band of over 20 detectives from the Eastern Transvaal division of the South African Police, under the direction of Major J. A. Coetzee, smashed the biggest illicit liquor organisation operating on the East Rand.

Expulsion of Rabbi

religion and it is my duty to take what I consider to be a "word approach to all action that concerns the life and rights and welfare of my people."

"It is not that they are Nationalists that worries me, but in their policies, I consider there have been certain actions the ethical principles of which all religions, not only mine, cannot accept."

It was the basic motives behind Government actions which he had opposed and those were mainly the separation and subordination of people. He thought the expulsion order was a result of his criticism of such policies as the refusal of a passport to an African scholar to study overseas, the Group Areas Act and the Bantu Education Act.

"What I criticised was not so much the individual acts of those in power, but the motive behind these acts," he said.

Duty of man

Dr. Ungar said: "I consider it the duty of all men of faith, especially of ministers of religion, to fight against prejudice, oppression and man's inhumanity to man wherever they are.

"Primarily it is with the problems of the society in which he lives that a religious man must grapple, but his moral responsibilities reaches beyond geographical confines."

Mrs. Ungar and their three-year-old daughter, Michaela, plan to leave South Africa this month. This had been arranged before the expulsion order was received.

Dr. Ungar, who has lately been assisting Hungary rebel efforts, is due to address the Publicity Club at Port Elizabeth on the present-day situation in his home country on Wednesday.

[Further continued]

WELL AND TRULY OUT

THIS is how men of the British Tank Corps in Port Said received the news that they would be out of Egypt and back to "Blighty" before Christmas.

Hungary cut off from the world

BUDAPEST, Sunday.

BUDAPEST was cut off following a defiant call for a two-day nation-wide general strike tomorrow. An appeal all over the world, to put in their protest against the regime...

Continued from Page 1

BIG PARIS TALKS START TODAY

Continued from Page 1

Mr. Dulles' statement today was cordial and positive. He emphasised the need to unite against Soviet truculence and specified again America's willingness to help oil-starved Europe with American supplies. But French opinion at least considers that more than this be needed completely.

What French diplomats want to know is the United States attitude on general Western policy in the Middle East and on Algeria, where France is heavily engaged in an effort to maintain her sovereignty.

Heavy agenda

The Nato session has a heavy agenda, of which the main items are:

■ Secret debate on the situation in the Middle East and Eastern Europe.
■ Number of troops needed by Nato for 1957.
■ Measures to compensate for absence of French Nato troops in Algeria and delay in producing a West German contingent.
■ Adaptation of Nato stategy and tactics to recent developments in thermo-nuclear weapons on both sides of the Iron Curtain.
■ Turkish proposal for extending benefits of Nato protection to Iran and Iraq, two members of the Bagdad Pact (which also includes Turkey, Pakistan and Britain.)

Leading Nato delegation members of various countries were agreed today that what matters in the coming week is the extent to which the various meetings and proceedings on the official schedule lead to a restoration of the Three-Power Western front between the United States, Britain and France.

Cameraman back from 'paradise'

From Our Correspondent
JOHANNESBURG, Sunday.

PHOTOGRAPHER JOHN EVERARD and his journalist wife, Jane, bounced their truck and caravan back over 15,000 miles of some of the worst roads in Africa and into Johannesburg during the weekend, with the news that they had "discovered a painless route to Africa's greatest paradise."

"One of the most splendidly scenic holiday resorts in the world and a real little bit of the Continent dropped in the heart of Africa."

City Rabbi ordered to leave country

RABBI DR. ANDRE UNGAR, head of the Jewish Reform Congregation in Port Elizabeth, has been ordered by the Minister of the Interior, Dr. T. E. Donges, to leave South Africa by January 15. No reasons were given in the brief letter telling Dr. Ungar of his expulsion.

Although the letter came as a complete surprise, Dr. Ungar regarded it with "some amusement" as he had already accepted an appointment in London and had planned to leave the Union at the end of January.

Although Dr. Ungar, an outspoken critic of the Nationalists racial ideologies, does not know the reason for his expulsion, he believes it is because of his frank condemnation of certain Government policies which he has made from the pulpit, on public platforms and in articles.

Born in Hungary, Dr. Ungar, who is 26 years old, studied at London University where he took his B.A. with honours in classical scientific languages and his Doctor of Philosophy in modern philosophy. A brilliant student, he took both degrees together and qualified as a rabbi at the age of 20.

Permit

He came to South Africa from England two years ago to become minister of Temple Israel. Because he was not born in Britain he could only enter the Union on a temporary permit and it is this that Dr. Donges has cancelled.

Immediately he arrived in Port Elizabeth, Dr. Ungar became an ardent church, welfare and race relations worker. He is a committee member of the Institute of Race Relations, acting hon. treasurer of the Child Welfare Society, a member of the Distressed Areas Committee, and a member of the Central Enclosure and of the S.A. Union for Progressive Judaism.

The letter notifying Dr. Ungar of his expulsion was addressed to the Secretary of the P.E. Jewish Reform Congregation and was signed by the Secretary for the Interior.

It read: "I have to inform you that the Honourable the Minister of the Interior has directed that the temporary permit issued to Dr. Andre Ungar be cancelled in terms of Sec. 8 (a) of Art. No. 1 of 1937 and that he be ordered to leave the country on or before January 15, 1957."

Dr. Ungar told the Herald yesterday: "I am not a politician and the politics of anyone are not my business as such. But, on the other hand, I am a minister of

Continued on Page 3

Dr. Andre Ungar

3

Syria said to be in hands of Communist dictator

NICOSIA, Sunday.—(Sapa-U.P.)

COLONEL SERRAJ, a 31-year-old military intelligence officer is today the virtual dictator of Syria, according to reports which has taken over the present Middle East...

FRESH CRISIS IN HUNGARY

Continued from Page 1

at Pecs, Tatabanya and Berkesabca.

Meanwhile travellers arriving in Vienna report that the Budapest population is becoming increasingly defiant and that the likelihood of further bloodshed was increasing hourly.

Summary courts

Budapest radio, quoting the Government's declaration of martial law, said new legal steps were necessary because "there are still quantities of arms in the hands of the people."

It said Mr. Istvan Dobi, President of the Republic, had ordered summary courts to be set up to deal with such offences as "armed actions, murder and looting." These would function at 6 p.m. on December 11. "Persons surrendering arms or ammunition by that time would be pardoned.

The Kadar Government has also ordered the immediate dissolution of the Budapest Central Workers' Council and the provincial workers councils.

Russians

Sources said the highly technical manner in which the pumping stations were destroyed led to the belief that the Russians might have been involved.

Strict military censorship has been imposed throughout Syria, Western correspondents being barred from entering.

Political opponents of Colonel Serraj have been imprisoned or forced into exile, while large quantities of Soviet arms are reported to have been imported.

A Western diplomat travelling through Syria early this summer was greeted by the manager of a Damascus hotel with the words: "Welcome, Tovarich" — half in English, half in Russian.

Eight Soviet army officers also recently appeared at an official Damascus reception. Nothing, however, is known of a large-scale influx of Soviet instructors and technicians, nor of any Russian "volunteers."

Modern arms

Experts in Cyprus said, however, that it was doubtful whether the 25,000-man Syrian army could handle the amount of modern arms which were reported to have been shipped to Russia.

These included 100 T-34 tanks, 200 armoured troop carriers, and an unknown quantity of Mig-jets.

Civil airline flights over Syrian territory have now been restricted to companies whose capital is mainly controlled by Arabs, and whose planes are manned by Arab crews.

Aircraft crossing Syrian territory are forbidden to carry British, French or Commonwealth citizens, and must touch down at Damascus for a security check. The only airline plying these regulations is the Egyptian. All other lines have been re-routed.

FOUR DIE OF STAB WOUNDS

CAPE TOWN, Sunday. — Four Coloured men died in Cape Town yesterday after having received stab wounds.

An unknown Native was found yesterday when the hut he was in was destroyed by fire. His body was found after a fire, which destroyed two huts at the corner of 12th Avenue and 3rd Street, Windermere.—(Sapa.)

LATE SMALLS

No Red forces in Syria says Soviet Press

LONDON, Sunday.

THE Soviet Army newspaper Red Star, said today that "there has not been, nor is there a single Soviet soldier or officer in Syria," according to the official Soviet news agency, Tass.

"On the other hand there are many American soldiers and officers in Turkey," an article by Mr. A. Leontyev said.

"There was no foreign military base in Syria, but in Turkey '15 big air bases and five naval bases are being built or reconstructed under the plans of the North Atlantic Treaty Organisation Command."—(Sapa-Reuter).

Visitor rule at Fort to be tested

From Our Correspondent
JOHANNESBURG, Sunday.

COLONEL D. J. SCHOLTZ, Superintendent of the Fort, must show cause tomorrow why Mrs. Helen Joseph, one of the "treason" detainees being held there, should not be allowed to receive visitors.

In the Rand Supreme Court yesterday, Mr. Justice Ramsbottom issued an order to this effect, following an urgent application by Mrs. Joseph.

It is understood that this is in the nature of a "test" case to obtain a ruling on visitors to the "treason" prisoners.

Ships' positions

Distances of ships from Port Elizabeth at midnight:

LEFT: *The Old Synagogue, Pretoria, site of the Treason Trial.*

BELOW: *Israel 'Issie' Maisels carried by jubilant supporters at the successful conclusion of the Treason Trial.*

OPPOSITE: *Police raid a Treason Trialists' party at the home of Joe Slovo, c.1958.*

without harming his position. Similarly, Louis Rabinowitz, the fiery Chief Rabbi of the (Transvaal-centred) Federation of Synagogues of South Africa, unequivocally condemned apartheid, branding it 'an abomination that desecrates the sanctity of life' without running into difficulty. The British-trained rabbi was critical of the lay leadership's mantra that the community should not take a collective stance on political issues. Rabinowitz, who on occasion participated in public protest alongside Christian clerics, expressed frustration with the repressive climate within which South African rabbis ministered. 'No matter how rigidly he confines himself to the purely ethical and religious implications of the prevalent racial policy,' Rabinowitz complained to the (London) *Jewish Chronicle*, 'the moment he utters a word which can be construed as a criticism of that policy he is immediately charged with "preaching politics".'

Unlike the timid and cautious lay leadership, who were cowed by the repressive and authoritarian 'McCarthyite' atmosphere, Rabinowitz refused to distance himself from those radical Jews who directly confronted the apartheid system. There are, he told his congregants in a *Yom Kippur* sermon in 1959, 'some Jews in the community who do attempt to do something and when, as a result, they fall foul of the powers that be, the defence put up by the Jewish community is to prove that these are Jews only by name, that they do not belong to any synagogue …'

Rabinowitz had in mind those Jewish radicals who were confronting the apartheid state. From 1948 Jews were conspicuous among the handful of whites who actively supported the freedom struggle of the black majority. The lawyer Sam Kahn, a communist who had been a member of Young Israel in his youth, was a 'Native Representative' in parliament till the proscription of the Communist Party at the start of the fifties. Jewish radicals took part in the Defiance Campaign of 1952 and were members of the clandestine South African Communist Party and of the (white) Congress of Democrats. The latter was allied to the African National Congress and the other progressive groupings that convened the Congress of the People in 1955 at Kliptown, Soweto, where the Freedom Charter was adopted. Lionel 'Rusty' Bernstein played a key role in drafting this historic statement of ANC policy.

Among the 156 activists arrested and accused of Treason in 1956, 23 were white and of these a disproportionate 14 were Jewish, 4 of whom were women. The protracted trial, which only ended in 1961, was conducted in the gracious 'Old Synagogue' building in Pretoria, vacated by a suburbanising local Jewish community a few years earlier. The victorious defence team was

Roads to Radicalism

Scholars agree that Jews were overrepresented in the ranks of radical opposition to apartheid. But they differ about the reasons for this.

Immanuel Suttner, editor of *Cutting Through the Mountain. Interviews with South African Jewish Activists*, argues that 'Jewishness frequently acted as a subtle catalyst' in determining the activists' political choices. Though often deracinated, their 'awareness of the historical dehumanisation of the Jews was the experiential ground in which blossomed the conviction that no one else should be dehumanised'. Moreover their dissent and iconoclasm were quintessentially 'Jewish'. The activists 'are all idol smashers, people who refuse to bow before the consensus. The aspect of Jewish tradition they link up to is the tradition of non-conformism, rebuke and solidarity with the underdog; a tradition

which manifested in biblical stories which established the dissenter … as the hero.'

Glenn Frankel, author of *Rivonia's Children. Three Families and the Cost of Conscience in White South Africa*, also identifies 'Jewishness' as an important factor informing Jewish radicalism. 'It was no surprise that many of the activists were openly hostile to Judaism and Jewish causes,' he writes. 'What none of them saw was that their alienation from Judaism and their radicalism were consistent with one wing of Jewish tradition – that even as rejectionists they were firmly within the larger family of their contentious and self-contradictory faith.'

Gideon Shimoni, author of *Community and Conscience. The Jews in Apartheid South Africa*, dismisses what he labels the 'Judaic values' theory, instead stressing the ethos

Ike Horvitch (left), Sam Kahn (centre), at the Grand Parade, Cape Town, 1950.

within particular families as a possible key to explaining Jewish overrepresentation in activist politics. The immigrant home, where there were communist sympathies or affiliations, was, he argues, a major factor. But Shimoni also observes that many radicals cut their political teeth in the Zionist movement which 'provided a stimulus for political awareness and sometimes a training ground for radical activism'.

James Campbell, an American scholar, discounts religious and cultural legacies and instead underlines the impact of migration and the consequent disruption and alienation. Immigration was a profoundly disruptive experience, he argues, and South Africa's celebrated Jewish radicalism may be less a product of community 'tradition', handed down from generation to generation, than a function of historically specific processes of dislocation and conflict. Drawing on a rich genre of South African Jewish autobiography, including the memoirs of Hyman Basner, Baruch Hirson, Pauline Podbrey and Joe Slovo, Campbell highlights common experiences of marginality and dislocation. Radical politics, he writes, 'and the Communist Party in particular, represented more than just a new political affiliation. It offered community, human contact, a warmth and solidarity otherwise absent from their daily lives.'

Albie Sachs (second from left) and Hymie Rochman being escorted from a 'non-Europeans only' entrance to the Cape Town Post Office during the Defiance Campaign, 1952.

Anyone for Revolution? (Standing from left to right) Harold Wolpe, Fred Schermbrucker, Ben Turok, Wilf East, Julius Baker, Ben Arenstein and Hymie Barsel. (Kneeling, left to right) Joe Slovo and Rusty Bernstein. All but East were later to become political prisoners.

led by Advocate Israel 'Issie' Maisels, assisted by Sydney Kentridge, son of the long-serving parliamentarian, Morris Kentridge. The prosecution team was led before his death by Oswald Pirow, leader of the wartime pro-Hitler New Order.

In the wake of the 1960 Sharpeville massacre of 69 peaceful demonstrators and of the subsequent banning of the ANC, resistance to apartheid turned from non-violent means to armed struggle. 'In 1961 history left us with no option but to engage in armed actions as a necessary part of the political struggle,' Joe Slovo later recalled. This new strategy was seriously disrupted in July 1963 when state security operatives carried out a successful raid on Lilliesleaf Farm in Rivonia on the outskirts of Johannesburg, which had been purchased by Arthur Goldreich as the headquarters for the underground SACP and as a safe house for political fugitives. Among the 17 arrested, all 5 of the whites were Jewish. At the 'Rivonia Trial' that led to the incarceration of Nelson Mandela, Jews were prominent on both sides. Besides those in the dock, the young Jewish lawyers Joel Joffe and Arthur Chaskalson formed part of the defence team, while Percy Yutar – Deputy Attorney General of the Transvaal province and a respected Jewish communal figure – led the prosecution.

Almost all the Jewish radicals were 'non-Jewish Jews' in Isaac Deutscher's classic formulation. With their Marxist allegiances, they were committed to a universalism that left little space for ethnic particularism. As Pauline Podbrey, an activist of the forties who went into exile in the fifties, reminisced, 'it now seems as if everybody was Jewish. But there was no sense of Jewishness amongst them. Nobody ever discussed their Jewishness or brought it forward as an issue, and it was quite irrelevant to the politics of the day.

I suspect that quite a few of us were not too anxious to be identified as Jewish, although nobody made a conscious effort to deny it. But it just wasn't allowed to impinge on Party work. It would have been seen as a concession to nationalism.'

The high visibility of Jews within the radical left was not lost on the state and the Nationalist press. It mattered little that these Jews were estranged from the community and a source of embarrassment to its leadership. 'Where does the Jew stand in the white struggle for survival?' asked Dirk Richard, editor of *Dagbreek*. 'The Jew is nowadays often the theme of a suspicious discourse. The suspicion is kindled by the numerous Jewish names among underminers, leftists, NUSAS [the liberal National Union of South African Students] leaders and the most poisonous journalists … When one is suspicious of a group, one judges it facilely by the deeds of its most extreme members.' Richard demanded that South African Jewry 'take a stand as a group' against those threatening the 'existing order'.

This broadside – one of a number in the sixties – was combined with an attack on Israel's support for the Afro-Asian bloc's condemnation of apartheid at the United Nations. At a time when 'liberal' and 'communist' were terms of opprobrium in the Nationalist lexicon, attacks of this sort reminded Jews of their vulnerability and spurred the mainstream to distance itself from the radicals. But while doing so, they were not wholly insensitive to the plight of the black countrymen.

Some took part in educational, healthcare and philanthropic endeavours. Encouraged by Rabbi Weiler, the Women's Sisterhood of the Progressive Congregation of Johannesburg set up and supported an elementary school in Alexandra

Opening in 1942 of the Cape Town Coloured children's crèche in Kensington by the Union of Jewish Women.

Township, and took under its wing a high school in Pimville. The Union of Jewish Women ran crèches in 'non-white' areas in Johannesburg and Cape Town and sponsored a non-racial bursary for nursing training, but carefully avoided taking any public stance. While not insignificant, such outreach activities were secondary to an inwardly-focused community's central concerns: the consolidation of communal institutions and support for Israel. Increasingly South African-born Jews took the lead in these matters.

The fifties and sixties were decades of growth and optimism for the Jewish community. By 1951 the Jewish population had expanded to 108 497; within two decades it had reached what would be its zenith, 118 200. Growth was slower than that of the wider white population, with the Jewish proportion shrinking from 4.1 per cent in 1951 to 3.1 per cent in 1970. The modest

Toni Saphra (standing), founder and first leader of the Union of Jewish Women of South Africa.

Function at MC Weiler School, Alexandra Township, Johannesburg.

expansion was largely due to natural increase with immigration hardly playing a role. (A trickle of Sephardi Jews began arriving after the Congo crisis in 1960.) Emigration was also limited in these decades, accelerating in the wake of the Sharpeville crisis.

Within the country, however, there was substantial movement. Like their black and Afrikaner neighbours, albeit for very different reasons, Jews in the countryside were moving to the larger centres. While the former were often propelled by rural poverty, Jews, and particularly the younger generation, were drawn to the cities by educational and career opportunities and by a wish to be part of a larger Jewish concentration. Parents sometimes followed their children while the elderly often retired to the cities. Between 1946 and 1970 the Jewish population beyond the metropolitan areas fell by roughly a third, from 15 137 to 9 570. During the same period, the Jewish population of Johannesburg grew from 50 371 to 61 325, Durban's from 4 132 to 5 990, while Cape Town's increased from 19 589 to 25 650, leaving many small-town communities substantially denuded.

Along the 'Great North Road' from Pretoria a string of once-thriving Jewish communities atrophied. Potgietersrus fell precipitously from 105 in 1951 to 9 in 1980, and Pietersburg from 323 to 178. Warmbaths – at one time a popular holiday destination for Jews from Johannesburg and Pretoria who stayed at its kosher hotels and supported a morning *minyan* before enjoying its hot springs – shrank from 172 in 1951 to 38 in 1980. Communities along the 'national road' to the north from the Cape suffered a similar fate. Worcester declined from 403 to 85; Beaufort West from 77 to 8; and Colesberg from 22 to 1, a solitary Jewish woman.

Jacob Newman, Rabbi to the Country Communities of South Africa.

Concern about the decline of these and many other small communities prompted the Board of Deputies to appoint a Rabbi to the Country Communities of South Africa in 1951. Rabbi Jacob Newman, the first incumbent, found that standards of religious education were low. 'A large percentage of ministers now serving rural centres are well beyond the age of retirement,' he observed. With 'very few exceptions, these ministers were trained only in one aspect of their sacred task, and that is Shechita [ritual slaughtering]. In regard to teaching, or pastoral work … they had no training and no guidance, except through experience won the hard way.'

Temple Menorah, Pretoria.

Newman also noted that relations between Jew and non-Jew on the *platteland* (countryside) were 'pleasant and cordial'. Clearly the tensions of the thirties and early forties had subsided. The *Boerejood* was fully bilingual in English and Afrikaans and comfortably integrated into a small-town life dominated by Afrikaners. Many children attended Afrikaans-medium elementary schools though they were often sent away for their secondary schooling to distant English-medium boarding schools in the larger centres. 'The prevalent attitude among members of the rural centres,' Newman wrote, 'is that all that matters is the future of their children.'

The drift to the cities was matched by movement within the cities. With growing prosperity, Jews moved increasingly from the inner to the outer suburbs where they concentrated in particular middle-class neighbourhoods. In Johannesburg, by 1970, 72 per cent of the total white

population in Killarney and Glenhazel was Jewish; 63 per cent of Cyrildene; 56 per cent of Sydenham; 54 per cent of Emmarentia; and 53 per cent of Highlands North. At this time in Cape Town, 52 per cent of Fresnaye's total white population was Jewish; 36 per cent of neighbouring Sea Point; 23 per cent of Oranjezicht; and 11 per cent of Claremont. In Durban, Jews moved up to the Berea, while in Pretoria they migrated eastwards to the leafy suburbs.

With suburbanisation went building: *shuls*, schools and sports clubs. The post-war decades saw an energetic surge of construction, concrete testimony to the community's vigour and confidence in its future. A spate of new synagogues catered to the changing demographics. Their architectural style was modernist and far removed from the 'oriental' features of some of their grand predecessors, reflecting the community's South Africanisation. The elegant and

Great Synagogue, Durban.

functional Temple Menorah in Pretoria was built on the fringe of the city's opulent Waterkloof suburb. Claremont in Cape Town's affluent southern suburbs replaced its poorly-ventilated modest old *shul*, stifling on the crowded High Holidays, with a large and airy modern edifice. Durban sold its historic St Andrew's Street *shul* in the downtown and built the elaborate and spacious Great Synagogue on the Berea, over the objections of a minority of congregants that such a large structure was hardly justified by the poor synagogue attendance outside of the High Holidays.

Alongside the new synagogue, the other major building project of the fifties and the sixties was the Jewish day school: in Johannesburg, the King David schools in Linksfield and Victory Park, and Menora and the Yeshiva College in Glenhazel; in Cape Town, Weizmann in Sea Point and Herzlia on the slopes of Table Mountain; in Durban, Sharona and Carmel; in Port Elizabeth, Theodor

Herzl; in Benoni on the East Rand, Hillel; and in Pretoria, Carmel. Almost all these schools were sited on attractive and expansive suburban campuses and were modelled on the prestigious government and private schools with which they competed for the enrolment of Jewish children. To satisfy parental expectations ample sporting facilities were a *sine qua non*. For many Jewish fathers who shared the sports-mania of other South Africans, and who subscribed to a latterday South African version of 'muscular Judaism', the cricket bat and rugby ball were at least as important as the *siddur* (prayer book).

The parents' own sporting as well as social needs were catered for by the founding of predominantly Jewish sports and country clubs: among them, King David and Keurboom in Cape Town, Wingate in Pretoria, Beaconsfield, Reading and Kyalami in Johannesburg, and David Hillman Park in Durban. These were

From 'cradle to matric': educating Jewish South Africans

In the wake of the Holocaust and the creation of the state of Israel, Jewish education in South Africa underwent a sea change in the fifties and sixties. A network of nursery schools was established to cater for an increasing demand for pre-primary Jewish schooling. There was also a significant shift from the afternoon school, the *Talmud Torah*, colloquially know as the *cheder*, to the newly established 'day school'. By 1964 the Jewish day schools were attracting close to 4 500 pupils and were beginning to redress the previous gender imbalance in Jewish education; in earlier decades the Jewish education of females had been a low priority. Despite the growth of the day schools, the *Talmud Torahs* survived, albeit uneasily.

Among the key figures in the rise of the Jewish day school were Isaac Goss and Norman Sandler in Johannesburg and Myer Katz in Cape Town. The South African-born Goss built on the legacy of his mentor and predecessor at the South African Jewish Board of Education, Rabbi Judah Leib Zlotnik. The guiding formula, devised in the mid-1940s, was that Jewish education would be based on a 'national-traditional' approach, a compromise between the requirements of religion and of secular Zionism. 'Equal emphasis was to be placed on the national content of Judaism as on its religious,' explained Chief Rabbi Louis Rabinowitz some years later. 'Hebrew and "Yiddishkeit," Israel and the Torah, the values of each would be stressed equally …'

King David School, Linksfield, Johannesburg.

Herzlia School, Cape Town.

The nursery and day schools provided a 'cradle-to-matric' Jewish education, comfortably integrated with secular studies and sport, so valued by South African-born Jewish parents. Many of these, members of the so-called 'lost generation', felt ill-equipped to impart Jewish knowledge to their offspring and preferred to delegate this task to the day school. But other parents feared what Isaac Goss termed the 'bugaboo' of segregation, that the day schools problematically separated young Jews from their gentile peers. To this Goss countered that the products of the schools 'mixed easily' and 'accepted their Jewishness naturally, and without evasion'. The King David schools – like their sister schools – prided themselves on their 'ideal of bi-cultural education' and on 'the splendid achievements by their children and students in every field of education and sport'.

Adding impetus to the movement towards the private day schools was

Norman Sandler.

Isaac Goss.

Judah Leib Zlotnik.

Myer Katz.

Weizmann School, Cape Town.

fear of Christian National Education, the policy elaborated in the late sixties which aimed to promote a Christian ethos in state schools and a Christo-centric education. But even without this threat, the day schools attracted growing numbers because of their evident success. They were perfectly pitched towards a parental mood which combined a pride in Jewishness and a fervent Zionism with a strong sense of (white) 'South Africanness'. They were also true 'community' schools, inclusive of all income groups and of all shades of Jewish identification. Some found them too religiously tepid and chose instead the more observant Yeshiva College, a modern Orthodox school in Johannesburg founded in 1951 by Rabbi Michel Kossowsky and led energetically from the mid-sixties by Rabbi Avraham Tanzer.

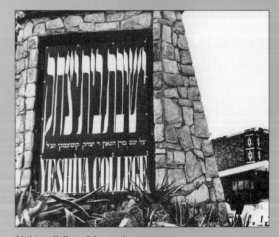

Yeshiva College, Johannesburg.

Smous *to sports hero*

Between 1930 and 1970 South African-born Jewish sportsmen were responsible for some of the great moments of South African sporting history. Louis Babrow scored two tries in the decisive Third Test of the 1937 Springbok Rugby tour of New Zealand to help seal an historic series victory against the All Blacks, South Africa's greatest rugby rivals. Aaron 'Okey' Geffin – 'The Boot' – kicked five penalties, scoring all the points, to win the First Test against the touring All Blacks in 1949. Syd Nomis's intercept try against the All Blacks at Loftus Versfeld in 1970 was accompanied by cries of 'Sydee, Sydee' over the public address system by the renowned Afrikaans rugby commentator, Gerhard Viviers. In the same year Aaron 'Ali' Bacher led the Springbok cricket team to a famous clean sweep over the touring Australians.

Babrow, Geffin, Nomis, Bacher and other Jewish sporting heroes – among them, Abe Segal in tennis, Sylvia Dyne in bowls, Morrie Jacobson in football, and Sid Kiel in athletics – pointed to the acculturation of a South African-reared generation, as did a host of Jewish sports fans and administrators such as Harry Getz in swimming and Lubbe Snoyman in football. South African Jews were as passionate about rugby, cricket and soccer as American-born Jews were about baseball. In

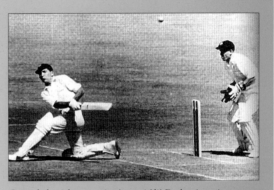

Springbok cricket captain Aaron 'Ali' Bacher in action.

Cape Town Jewish fans rushed on Friday nights from the Sabbath table to soccer at Hartleyvale, where in the 1960s Walter Gradner, one-time president of the Cape Town Hebrew Congregation, presided comfortably over Cape Town City, the local team.

The elevation of Jews to South Africa's sporting pantheon was indicative of their increasing acceptance by the wider society. Jewish sporting greats, whose 'alien' parents might have been treated with disdain, were now embraced as national heroes. Some supporters even joked that the success of a Springbok rugby team depended on having a Jewish member.

partly responses to a residual social exclusion of Jews by some elite English-speaking South Africans, practised by the likes of the Pretoria Country Club, Kelvin Grove and the Royal Cape Golf Club in Cape Town, and the Royal Johannesburg, Parkview and Kensington in Johannesburg. But the formation of these 'Jewish' clubs was also indicative of a desire for ethnic companionship in one's leisure time, with the Saturday morning 'four ball', or the Saturday afternoon 'rinks', trumping the morning *minyan* or afternoon *shiur*.

The sports club was a measure of spreading

affluence within the community. The trends identified by Sonnabend in the 1930s had strengthened with Jews opting for self-employment and entering the professions in ever-larger numbers. Between 1936 and 1960 there was a leap in the proportion of Jews in professional positions, from 9.7 per cent of the economically active Jewish population to 20 per cent. There was an equally dramatic shrinkage in the percentage in the 'sales' category from 48 per cent in 1936 to 29.1 per cent in 1960.

By 1970, 28 per cent of Jews who were economically active were employers of whom just

Golda Selzer and 'Frankie' Forman, distinguished medical academics of the University of Cape Town.

Isidor Gordon, Dean of the Medical School of the University of Natal.

Phillip Tobias, renowned palaeo-anthropologist of the University of the Witwatersrand.

under half were in commerce. This was in marked contrast to the 12 per cent who were employers in the economically active wider white population. Jewish women were less actively engaged in the work force than Jewish men. Of those aged 15 and over, 26 per cent were economically active as opposed to 59 per cent of the men. One in five of the working women were in 'sales', one in two in clerical occupations, and one in five in the professions, a huge jump since the pre-war years.

As elsewhere in the modern world, Jews preferred the independent professions. 'Jewish' accounting and law firms featured conspicuously in the central business districts of South Africa's cities. The Medical Centre on the Foreshore in Cape Town, like its Johannesburg and Pretoria counterparts, housed a legion of Jewish doctors. In 1960 approximately 23 per cent of all practising doctors registered in South Africa

Raymond 'Bill' Hoffenberg departs at
DF Malan airport, Cape Town, for exile.

were Jewish. The percentage among medical specialists was even higher, nearly one in three. Jews were also prominent in academic medicine, among them Golda Selzer, 'Frankie' Forman, Harry Zwarenstein and Raymond 'Bill' Hoffenberg at the University of Cape Town, Leo Schamroth, Harry Seftel and Phillip Tobias at the University of the Witwatersrand, and Isidor Gordon, Dean of the Medical School of the University of Natal. (Phillip Tobias, who, as an adolescent, considered becoming a rabbi, was to become an internationally renowned palaeo-anthropologist.) 'Bill' Hoffenberg was driven into exile in 1967 following his banning by the government for his opposition to apartheid and was later knighted for his services to medicine in the United Kingdom.)

Beyond the professions, a new breed of South African-born Jewish entrepreneur, often well educated, achieved prominence from the 1950s onwards, transforming particular sectors of the

The Arts

As elsewhere in the twentieth century, Jews in South Africa have played a conspicuous part in cultural life – as artists and performers, as patrons, dealers and impresarios, and as audiences, critics and devotees. Spanning generations, this energetic engagement has involved both immigrants and the locally born, and has drawn creatively from a range of European sources.

The German-born mining magnate Max Michaelis donated his collection of Flemish and Dutch masters to the country shortly after Union and financed the creation of the Michaelis Art School at the University of Cape Town in 1923. His contemporary, Alfred de Pass – grandson of the coastal shipping magnate, Aaron – similarly enriched South African art collections.

The acclaimed Lithuanian-born sculptor, Isaac 'Lippy' Lipschitz, was professor of Fine Art at the Michaelis School, and at one point shared a studio with the Polish-born artist, Wolf Kibel, who played a pioneering role in the introduction of Expressionism into South African art. Similarly, the sculptor Moses Kottler, born in Lithuania but trained in Munich, introduced European modes of expression.

Irma Stern, born to German Jewish parents in the remote western Transvaal town of Schweizer-Reneke, returned to the 'fatherland' to study art. She later made Cape Town her home which she used as a base for forays into Africa. Stern gained an international reputation for her expressionist work which drew inspiration from African subjects and artefacts.

The German Jewish refugees of the thirties brought with them their enthusiasm for *kultur*, in particular their love of classical music. Hans Kramer founded the Concert Club in Cape Town in 1955 which, together with Hans Adler's Johannesburg Musical Society, introduced South African audiences to international maestros. Earlier, Eastern European immigrants had transplanted a passion for theatre. Throughout the century, Jews contributed to the development of the dramatic arts in South Africa with people like Muriel Alexander founding the Johannesburg Repertory Players, and Cecilia Sonnenberg and Rene Ahrenson the open-air Shakespearian theatre at Maynardville in Cape Town.

Stanley Glasser, musical director of King Kong, *and below, Leon Gluckman, directing* King Kong.

Jews also contributed to broadening South African theatre beyond narrow racial confines. Ian Bernhardt, Harold Bloom, Leon Gluckman, Arthur Goldreich and Stanley Glasser played key roles in the 1959 production of the 'jazz opera', *King Kong*, with its all-black cast. Seventeen years later Barney Simon and Mannie Manim founded the Market Theatre in Johannesburg which played an heroic part in cultural resistance to apartheid. Its production of *Woza Albert*, directed and co-written by Simon, was riveting protest theatre. Jewish theatregoers, like other white members of the audience, might have felt more comfortable with the productions of Taubie Kushlick, the 'grande dame' of South African theatre, and Leonard Schach.

Irma Stern in her studio.

Barney Simon, co-founder of the Market Theatre, Joahnnesburg.

Taubie Kushlick, 'grande dame' of South African theatre.

Donald Gordon, founder of Liberty Life.

economy. Pre-eminent among these were Donald Gordon, Raymond Ackerman and Sol Kerzner. Ackerman, son of the retailing pioneer, Gus Ackerman, was schooled at the prestigious Diocesan College (Bishops) in Cape Town, while Gordon and Kerzner, both children of Eastern European immigrants, attended government schools in Johannesburg. Gordon and Kerzner qualified as chartered accountants at the University of the Witwatersrand, while Ackerman graduated with a commerce degree from the University of Cape Town.

In 1958, the 27-year-old Gordon founded a life assurance company, Liberty Life, which was floated four years later on the Johannesburg Stock Exchange. Through its business innovations, initially derided by critics, Liberty Life was to revolutionise the South African insurance industry. Raymond Ackerman had a more chequered career. He entered retailing, working for his father before playing a key role in building the pioneering Checkers supermarket chain. After his bruising dismissal in 1966, at the

Raymond Ackerman of Pick 'n Pay, chain store innovator.

Hotel magnate Sol Kerzner, the 'Sun King'.

age of 35, he bought a trio of stores in Cape Town, trading collectively as Pick 'n Pay. (The seller, Jack Goldin, went on later to found the Clicks 'health and beauty' chain.) Pick 'n Pay was floated in 1967 and proceeded to transform food retailing in South Africa, overshadowing the chain from which he was fired.

Sol Kerzner, the 'Sun King', was to the hotel industry what Gordon was to insurance and Ackerman to food retailing. Kerzner was introduced to hotel-keeping at the modest family-owned Menorah kosher hotel in Durban. At the age of 29 he built South Africa's first five-star hotel, the luxurious Beverley Hills, overlooking the warm Indian Ocean at Umhlanga Rocks north of the city. Within a few years he launched the Southern Sun hotel group, setting a new di-

rection for hoteliering in South Africa, and later still built Sun City, a resort in the apartheid-created 'homeland' of Bophuthatswana. This resort was known for its casinos and risqué entertainment, catering to escapees from the puritanism of apartheid South Africa.

Among the many visitors were Jews who, in their recreational preferences and in many other ways, were very much part and parcel of white South African society. By education and broad socialisation, Jews in the post-war decades largely shared the world-view, values and interests of their fellow English-speaking white suburbanites. But at the same time they were distinctive. By and large Jews continued to cluster in certain neighbourhoods and occupations, and marry other Jews. They had a powerful sense of

Chief rivals: Rabbis Rabinowitz and Abrahams

Shortly after the Second World War, Jewish leaders in Johannesburg attempted to create a Union of Orthodox Hebrew Congregations for Southern Africa. Louis Rabinowitz was proposed as the first chief rabbi of the country. Cape Town sharply objected. The Western Cape feared northern domination, testimony to a lingering provincialism within South African Jewry. When in 1949 the Transvaal announced the appointment of Rabinowitz as its Chief Rabbi, the Cape retaliated by naming Israel Abrahams as theirs.

Behind the provincial quarrel lay a longstanding personal rivalry between two powerful rabbinical figures. Louis Rabinowitz and Israel Abrahams had tracked each other's lives from their early years. Both grew up in Britain: Rabinowitz, the son of a rabbi with a lineage stretching back to the illustrious Rashi, was born in Edinburgh in 1906; Abrahams was born in Vilna in 1903 but came to England as a young child. Both were educated at the University of London and at Jews' College, London. Abrahams succeeded Rabinowitz in the late 1920s as minister to the Shepherd's Bush Synagogue in London. After further service in Manchester, Abrahams succeeded Reverend Bender as spiritual leader of the Cape Town Hebrew Congregation in 1937. Eight years later Rabinowitz was appointed to the equally prestigious United Hebrew Congregation of Johannesburg after distinguished war service as principal Jewish chaplain to the Eighth Army.

Both Abrahams and Rabinowitz were scholars of note. Rabinowitz, who held a doctorate, produced important work on medieval Jewish history, while Abrahams was the acclaimed translator from Hebrew to English of the biblical exegesis of the Italian Umberto Cassuto. Both held university chairs in Hebrew: Rabinowitz at the University of the Witwatersrand and Abrahams at the University of Cape Town. Both were Zionists and both had a passion for promoting Jewish education.

They differed, however, in temperament and in public profile. While the combative Rabinowitz spoke out unequivocally against apartheid, the reserved and somewhat cautious Abrahams was more circumspect. He sought harmony between the Jewish community and the Nationalist authorities. Token of this was the prayer he composed for the welfare of the government that drew criticism since it patently ignored the lot of black South Africans.

For all their personal and political differences, these dominant figures were both bearers of the Anglo-Jewish rabbinical tradition, and broadly shared the religious outlook of their predecessors, Hertz, Landau and Bender. Separately, each reinforced the prestige of the office of Chief Rabbi which remained divided till their departure from South Africa (and for some years after). Both these long-term rivals retired to Jerusalem in the 1960s where they became friends.

Israel Abrahams.

Louis Rabinowitz.

being Jewish. This ethnic consciousness came at little cost in a society that placed a premium on ethnicity. In a country where the English-Afrikaner divide persisted among whites, and where 'grand apartheid' made great play with ethnic origins (often invented and distorted), Jews were not pressed to shed their identity in service of any 'melting-pot' ideal. In South Africa the politics of assimilation, so potent in the modern European and American Jewish experience, was muted.

Ethnic awareness did not necessarily translate into rigorous religious observance. Though South African Jews generally affiliated to Orthodox *shuls*, on the whole they 'practised' a diluted form of orthodoxy. As in earlier years, the High Holidays were generally observed, sometimes leaving the commercial main street eerily deserted. In a singularly South African style, Friday-night services were much better attended than those on the Sabbath day. Jews, including the lay leaders of congregations, were unembarrassed about driving to these services and parking in plain sight of the synagogue. *Kashrut* (dietary law) was often honoured in the breech: it was not uncommon to keep *kosher* at home and to eat *treyf* out. Few brides went to the *mikvah* (ritual bath) on the eve of their wedding, and some divorced couples did not seek a *get,* a religious divorce.

This lack of rigour or of obligation, and its pragmatic toleration by the Orthodox rabbinate, minimised any wholesale drift towards Reform Judaism and stifled the introduction of American-style Conservative Judaism. For all their lack of observance, most South African Jews felt more comfortable within the familiar confines of the Orthodox *shul* of their parents rather than within the Reform temple. Unlike the United States where Conservative and Reform Jews greatly outnumbered the Orthodox, there were only five Reform Temples in the late 1960s in Johannesburg and Cape Town as opposed to 44 Orthodox synagogues.

Beneath this tepid observance there were signs of religious revival, particularly among the youth, who were increasingly attending the Jewish day schools. Youth and students' services attracted growing numbers as did *Bnei Akiva*, the Orthodox youth movement. In contrast to his pessimistic predecessor, Rabbi Landau, Chief Rabbi Louis Rabinowitz was optimistic about the future. 'At no time in the history of the South African Jewish

Continued on page 170

Reform Judaism in South Africa: 1930s-1960s

Reform Judaism arrived belatedly in South Africa, long after its establishment in Germany, the United States and Britain. A family visit to Johannesburg in 1929 by Professor AZ Idelsohn of the Hebrew Union College in Cincinnati, the seminary of the American Reform rabbinate, stirred local interest in Reform Judaism and led to the formation of a small group that held services in the homes of its members. Idelsohn persuaded Moses Cyrus Weiler, a 26-year-old graduate of the Hebrew Union College, to serve as minister to the fledgling congregation.

In September 1933, one month after his arrival, Rabbi Weiler conducted the first Reform High Festival service in South Africa. This was held in a Freemason's Hall because no Jewish organisation would allow the use of its facilities, foreshadowing the antagonism Reform Judaism would encounter for decades thereafter from those opposed to its mode of worship and theology.

From its inception Reform Judaism in South Africa differed in important respects from its American parent, adapting to the more conservative and traditional local milieu. Most notably, it aligned itself unequivocally with Zionism. (Weiler was a committed Zionist, unlike some of his American peers, and would later introduce a prayer for Israel, an innovation subsequently adopted elsewhere.)

Reform appealed to those seeking a more accessible form of service, much of it in English rather than in Hebrew. It also drew support from German Jewish refugees and from those who had encountered the Reform movement in England. Within two decades of its founding in South Africa membership had grown to almost 8 000 with congregations in Johannesburg, Cape Town, Durban, Port Elizabeth, Pretoria, Springs and Germiston along the Rand.

Despite Rabbi Weiler's conciliatory overtures on his arrival and his expressed desire not to divide the community, he met fierce opposition from the start. This did not even abate during the dark years of the Second World War when Orthodox voices objected strenuously to Weiler's appointment as representative of the Board of Deputies at the Day of Mourning gathering in Johannesburg in 1943. Shortly after the war, David Sherman, the newly appointed Reform Rabbi in Cape Town, faced similar hostility: 'I was shown a leaflet put out by the Board of Jewish Education, a solemn warning to those good and innocent people who might be enticed by the glitter and glamour of this new-fangled heresy, informing them that the main purpose of Reform was to lead their children to the baptismal font.'

Chief Rabbi Israel Abrahams, the spiritual leader of the Cape Town Hebrew Congregation, held a series of meetings on the 'Perils of Reform'. His counterpart in Johannesburg, Chief Rabbi Louis Rabinowitz, had sought 'a modus vivendi if possible' with Rabbi Weiler at a 'confidential meeting' at the Carlton Hotel in Johannesburg. 'I ... suggested,' Rabinowitz recalled years later, that 'if he would agree to leave ... matters of personal status to the recognised Orthodox Community I would be prepared to recommend recognition of the Reform Movement.' This proposal had foundered when news of the meeting had leaked out.

In the 1960s, after Weiler and Rabinowitz had both retired to Israel, their successors, Rabbi Arthur Saul Super and Chief Rabbi Bernard Moses Casper, negotiated a 'Concordat' designed to reduce tensions between Orthodox and Reform. Again the attempt at rapprochement floundered, this time because Super had failed to consult his rabbinical colleagues.

In Cape Town, the *Av Beth Din*, the Hungarian-born head of the ecclesiastical court, Rabbi Eugene Jacob Duschinsky, was more conciliatory than Chief Rabbi Abrahams who departed for Israel in 1968. In that year Duschinsky shared a public platform with Rabbi David Sherman to condemn the persecution of Iraqi Jews.

Throughout the rancorous quarrel between Orthodox and Reform, the lay leadership of the community, especially the Board of Deputies, sought to calm the waters. For the community at large, ethnic solidarity and cohesion trumped denominationalism.

The 'Concordat'

With a view to clearing up the confusion and misunderstanding that seem to be rife in some communal circles, the Orthodox Chief Rabbi BM Casper and the Senior Reform Rabbi AS Super have agreed as follows:

1. From the religious point of view there is an unbridgeable gulf between Orthodoxy and Reform. Therefore there can be no question of Orthodox Rabbis, Ministers or Chazonim [cantors] participating in any Reform services, or vice versa; nor can there be any joint Orthodox Reform religious services.

2. At public communal functions such as banquets, dinners or luncheons, Grace before and after meals will be recited completely by an Orthodox Chazan.

3. At the Annual Memorial Meeting at West Park Cemetery, organised by the Board of Deputies, as an Act of Mourning and Homage representative of the entire Community, the traditional Memorial Prayers will be recited by an Orthodox Chazan; and an Orthodox Minister and a Reform Minister will both be seated on the platform.

4. With regard to Chaplaincy at Military Camps, the duly appointed Orthodox visiting Chaplain will use his good offices with the local camp Commander to facilitate visits by a Reform Minister to the Reform personnel who happen to be there. In other words, the Orthodox appointed Chaplain would ask his local Commander if a Reform Minister would be allowed to visit the Reform boys.

5. In social, welfare, and other non-religious matters, Orthodox and Reform should co-operate (as is indeed already the practice) in the general communal interest. Where religious issues become involved, the principles stated in paragraphs 1 and 2 of this letter would apply.

6. It has long been the custom for the Chief Rabbi to recite a Prayer at the opening of Conferences of the Board of Deputies and of the Zionist Federation. This has become an accepted 'minhag' [custom] of the South African scene; and it is therefore agreed that the Chief Rabbi or his representative shall continue to offer the Prayers on such occasions.

Signed: *BM Casper, AS Super*

Arthur Super.

Bernard Casper.

SOUTHERN AFRICAN JEWISH TIMES, FRIDAY, JUNE 9, 1967.

DRAMA OF DEPARTURE: Tense faces in the crowd of 2,000 people who thronged Jan Smuts Airport last Saturday night to say goodbye to the volunteers.

FIRST GROUP OF S.A. VOLUNTEERS LEAVE FOR ISRAEL

2,000 people crowd airport to see them off

("Jewish Times" Reporter)

Unprecedented scenes were witnessed at Jan Smuts Airport last Saturday night when the first group of 50 South African Jewish volunteers left by El Al plane to render personal service in the crisis which Israel confronts today. A crowd of over 2,000 people came to see them off — parents, relatives, friends and others who wished to show, by their presence, their solidarity with these eager young people going to help Israel in her hour of need.

The contingent — young men between the ages of 18 and 30, and a couple of girls of 18-19 — was under the charge of Mr. Joseph Daleski, veteran vice-chairman of the South African Zionist Federation, who got many a warm greeting as he moved among the group, seeing to it that all was set for departure. The young people will go to non-combatant work, replacing Israelis called up by the army.

They offered their services in any capacity, but today's highly technicalised Israeli army is too specialised to assimilate foreign volunteers. So those who come to give their help will be posted for work in the factories and fields, hospitals, offices; there, while the army confronts the Arabs, they will help Israel carry on.

HIGH MORALE

I weave through the crowd, watching faces, listening to conversations. Parents try to control their emotions — anxiety struggling with pride. Younger brothers and sisters look enviously on. Friends slap backs, shake hands. "Hallo Dave!" "Lo, Joe!" "See

you soon — I'll be along in the next group!" Laughter interleaves the conversation — a joke here and there. Morale is high — these youngsters are full of determination.

I ask what prompted them to go.

John Malcow tells me: "Every generation has to face its crisis. This is ours. I am a Jew. How could I stand aside?"

Alan Caplan says: "Israel needs us. I couldn't stay behind".

David Goss (former head boy of King David School) says: "It's a test for every young Jew".

Hilton Sacks, another former King David pupil, says: "I'm going to uphold my Jewish heritage. What's the point of a Jewish education unless I put into action?"

To Mr. Norman Sandler, Principal of Linksfield's King David High, this is a momentous occasion. "There are six former King David boys in this group", he tells me. "Four of them were in the 1963 Ulpan group. Can you have a better testimonial for the Ulpan or the King David Schools?"

Some of the fellows are university students, interrupting their courses in the firm conviction that this is a duty they owe. "Israel needs whatever I can give at this moment", says Ian Browde, Martin Glatt tells me: "I always promised myself that, whatever I

was doing, I would make myself available when Israel would have her back to the wall".

There's a warm feeling in this group; the sense of expectancy; the glint of determination. No heroics: these young people are going to do a job.

Mr. Leon Segal, well-known welfare worker, moves through the group, giving each a "South Africa" badge to sew on his coat. "I'm going to do this for every group", he tells me.

TENSE FAREWELLS

I button-hole Mickey Glass, Secretary of the Zionist Federation, who says: "Sorry — too busy to answer questions now". But I manage to get from him that the number of volunteers has been "fantastic" — a spontaneous response from young Jews all over the country — and some non-Jews, too. The volunteers are going for at least six months' service. They get their tickets and their keep in Israel, but no pay. It is part of their contribution that they want to serve without being paid.

The loudspeakers cuts across the conversation, "calling all passengers". The crowd sweeps forward. There are tense farewells. Zionist Youth form a guard of honour, singing, "Shalom Aleichem". Many a parent's voice is strained. Eyes are glistening with held-back tears. "Goodbye!" "God bless you!" "Look after yourself!"

Relatives and friends crowd the gallery, cram the cafeteria, watching the duffle-cloaked figures trundle over the apron, up the gangway, into the plane.

Haikvah throbs from two thousand throats ... a benediction and a hope. The aircraft swings slowly out, sombre in the harsh artificial light, and like a phantom spreads its wings in the night ...

"GOODBYE, ALL . . .": A volunteer is overcome by emotion as she says farewell to her family.

"LEHITRAOT!" Expressions vary as brothers, sisters, parents take farewell of members of their families going to help Israel.

The Six Day War and South African Jewry

The Six Day War of June 1967 demonstrated the depths of South African Jewry's attachment to Israel. In the tense weeks before the war, offers of assistance – even from people not previously involved in communal work – began to arrive at the offices of the South African Zionist Federation (SAZF) and the Board of Deputies. The community launched an Israel Emergency Campaign at the end of the month to raise funds for the beleaguered state and the SAZF put together a programme for those wishing to volunteer for six months of non-combatant service in Israel. The volunteers would replace mobilised soldiers in the towns and kibbutzim, helping to gather the harvest and maintain industries and vital civilian transport and medical services.

Some 1 800 individuals applied for the programme, with an initial contingent of 782 volunteers setting out two days before the outbreak of the war. In relative terms, the South African group was the largest of any Diaspora Jewish community. Among the volunteers were nearly 100 university students who were sacrificing an academic year for the Jewish cause. South African Jewry also led in the realm of fund-raising. Within weeks, R20 million (at that time the equivalent of more than $27 million) had been collected from some 25 000 contributors. Israel's *Magen David Adom* made an arrangement with the South African Blood Transfusion Services to have blood plasma sent to Israel on condition that the South African Jewish community would rapidly replace it. The response was enormous.

With the outbreak of war, 'a wave of public sympathy for Israel swept over South Africa', reported the *South African Jewish Times*. Jews were glued to their radios, anxiously awaiting the news bulletins. All Hebrew congregations were requested to hold special prayer services – the first one taking place at Temple Israel in Johannesburg two days after the outbreak of the war. Huge crowds heard Rabbi Arthur Super announce that Israeli forces had taken Jerusalem's Old City and that the chief chaplain of the Israeli army, Rabbi General Shlomo Goren, had sounded the *shofar* (horn) at the Western Wall. 'In

kinship with our brethren in Israel,' exhorted Rabbi Super, 'it is proper that we start this service today with the blowing of the shofar.' These were electrifying times for South African Jews, who flocked to thanksgiving services throughout the country. In Cape Town alone, 26 hugely attended services were held simultaneously.

Although South African government policy was formally neutral, many non-Jews made contributions to the SAZF's fund-raising effort. More importantly, the government responded sympathetically to a joint Board and SAZF delegation that requested special permission to transfer the proceeds to Israel. This was agreed to, on the condition that the funds would be used by charities solely for humanitarian purposes.

'Israelis Fight for Peace,' as an editorial in the Board's journal, *Jewish Affairs*, put it, had rallied world Jewry as never before. Jews realised, the editorial continued, 'that the Arab threat to Israel was in fact a challenge to the right of Jews everywhere to exist as free men'. Notwithstanding its melodramatic tone, the editorial was correct in its assessment that the war had been perceived by Jews worldwide in apocalyptic terms. It had conjured images of destruction that, for South African Jews at least, had resonated powerfully; they shared with world Jewry a sense of cataclysm.

Few South African Jews remained uninvolved in the war. Fund-raising activities were extensively publicised and lavishly illustrated by photographs in the popular press. The war eroded the tensions surrounding Israel's participation in anti-apartheid actions at the United Nations. The obvious sympathy of the white population in general, and of Afrikaners in particular, also ended any lingering bitterness of the memories of the 1930s and early 1940s. (Helen Suzman, arch-critic of the Nationalist government, was greeted in parliament with the words, 'Mooi skoot, Helen' (Well done, Helen). The South African government's gesture to facilitate the transfer of funds was viewed by *Jewish Affairs* as a particularly hopeful sign that 'a new chapter [would] be opened in relations between Israel and South Africa'.

Habonim members (in scarves), early 1950s.

Continued from page 165

community,' he wrote in 1960, 'has so much attention been paid to the needs of youth and the results have been so gratifying as to show that there is a real desire for religious expression among our youth.'

Alongside formal religion (however compromised), Zionism remained a key component of South African Jewish identity: the civil religion of the Jewish community. In the decade following the creation of the Jewish state, South African Jews contributed more per capita to Israel than Jews anywhere else. (There was a hiccup in the sixties when the South African government severely restricted the transfer of funds in retaliation for Israel's hostility to apartheid at the United Nations.) Through these years Zionist organisations flourished. Branches of the *Bnoth Zion* (Daughters of Zion) attracted record numbers, while the Women's Zionist Organisation had a membership of almost 17 000 in 1967.

The Zionist youth movements – *Habonim, Betar, Bnei Akiva* and a waning *Hashomer Hatzair* – successfully recruited over 40 per cent of all Jewish youngsters between the ages of 10 to 18; by 1969, 8 535 belonged to these organisations. These provided a safe alternative focus for youthful idealism at a time when political protest was risky. And yet, despite their concern with matters far away, the youth movements, and in particular the socialist-oriented *Habonim*, introduced a younger generation, many from conservative homes, to issues of social justice, conspicuously absent in apartheid South Africa.

Anxieties about the future stability of a racially polarised society added a peculiarly South African dimension to local support for Zionism: Israel was seen by some as a place of refuge if needed. But the general enthusiasm for Zionism went much deeper than simple expediency, with deep roots reaching all the way back to the *shtetl*. This enthusiastic commitment was reinforced by the birth and subsequent success of the young Jewish state. However, this did not lead to mass *aliyah* in pursuit of the Zionist ideal. Most were content to remain at home though there was a steady if limited stream of emigration for Israel: approximately 100 annually in the fifties, increasing to almost 300 in the sixties.

All these activities were coordinated by the South African Zionist Federation which, together with the Board of Deputies, provided a centralising lay leadership that contributed significantly towards the community's distinctive coherence.

Though there were regional tensions – particularly between the old rivals, Johannesburg and Cape Town – South African Jewry at the end of the sixties was proudly cohesive and well organised, with a dense network of educational, welfare and philanthropic institutions. Even the charged denominational differences between Orthodox and Reform were of little practical consequence to most South African Jews.

In 1970 the Jewish population of South Africa reached its all-time numerical peak. Jews were comfortably integrated into white South African society. Accusations of dual loyalty directed against them a few years earlier because of Israel's stance at the United Nations had subsided. Antisemitism had largely abated, except for the rare ugly incident emanating from the far right such as provocative celebrations of Hitler's birthday in a Hillbrow beerhall in Johannesburg. Despite the political upheavals at the beginning of the sixties and the years of severe repression that followed, at the end of the decade Jews were optimistic about the future of their community. They had no sense that they were on the brink of a new and challenging era.

CHAPTER 4

JEWISH SOUTH AFRICANS

CHALLENGES AND RESPONSES, 1970–1990

THE GRUESOME DEATH OF MELVILLE EDELSTEIN in Orlando West on 16 June 1976, the first day of the Soweto revolt that was to shatter the complacency of white South Africans, dramatised the racial anger that lay beneath the calm facade of apartheid society. Ironically, Edelstein, a social worker employed by the West Rand Administration Board who was deeply committed to black communal upliftment (and one of only two whites to die in the bloody uprising), had warned in the years preceding that reform was a necessity if racial confrontation was to be averted.

Three years earlier, black workers in Phillip Frame's textile factories in Natal had gone on strike against low wages in defiance of apartheid proscription of black collective bargaining. After years of labour repression and apparent quiescence, the workplace had once again become a site of struggle. Alongside the workers, a new generation of black students and intellectuals sought liberation though the ideology of Black Consciousness. Steve Biko, the charismatic leader of the movement, died in police detention in September 1977. Two Port Elizabeth district surgeons, doctors

Morning prayers at Yeshiva College, Johannesburg.

M. L. Edelstein

THE ATTITUDE OF AFRICANS AND COLOUREDS TO JEWS

The writer is a well known South African Sociologist whose 1971 survey on the attitudes of young Africans provoked world-wide interest. The results were published in book form in 1972 by the S.A. Institute of Race Relations under the title "What Do Young Africans Think?" In 1973 Dr. Edelstein completed a survey on Coloured attitudes. This research work is being used to guide the Government Commission of Enquiry into the future of the Coloured People of South Africa.

WHEN 200 African matric students resident in Soweto, Johannesburg's African Township were tested by means of a social distance test in 1971 their reactions seemed to indicate that they associated most readily with Africans and least readily with Afrikaners.

The order of ease of their association with the various South African racial groups towards whom their attitudes were tested was:

Ethnic Group	Score
1. Africans	1,9 (average for eight tribes)
2. South African English and Coloureds	3,0
3. Indians	3,4
4. Jews	3,6
5. Afrikaners	4,0

Thus it can be seen that their feeling towards Jews was only slightly less hostile, or more friendly than towards Afrikaners.

When 500 adult Coloureds residents of Johannesburg were tested by the same test in 1973 their reactions seemed to indicate that they associated most readily with Coloureds and least readily with Africans.

The order of ease of their association with the various South African ethnic group was as follows:

Ethnic Group	Score
1. Coloureds	1,1
2. Indians	2,7
3. English-speaking South Africans	2,8
4. Jews	3,2
5. Afrikaners	3,5
6. Africans	3,6

□ *Dr. M. L. Edelstein.*

LEFT: : *Helen Suzman (centre, standing) with Progressive Federal Party workers, including Tony Leon, future leader of the offical opposition in the 'New South Africa'.*

Ivor Lang and Benjamin Tucker, failed to protect him against police brutality, as was subsequently revealed at an inquest where advocate Sydney Kentridge, son of the politician Morris, masterfully unravelled the web of deception and exposed the tissue of official lies surrounding Biko's death.

That Edelstein, Frame, Lang, Tucker and Kentridge all played cameo roles in the great drama of South Africa in the 1970s illustrates the close integration of Jews into the fabric of the society. Well-meaning social worker, hardboiled industrialist, fearful doctors and courageous lawyer, they personified to a degree the different ways Jews behaved in a turbulent South Africa.

Some chose to leave. During the three years after 1976 more Jews emigrated from South Africa than had done so during the seven years preceding the Soweto crisis. Through the combined impact of political uncertainty and economic recession, the rate accelerated from about 1 000 to more than 3 000 per year. The premier destinations were Israel, with its open-door policy to Jewish immigration, and the United States. The former attracted nearly 40 per cent of the emigrants and the latter 25 per cent. Smaller

From *chazanut* to charcoals:
four generations of the Kentridge family

Sydney Kentridge.

Morris and May Kentridge.

Few South African Jewish families compare with the Kentridge dynasty in the extent of their sustained contribution to South African public life – in politics, law and art. On arrival in South Africa before the turn of the century, the family first settled in Vryheid, then a small town in Kruger's South African Republic. The founding father, the Lithuanian-born Wolfe Kentridge (originally Kantrovitch, literally – and in reality – the son of a cantor) had served as a *chazan* in Sunderland in the north of England before coming to South Africa. Besides his Hebraic and Talmudic knowledge, he was, as his son later recalled, an omnivorous reader of English literature and an enthusiastic participant in Sunderland's musical life. This *maskilic*

bent evidently set the tone for his descendents, his son Morris, grandson Sydney and great-grandson, William.

Born in Lithuania, Morris Kentridge grew up in Sunderland and studied at St Andrew's University, before joining his father who was ministering to the Vryheid Hebrew Congregation. After serving his articles as an attorney Morris moved to Durban where he played an active part in both Jewish and civic affairs. He was elected to parliament as a member of the Labour Party, first for Durban Central and later for Troyeville, Johannesburg. Kentridge gained notoriety during the Rand Rebellion of 1922 when he powerfully championed the strikers' cause. He vociferously opposed the Quota Bill in 1930 and subsequent efforts to restrict Jewish immi- gration. Morris Kentridge combined his political activ- ism, first in the Labour Party and then in Smuts's United Party, with a deep engagement in South African Zion- ist affairs, serving as vice-president of the South African Zionist Federation.

Sydney followed his father into law where he attained great distinction. He was educated at the University of the Witwatersrand and at Oxford, with war service in between. While establishing a fine reputation at the Jo- hannesburg Bar, he took on cases of political importance, including appearances for 'Solly' Sachs's Garment Work- ers' Union. He also appeared for the local community at the commission of inquiry into the Sharpeville shootings of 1961, and for the Biko family at the inquest into the death in police custody of the Black Consciousness lead- er in 1977. His relentless and damning cross-examination of the security policemen involved was memorably por- trayed by the British actor, Albert Finney, in a docudrama based on the inquest. Kentridge's subsequent success as a Queen's Council in England and his service as a judge in South Africa's post-apartheid Consitutional Court culmi- nated in a knighthood in 1999 for 'services to internation- al law and justice'.

William, the fourth generation of the Kentridge clan in South Africa, chose a less conventional but no less distin- guished path. Merging a fine-art and theatre training in Johannesburg and Paris, he converted charcoal drawings into a series of internationally acclaimed short animat- ed films, centred on the dubious exploits of Soho Eck- stein, a property developer and mine magnate competing with a business rival, Felix Teitlebaum, for the affections of Mrs Eckstein. His choice of identifiably Jewish characters provoked some controversy, possibly because of the reso- nance with older stereotypes of the Jewish plutocrat. Ken- tridge adamantly denied the charge of antisemitic cari- caturing: 'The accusation saddens me because that's not how I want people to be looking at the work …'

William Kentridge.

Lone 'Prog' Johannesburg City Councillor Selma Browde calls upon a protest meeting to oppose the removal of the city's black citizens into prison-like hostels.

numbers went to Australia, the United Kingdom and Canada.

For those who chose to stay – the vast majority – there was a decided shift in political allegiance. In the general election in the year after the Soweto revolt, Jewish voters moved in opposite directions. Many abandoned their traditional political home, the floundering United Party, and voted for the liberal Progressive Federal Party; a minority shifted rightwards and joined a growing number of English-speaking whites in the shelter of the National Party laager. A poll by the Afrikaner weekly, *Rapport*, indicated that almost 60 per cent of Jewish voters supported the 'Progs' and just over 30 per cent the 'Nats'. The direction chosen was more a function of social class, education and age than of 'Jewishness', explained Henry Lever, a contemporary analyst. 'The Jewish voter who supports the National Party is likely to be elderly, of low income

and with a low level of education ... The Jewish voter supporting the Progressive Federal Party is likely to be young with a high level of education.'

Some of those Jews who voted for the 'Nats' were attracted by the budding relationship between Pretoria and Jerusalem. Two months before the Soweto uprising, Prime Minister Balthazar John Vorster – interned during the Second World War as a member of the pro-German *Ossewabrandwag* – had visited Israel and signed trade (including military weaponry) and technical cooperation agreements. On his return he was fêted at a banquet by the Board of Deputies, much to the chagrin of many liberal Jews, especially students.

The charismatic Rabbi David Rosen of Cape Town's Green and Sea Point Hebrew Congregation, one of the largest in the country, boycotted the banquet. Writing in *Strike*, a Jewish student publication of the University of Cape Town, Dennis Davis wondered how the supposedly politically neutral Board could 'pay homage to the leader of a party whose entire political manifesto is alien to the tenets of Judaism'. Critics were not assuaged by a guarded appeal for racial justice by the Board's chairman, David Mann, at the banquet.

Young Jews continued to challenge the circumspection of the Jewish leadership in the turbulent years that followed. During the early 1980s, Vorster's successor, PW Botha, attempted to modernise racial domination through the co-optation of Indians and Coloureds into a Tricameral Parliament. Instead of securing greater stability, Botha's initiative provoked widespread resistance led by the United Democratic Front. The mid-eighties witnessed a new wave of popular resistance in the townships, culminating in

The Pretoria-Jerusalem Axis

Israel's growing ties with apartheid South Africa from the early seventies were a consequence of the dramatic collapse of its longstanding diplomatic initiatives in Africa. In the years before and after the Yom Kippur War of 1973, state after state in sub-Saharan Africa cut its links with Israel. In November 1975 most of these supported a UN resolution equating Zionism with racism. These developments drew Israel closer to an even more isolated South Africa.

The two countries strengthened their diplomatic relations, significantly upgrading the status of their diplomatic missions. Visits were exchanged at a senior level. Trade expanded exponentially with Israel helping South Africa on occasion to bypass economic sanctions. The most controversial aspect of the relationship was the military cooperation in defiance of the imposition of an international arms embargo on South Africa in 1977. Israel supplied South Africa with equipment and expertise. This collaboration might have extended to the nuclear sphere; in September 1979 a flash over the South Atlantic led to conjecture about a joint nuclear experiment.

For all the closeness between the two countries, there was a certain reticence on both sides to publicise the relationship. Israel continued to criticise apartheid, albeit in a muted fashion, and refused to recognise the 'homelands' despite the investment by individual Israeli businessmen in these apartheid creations. South Africa, dependent on oil supplies from the Middle East, was similarly reluctant to advertise its intimacy with Israel.

Many South African Jews, who had been discomforted by the earlier estrangement of the 1960s, welcomed the closer ties with Israel. Others were embarrassed by what the British journalist James Adams labelled 'the unnatural alliance'.

John Vorster (second from right) with Menachem Begin (left), Moshe Dayan (second from left) and Yitzchak Rabin (right).

Prime Minister John Vorster (centre) with Israeli premier Yitzchak Rabin (right) and Defence Minister Shimon Peres (left).

LEFT: *Jews for Justice protest meeting, Cape Town, 1987.*

BELOW: *Rabbi Selwyn Franklin (with cap), Rabbi Ady Assabi (front, left) and Rabbi Scott Saulson (front, right) visit a Cape Town squatter camp, 1985.*

repeated states of emergency and harsh repression.

Jews for Justice and Jews for Social Justice, founded in Cape Town and Johannesburg respectively, with the support of Rabbis Selwyn Franklin of Sea Point and Norman Bernhard of the Oxford Synagogue, aligned themselves vocally with the broad anti-apartheid struggle.

Both organisations sought to educate their fellow Jews about South African realities, to reach out to black organisations, and to engage fully in changing South African society. Their predominantly youthful membership shunned the bystander role and vigorously advocated a direct and explicitly Jewish engagement with the politics of the day.

Though their numbers were small, they nevertheless brought significant pressure to bear on the communal leadership. In 1985 the Board passed a resolution which for the first time unequivocally condemned apartheid: 'Congress records its support and commitment to justice, equal opportunity and the removal of all provisions in the laws of South Africa which discriminate on grounds of colour and race, and rejects apartheid.' The Board's pronouncement came at time when even the supporters of apartheid had begun to question publicly its claims, moral and otherwise.

The renewed political instability in the mid-eighties and the associated economic turbulence, exacerbated by international financial and trade sanctions (which most South African Jews, like other whites, abhorred), fuelled a fresh tide of Jewish emigration. So did the threat of military service in suppressing the township revolts and in South Africa's border war. Young Jews were prominent in the campaign against conscription.

David Bruce, draft resister.

BELOW: *'Laurie' Nathan, national organiser of the End Conscription Campaign.*

From Rhodes to Regent Road: Sephardi Jews in South Africa

Sephardi Jews were among the early Jewish settlers in South Africa in the nineteenth century. Best known of these was the apostate, Joseph Suasso de Lima, self-styled 'father of the Dutch press in South Africa'. The son of Portuguese Jews, De Lima had converted into the Reformed Church in the Netherlands before arriving at the Cape in 1818.

There was no distinctive Sephardi presence until the early twentieth century when Sephardis, originating from Salonica, Smyrna (Izmir) and Aydin, founded a welfare organisation in Johannesburg that mutated into the Transvaal Sephardi Hebrew Congregation. Small in numbers, the community limped on till the arrival of Egyptian, English and Iraqi families in the wake of the Second World War. In 1951 the congregation was renamed the Johannesburg Congregation of Spanish and Portuguese Jews.

The Sephardi presence remained modest till the influx of Jews in the early sixties from the newly-independent Congo, which had dissolved into civil strife. Most of these refugees had come originally from the island of Rhodes of whom some were survivors of the Holocaust. Jewish welfare organisations provided support to the newcomers, most of whom settled in Cape Town. At first the 'Rhodeslies' affiliated to the Ashkenazi Green and Sea Point Hebrew Congregation, but soon opted for their own Sephardi-style of worship with the full support of the parent congregation. 'Courteously they gave us a hall,' explained Moïse Israel, 'with all the religious objects so we could now pray in the Sephardi *nusach* [style of service], employing tunes and rites from Salonica and Rhodes. We wanted to sing and chant the same songs and melodies in the Sephardi style which we had heard in our parents' home.'

The new community, like their Ashkenazi counterparts, was more traditional than strictly Orthodox in practice. Many were not fluent in English and formed a tightly-knit minority within the larger Jewish population. Over time there has been been extensive intermarriage with Ashkenazis but the non-Sephardi partners typically join the Sephardi congregation, known for its warmth and intimacy.

Rabbi Ruben Suiza officiating at the Sephardi Synagogue in Sea Point.

David Bruce, son of a pre-war refugee from Nazi Germany, was sentenced to six years' imprisonment for draft refusal. At his trial he insisted that with his family's experience of persecution, he could not serve in a racist cause.

Between 1970 and 1990 close to 38 000 Jews left South Africa, though some 4 000 returned, many of these from Israel. In the eighties, as many went to Australia as to the Jewish state. A popular joke had it that 'PFP'– the acronym for the Progressive Federal Party so many Jews supported – now stood for 'Packed for Perth'. Partly compensating for the losses were fresh arrivals from Israel and from a troubled Rhodesia/Zimbabwe, among them Sephardi Jews with their origins on the Mediterranean island of Rhodes. By the beginning of the eighties there were about 1 200 Sephardis in South Africa, of whom two-thirds lived in Cape Town where they consecrated a synagogue, *Kehillah Shalom*, named after the only remaining synagogue on Rhodes.

While the Sephardis maintained their distinctiveness, they nevertheless played a full part in the life of the broader community. By contrast, the Israeli newcomers – some 9 500 strong by the end of the eighties – kept their distance. Despite their not insignificant numbers, they added little to Jewish communal life, though they did alter the gender balance somewhat, since many came as young bachelors. The Israelis saw themselves as very different from the locals. 'The South Africans, when they hear I'm Israeli, they're immediately friendly,' noted a recent arrival. 'They are sure we're on the same wave-length just because we're Jews. But we're not; we're not even similar – [we] simply don't relate to the world in the same way.'

The net loss through emigration substantially altered the age profile of the community. With the departure of many young (and often professional) people, including families with children, the median age rose from 31.9 in 1970 to 38.9 in 1991. Reinforcing the ageing of the community was the low birth rate and the extended life expectancy of Jews. Whereas the average white male in Johannesburg in 1970 could expect to live to 61.1 years, a Jewish male in 1991 could expect to live to 71.9. The comparative figures for women were 71.1 and 73.4 years. Jewish women also had fewer children than their white gentile counterparts, began childbearing later, and ended it earlier.

The effects of emigration were felt more severely in the smaller centres. Between 1980 and 1990, Port Elizabeth lost half its Jewish population and Bloemfontein suffered similarly. By contrast, numbers in Johannesburg and Cape Town were buoyed by an influx from the rest of the country. By 1990, some 60 per cent of the total Jewish population of South Africa lived in Johannesburg while 22 per cent lived in Cape Town. Many country communities had simply ceased to exist.

Despite the exodus and the haemorrhaging of young professionals, the South African Jewish community remained vibrant.

Bernard Kantor (left) and Stephen Koseff of Investec bank.

Ian Kantor, founder of Investec.

Issie Kirsh, 'talk radio' pioneer.

Barney Hurwitz of Clinic Holdings.

Communal institutions continued to flourish. Jews continued to enter the professions in large numbers and to make their mark professionally as judges and as professors. Businesses often grew and thrived, even in the adverse climate of the eighties. As before, Jewish entrepreneurs identified new opportunities. Issie Kirsh, a proud product of Potchefstroom, pioneered independent 'talk radio' with the establishment of Radio 702. Brothers Ian and Bernard Kantor of Pretoria and Stephen Koseff from Benoni on the East Rand steered Investec, a small finance company, towards banking renown. The 'hospital king', Barney Hurwitz, established a private hospital group, Clinic Holdings, which helped to transform the private health sector.

The sustained vibrancy of the Jewish community was especially evident in the field of education. Attending a day school increasingly became the norm, with one in two Jewish children of school-going age enrolled by the early eighties. In 1983, 4 869 attended 13 primary schools and 3 768 were enrolled in 13 high schools. This growth was testimony to the academic success of these schools and to the evaporation of earlier parental fears of 'ghettoisation'. Expansion came at the expense of the afternoon

Rabbi Mendel Lipskar, founder in Johannesburg of a branch of the Chabad movement.

Rabbi Avraham Tanzer, head of Yeshiva College, Johannesburg.

schools, a few of which closed their doors.

With the exception of Reform supplementary schools and ultra-Orthodox day schools, Jewish education, including religious instruction in state schools, was serviced by an umbrella body, the South African Board of Jewish Education. With only very limited financial support from the state, schooling made heavy demands on communal funds and donors. Catering for all meant underwriting the costs of many who could not afford the high fees of the day schools.

The 'national-traditional' schools were sometimes accused of insufficient attention to religious education. Detractors claimed they were 'schools for Jews' rather than 'Jewish schools'. Efforts were made to counter these charges

through special programmes including *Shabbatons* or weekend retreats, but these failed to appease the critics. Those who sought a deeper religious education for their children preferred to send them to the modern Orthodox Yeshiva College schools in Johannesburg, or to their ultra-Orthodox counterparts, the Kollel Schools and the Lubavitcher Torah Academy. By 1983 some 11 per cent of the total Jewish day school enrolment in South Africa attended these, mainly at the primary school level.

The rise of these religious schools was indicative of a turn towards increased observance which would transform the face of South African orthodoxy within a couple of decades. This revitalisation had its modest beginnings years before in the efforts of Rabbis Kossowsky and

Rabbi Michel Kossowsky, founder of Yeshiva College, Johannesburg.

kept strictly kosher. Synagogue attendance was low, with 50 per cent of respondents attending less than 7.6 times per year. Only 20 per cent of males and 13 per cent of females attended synagogue weekly, while 15 per cent of males and 20 per cent of females did not attend at all.

This had changed significantly by 1991 when the community's religious behaviour was next surveyed. Now 37.7 per cent of respondents kept strictly kosher. The younger members of the community, those aged between 18 and 44, were twice as likely to attend synagogue as their equivalents in 1974. Increasingly they *davened* (prayed) at *shtieblech*, small and intimate places of worship, an emerging feature of Johannesburg Jewish life as was the growth of religious schools. In 1983, 763 children attended the Kollel schools and the Torah Academy in Johannesburg, while a further 698 attended the modern Orthodox Yeshivah College. With the intensification of Orthodox practice, particularly in Johannesburg, went a relative decline in affiliation to Reform. In 1974 the ratio of Orthodox to Reform had been 4.81:1; in 1991 this had widened to 6.6:1.

Accompanying Johannesburg Jewry's 'great awakening' was a geographical shift. Jews were increasingly concentrated in the north and the northeast with the recently developed and fashionable Sandton expanding its share of the Jewish population from 10.6 per cent in 1980 to 16.6 per cent in 1991. Similarly, Glenhazel, emerging as the epicentre of Orthodox observance, grew from 12.2 per cent in 1980 to 17.4 in 1991. In Cape Town in 1991, one out of every two Jews lived on the desirable Atlantic seaboard. By then the outlying northern-suburb congregations had effectively disappeared; Parow synagogue 'lived on' in Israel through the transplantation of its *bimah* (platform) and pews to Ra'anana, jocularly

Tanzer of the Yeshiva College. It gathered momentum with the establishment in 1969 of a *kollel* – an intensive Torah study centre – in Yeoville, Johannesburg, and with the founding in 1972 of a branch of the *Chabad* movement in South Africa by Rabbi Mendel Lipskar, an emissary of the Lubavitcher Rebbe. However, in the mid-seventies the great majority of South African Jews could still be described as 'non-observant' Orthodox.

Central to their diluted practice were fasting on *Yom Kippur* (the Day of Atonement), observed by 90 per cent of households surveyed in a communal study in 1974; the lighting of candles on the Sabbath eve, observed by 83.9 per cent; and marking the Passover festival, observed by 94 per cent. (Unlike among American Jews, *Chanukah* was less observed.) Only 27 per cent

THE KOLLEL YAD SHAUL
The first Institute for Higher Torah Studies in S. Africa

Rabbi Yaakov Salzer, Rav of the Adass Jeshurun Congregation, spiritual head of the Kollel, speaking. Centre seated: Chief Rabbi B. M. Casper, hon. president, and Rabbi A. H. Lapin hon. vice-president.

known as Ra'ananafontein because of its concentration of South African *olim* (immigrants).

In these 'Jewish' suburbs Jews continued to mix primarily with other Jews. A sociological survey of Johannesburg Jewry, published in 1977, revealed that eight out of ten had only Jews as 'close friends', and a mere 4 per cent 'mostly or only non-Jews'. This social exclusiveness extended to a degree to business relationships. Forty-five per cent reported that all their business associates were Jewish while only 13 per cent had a balance between Jews and non-Jews. By and large Jews married other Jews. The communal survey of 1974 reported that only 10 per cent of the children of respondents had married 'out'. By 1991 this had grown to 15 per cent, suggesting a very low rate of intermarriage compared with many other Jewish communities, most notably the United States, where a national survey at this time controversially estimated the 'out'-marriage rate at one in two.

All this spoke of an abiding ethnic consciousness and cohesiveness. In a society which continued to attach great importance to ethnicity, where whites were sharply separated from the black majority, and where the Afrikaner/English divide still lingered, Jews could comfortably maintain their distinctiveness.

Besides religion, which was still more honoured in the breach than in practice by many, Zionism remained an essential ingredient of South African Jewish identity. Most felt a deep sentimental attachment to Israel and were willing financial contributors to the Jewish state, but only a minority contemplated *aliyah*. Support for Israel was largely uncritical, although a few were disquieted by Israel's incursion into Lebanon in 1982 and by its tough response to the Intifada that broke out in 1987. Jerusalem's close ties with Pretoria were welcomed by many, though there were some who were acutely embarrassed by the Jewish state's intimacy with the apartheid government.

Young Jews in particular – especially the high proportion who attended university – were troubled. They were confronted at the Universities of Cape Town and of the Witwatersrand by Muslim and black student organisations that condemned Israel and associated Zionism with apartheid. While vigorously defending the Jewish state, some were uneasy at the turn in Israeli politics and at the apparent similarities between the two 'pariah' states, especially with regard to the un-

'Hullo, howzit': the 'kugel', the South African Jewish princess

How to spot a kugel:

> She's well dressed.
> She wears diamond studs in her ears.
> She smells expensive.
> She speaks through her nose.

The late twentieth-century stereotype of the 'kugel' was more benign than the Hoggenheimer stereotype of the early century. She was the transatlantic counterpart of the JAP – the Jewish American Princess. Far removed from her immigrant forebears, she confidently bestrode the shopping malls of Johannesburg's affluent northern suburbs. She was regularly parodied on stage by the likes of Pieter-Dirk Uys, South Africa's master satirist, and was the subject of countless 'kugel jokes', enjoyed by both gentile and Jew. This shared mirth was a barometer of the comfortable place Jews enjoyed in late twentieth-century South African society. Eventually the 'kugel' stereotype escaped ethnic bounds and became a generic term for materialistic and ostentatious suburban women of leisure.

Holocaust commemoration at West Park Cemetery, Johannesburg, 1984.

resolved question of the 'West Bank'. These concerns did not erode the vitality of Zionist youth activities which continued to flourish, albeit without the same level of ideological fervour as in the fifties and sixties. The youth movements' annual summer camps at the sea remained immensely popular, as much, if not more, for their social activities.

Together with Zionism, Holocaust memorialisation served as a central pillar of South African

Jewry's civil religion. She'erith Hapletah, a survivors' organisation numbering more than 200 members at its height, dedicated itself to keeping the memory of the Holocaust alive. *Yom Hashoah*, the annual commemoration of the Holocaust, had become an important day in the communal calendar, attracting large numbers to memorial ceremonies. Holocaust education was integral to the curriculum of the day schools and to communal adult education. South African Jews joined world Jewry in commemorating the fiftieth anniversary of *Kristallnacht*, the 1938 Nazi pogrom against the Jews.

Counterbalancing the cohesion and vibrancy of the Jewish community were nagging anxieties about the state of the nation. Township uprisings, states of emergency, international sanctions and a faltering economy preoccupied Jews as it did all whites. But for all the gloom and doom of the late seventies and eighties – with one communal notable even predicting that by 2000 there would be no Jews in South Africa – and for all the dinner-table talk of fresh pastures in Sydney and San Diego, South African Jewry was nevertheless sufficiently self-assured, resilient and robust to engage productively and creatively with the new political and social realities ushered in by President de Klerk's watershed speech of 2 February 1990.

INTO THE 'NEW SOUTH AFRICA'

South Africans of all races were stunned when President de Klerk announced to a hushed parliament the unbanning of the African National Congress (ANC), the South African Communist Party (SACP) and the Pan Africanist Congress (PAC), as well as the forthcoming release of the icon of 'the struggle', Nelson Mandela, who had been imprisoned for 27 years. De Klerk's speech heralded the normalisation of South African political and social life. A raft of segregationist legislation was rapidly repealed in the months that followed and the government opened formal negotiations with its longstanding enemy, the ANC. Among the principal negotiators for the ANC was Joe Slovo, general secretary of the SACP.

Jews generally welcomed de Klerk's bold initiative. The Board of Deputies praised his historic speech and his desire to pursue 'dialogue and negotiations to bring about peace and harmony in South Africa'. The Board anticipated that 'an atmosphere for the establishment of genuine democracy for the benefit of the country and all its peoples' would be established. As its Board's National Vice Chairman, Mervyn Smith, tellingly put it, '… the logjam has been broken and the government and the ANC are prepared

to come to the negotiating table. The Jewish community stands four-square behind negotiations.'

The Board's enthusiasm was shared by those it represented. When President de Klerk attended the 150th anniversary celebration of the founding of the Cape Town Hebrew Congregation as guest of honour in 1991, he was given a standing ovation,

Nelson Mandela visits the Green and Sea Point Hebrew Congregation, 1994. (Left to right) Rabbi Jack Steinhorn, the Israeli Ambassador to South Africa, Alon Liel, Chief Rabbi Cyril Harris and Mervyn Smith, National Chairman of the South African Jewish Board of Deputies.

African voices on the Jew

Since the birth of the 'new South Africa' in 1994 it has been obvious to Jews that their wellbeing is essentially dependent upon the black majority. Historically, blacks have never focused specifically on the Jews when articulating grievances and aspirations. During the late nineteenth and early twentieth centuries – when Eastern European Jews were the subject of hostile attention in the 'white' press – Jews hardly figured in the African press. The cardinal divide in South Africa was always one of colour. But anti-Jewish sentiment was not totally foreign to the black population. In a rare mention of Jews in the early African press, JK Masike, a Batswana writing in 1891, warned travellers to Johannesburg:

> I say, you should guard yourself well. There are Jewish European men there who are very deceptive. Those people have cheated many people … upon arriving they put you in their house. They say, "What would you like to eat, do you like beer?" If you say no, they say that you like wine and they give it to you to drink. After they give you wine, they say, "Do you want to play?" And when they say that, you are likely already confused and not knowing what has taken place. You simply give them all your money. They say "play cards" so that they might take all of it. So friends, I say be well aware of this activity in Johannesburg.

In more recent times 'Jewish capitalists' were singled out in some industrial protests and antisemitic placards were displayed at a number of strikes around the country. At a strike by black Volkswagen car workers in 1994, a pamphlet accused Jews of controlling the country and called for the killing of the 'capitalist Jew pigs'. 'Away with the Jewish settlers', 'Jews dismiss innocent workers' and 'Jews are union bashers' were displayed on another placard. 'Mr Ackerman, remember Adolf Hitler' was the comment on a placard during a Pick 'n Pay strike.

Clearly some blacks had imbibed well-worn anti-Jewish stereotypes. There is evidence of this in a study of matriculation students in Soweto, conducted in 1971 by Melville Edelstein, later a casualty of the Soweto uprising. The survey revealed that blacks experienced a greater 'social distance' in relation to Jews than toward English speakers in general, although less than towards Afrikaners. Those interviewed told Edelstein that an African who was loath to part with his money was described as being as 'stingy as a Jew', a trope affirmed by the anti-apartheid activist, Saths Cooper, in an interview conducted in the late 1980s: 'The common reaction, and this is throughout the black community – is to classify any exploiter as a Jew, even if he happens to have a black skin, he appears to be in the Shylock mould.'

In Edelstein's view the prejudice of the black matriculants arose from New Testament teaching in school and church. An additional factor Edelstein might have considered is the historic resentment against Jewish traders in town and country. A survey conducted two decades after Edelstein's among urban South African 'elites' showed that black 'elites' harboured substantial antipathy towards Jews with almost one in five saying that the Jewish community 'irritated' them because they were parasites, snobs, racists, anti-Christ, and unpatriotic.

This was a methodologically questionable survey, the findings of which need to be balanced against philo-Semitic sentiments expressed on other occasions by important voices. Interviewed in the sixties, Bloke Modisane, an exiled writer, asserted that 'there exists a bond, a kind of affection for the Jews on the part of the Africans'. Similarly, the author Lewis Nkosi recalled: 'If one was foolhardy to have girl friends across the colour line, they were likely to be Jewish; if one had white friends of any sort they were most likely Jewish; almost eighty percent of white South Africans who belonged to left-wing and liberal organizations were Jewish …' In his autobiography, *Long Walk to Freedom*, Nelson Mandela, was equally complimentary: 'I have found Jews to be more broadminded than most whites on issues of race and politics, perhaps because they themselves have historically been victims of prejudice.'

Arthur Chaskalson at a 1990 rally welcoming Nelson Mandela to Johannesburg. Chaskalson later became the first president of the Constitutional Court, serving with, among others, Richard Goldstone, Sydney Kentridge and Albie Sachs.

an unthinkable honour for his Nationalist predecessors. But for all their enthusiasm, Jews shared the apprehension of other whites about the impending far-reaching changes, succinctly articulated by the Johannesburg *Sunday Times*. 'What guarantee is there,' asked the editor, 'that an ANC-led South Africa will be any different from the benighted states to the north? Can safeguards be built into a new constitution?'

In addition to their anxieties as white South Africans, Jews had their own specific concerns, particularly about the prospects for Zionist activity in a new South Africa and the country's future relationship with Israel. Their worst imaginings were seemingly realised a fortnight after Mandela's release when he hugged Palestine Liberation Organisation (PLO) leader, Yasser Arafat, at a meeting in Lusaka in Zambia. Matters were not helped when Mandela peremptorily dismissed anticipated Jewish criticism of this embrace with the words: 'Too bad.' In the wake of this, mass meetings were held in Cape Town and Johannesburg where

Mandela's Rabbi

'Shalom, dear brother, shalom.' Chief Rabbi Cyril Harris's tribute at the memorial service for the communist Joe Slovo at the Orlando Stadium in Soweto in January 1995 captures the character of his forceful tenure as Chief Rabbi of South Africa at a time of momentous transformation. The Scottish-born and English-educated Chief Rabbi continued in the tradition of his predecessors who combined secular and religious learning, and were committed to the Zionist idea and to modern Orthodoxy. Prior to his departure for South Africa in 1988 he occupied the pulpit of the prestigious St John's Wood Synagogue, close to the 'hallowed' Lords cricket ground. As he told his English congregants, 'I come here to bring you closer to the Lord – and me closer to Lords!'

His arrival in South Africa to take up the office of Chief Rabbi of the Union of Orthodox Synagogues of South Africa – formed only a few years earlier – coincided with a period of political turmoil. The new incumbent was fully aware of the inequities of his new domicile. Five months previously, on an exploratory trip, he had visited the 'Crossroads' squatter camp on the Cape Flats, situated on the doorstep of 'white' Cape Town. The sight had proved quite shocking: 'I have never seen such squalor in my life,' he later wrote in his memoirs. 'Anywhere else in the civilized world these dilapidated, ramshackle "living quarters" would have been condemned outright and demolished. But this was home to thousands, with broken planks of wood, empty tins, bits of wire, black plastic bags and the odd brick put to constructive use. Rain was pouring down that morning and the whole settlement was a miserable soggy mess.'

Unlike his immediate predecessor, Chief Rabbi Bernard Casper, Harris (together with his wife Ann) energetically engaged with the broader society, dramatically raising the public profile of his new office. His memorable appearances – and eloquence – at the inauguration of President Mandela, at the Slovo obsequies and before the TRC, made a striking impact well beyond the Jewish community.

Some members of his own community were less im-

Chief Rabbi Harris at President Mandela's inauguration, 1994.

pressed. His eulogy to Slovo, which included an apparent rebuke to those 'religious people who acquiesced, passively or wrongly, with the inequalities of yesteryear', touched a raw nerve, though Harris subsequently denied that he had his co-religionists in mind. Most, though, were proud of his public stature and were especially warmed by his intimate relationship with President Mandela who affectionately referred to Harris as 'My Rabbi'. Mandela served as the honorary president of MaAfrika Tikkun, a Jewish community initiative founded by Rabbi Harris and Bertie Lubner, a Jewish industrialist, to help the disadvantaged in South Africa.

After his untimely death in 2005, shortly after his retirement to Hermanus on the southern Cape coast, Harris was awarded a posthumous Order of the British Empire for his services to Jewish communities and to inter-communal relations in South Africa. 'Rabbi Harris,' wrote the *South African Jewish Report*, 'you came to us from distant Scottish shores, and you were the right man for our time. You made us proud, as Jews and South Africans.'

Chief Rabbi Cyril Harris.

communal leaders, including the new Chief Rabbi, the Glaswegian Cyril Harris, appointed only two years earlier, sought to assuage Jewish anxieties and promised that the Board would closely monitor developments.

The Board did more than simply monitor the situation. From 1990 it became more outspoken and engaged, moving closer to 'progressive' Jewish opinion. The Board reversed its traditional stance of non-involvement in politics and instead pursued constructive engagement with the unfolding political process. Some Jews demurred, preferring that the community maintain a low profile and a focus on Jewish needs.

Siding with the underdog, they warned, would go unappreciated as had been the case in the United States where relations between Jews and blacks were poor despite Jewish contributions to the Civil Rights struggle. Ady Assabi, a Reform rabbi, disagreed. 'Sitting on the fence,' he argued, 'is not a Jewish option.' Chief Rabbi Harris similarly advocated a broader engagement rather than an exclusive concentration on matters Jewish. 'There is all the difference in the world between exclusivity and priority,' contended Harris. 'I give priority to the Jewish community. I will not give exclusivity to the Jewish community because my religion, my beloved Torah, won't allow me to do that.'

In their efforts to safeguard the rights and interests of Jews in a changing South Africa, Jewish leaders maintained contact with politicians and government officials, and briefed opinion makers and the press on issues of concern to the Jewish community. A special committee, incorporating Jewish communal leadership and legal experts, was convened to study the content of the proposed Constitution of the new South Africa. The committee made a submission on behalf of the community to the multi-party group working on a Bill of Rights. It focused on issues of racism and hate speech and proposed that the Constitution limit freedom of expression by outlawing the instigation of racial hatred, violence and discrimination. The Board of Deputies also made submissions to the Constitutional Assembly on freedom of religion, belief and opinion, separation of church and state, and religious observance in schools. These contributions played some part in shaping the character of the Bill of Rights.

In the first democratic elections of 1994, 11.1 per cent of Jews supported the ANC which, in

Grappling with the past

South African Jewish Museum, Cape Town.

During the apartheid era, Jewish collective memory, moulded by the seminal texts of Herrman, Saron and Hotz, and Abrahams, promoted a 'usable past' that encouraged conformism to the racial social order, political quietism, and a narrow focus on entrepreneurship. Since the demise of apartheid, South African Jewry has begun to grapple with its past, and collective memory has duly been modified. What was formally disquieting or even taboo has been recovered, valorised and often proudly publicised. In particular, Jewish radicalism, once embarrassing to the community and requiring explaining away, has been given pride of place in the search for a new 'usable past'.

Chief Rabbi Harris's submission to the Truth and Reconciliation Commission in 1996 drew attention to the prominence of Jews in 'the struggle', as did Im-

manuel Suttner's *Cutting Through the Mountain*, an edited collection of 'Interviews with South African Jewish Activists'. In 1998 a major exhibition, 'Looking Back. Jews in the Struggle for Democracy and Human Rights in South Africa' was mounted by the Kaplan Centre for Jewish Studies at the University of Cape Town.

More contentiously, a special issue in 1997 of *Jewish Affairs*, a journal published under the auspices of the Board of Deputies, grappled with the question of Jewish behaviour during the apartheid era. The debate spilled over into the weekly press because of the exclusion of an article dealing with Percy Yutar – prosecutor in the trial of Nelson Mandela – by Claudia Braude, a member of the editorial board.

The vexed question of Jewish behaviour under apartheid was the subject of a major scholarly study by the

Mendel Kaplan shows Nelson Mandela around the South African Jewish Museum.

South African-born Israeli scholar, Gideon Shimoni, published in 2003. Shimoni's judicious account, *Community and Conscience*, might reshape the South African Jewish collective memory, at least with regard to the way in which South African Jewry dealt with the moral conundrums of life under apartheid.

The concrete embodiment of the current understanding of the Jewish experience in South Africa is the 'Jewish campus' in the Gardens in Cape Town – what one observer has called 'South Africa's Jewish complex'. Within it are four important 'sites of memory': the 'Old Synagogue', built in 1863; the 'Great Synagogue', opened in 1905; a Holocaust Centre, with a permanent exhibition on the Nazi genocide; and the South African Jewish Museum, which incorporates the Old Synagogue as its entrance.

The museum, opened by former President Nelson Mandela in December 2000, was the 'brainchild' of Mendel Kaplan, a prominent industrialist, philanthropist and international Jewish leader. The museum presents traditional understandings of the South African Jewish experience – *shtetl* origins, modest immigrant beginnings, and entrepreneurial success, personified by the mining magnates, Barney Barnato and Sammy Marks, and Max Rose, the 'Ostrich Baron' – alongside an acknowledgement of Jewish political activism, stamped by an approving citation by Nelson Mandela. This new inclusivity, which frankly confronts opposing Jewish choices under apartheid, reflects South African Jewry's ongoing grappling with a problematic past.

alliance with its junior partner, the SACP, secured overwhelming support, with 63 per cent of the national vote and control of seven of the nine provincial legislatures. The rest of the Jewish vote was spread between the political successor to the PFP, the Democratic Party (56.4 per cent), which obtained less than 2 per cent of the national vote, and the New National Party (30.8 per cent) with 20.4 per cent of the total vote.

Chief Rabbi Harris was one of four spiritual leaders to deliver a prayer at the inauguration of Nelson Mandela as president on 10 May 1994. His presence reflected the 'new South Africa's' commitment to multiculturalism and the respect accorded to religious diversity in the self-styled 'rainbow nation'. Prior to the elections, the ANC had made overtures to the Jewish community, and on more than one occasion had praised it for its contribution in the struggle for human rights and democracy. In turn, the community expressed a willingness to help in constructing a democratic culture to contribute to the healing process after years of racial exploitation and oppression.

Jewish leaders generally supported the establishment of the Truth and Reconciliation Commission (TRC) that was charged with investigating crimes committed under the apartheid regime and considering applications for amnesty. Jews joined other 'faith communities' in making submissions to the TRC, reflecting on their past behaviour. Chief Rabbi Cyril Harris, by now widely recognised, appeared on behalf of South African Jewry at the behest of the Board of Deputies. In his oral submission he welcomed the work of the TRC: 'We must examine the past, must admit failings for the past – those failings must prompt us all to move forward in some way, to do something now and in the years ahead to build a better country for the millions of our brothers and sisters who live in this country and hope for a better future.'

Most members of the community, Harris acknowledged, had in one way or another benefited from apartheid, although they had not initiated the apartheid system and had mostly voted for opposition parties. Harris confessed on behalf of the community to 'a collective failure to protest against apartheid'. But he also reminded commissioners of the disproportionate role played by Jews in the struggle against apartheid. While recognising that many of the most prominent activists were not practising Jews, he suggested that 'they were moved by either Jewish and, more often than not, humanitarian motivations to speak out'.

Within the community, less attention was paid to Chief Rabbi Harris's *mea culpa* on its behalf for its historical omissions than to the more immediate and pressing challenges of daily life in the 'new South Africa': an escalating funding crisis afflicting communal institutions and a spiralling crime rate. 'There is hardly a member of the [Johannesburg] Jewish community,' noted the *SA Jewish Times* in October 1995, 'who is not personally acquainted with a victim of car hijacking, mugging, burglary or assault – or with families of those who have met violent deaths.' In 1997, as the tsunami of crime mounted, and the new ANC-led government seemed unable to contain it, Jewish religious leaders in Johannesburg convened a well-attended meeting billed 'Prayer, Protest and Plan'. 'We are living in a state of absolute anarchy,' exclaimed Rabbi Yossy Goldman, chairman of the Southern African Rabbinical Association. 'We are stretcher cases, ICU cases. Life support machinery is needed – and what does the government give us? Plaster and Panado.'

Nelson Mandela and Helen Suzman.

To meet this challenge the Board of Deputies participated in community police forums while Jews volunteered as police reservists and as members of neighbourhood-watch groups. Posttraumatic stress counselling services were also provided. Despite these efforts and official reassurances, there was widespread pessimism within the Jewish community about the government's handling of crime. A national survey in 1998 indicated that 'personal safety' was paramount in the decision of many to emigrate.

'Not in My Name'

In October 2001, Ronnie Kasrils, Minister of Water Affairs and Forestry in the ANC government and a veteran of the 'struggle', launched a fierce attack on Israel during a special Middle East debate in the National Assembly. Kasrils read a statement he had co-authored with an ANC member of the Western Cape provincial legislature, Max Ozinsky, that drew a comparison with apartheid South Africa and identified the fundamental cause of the conflict as 'the suppression of the Palestinians' struggle for national self-determination'. Kasrils argued that recognising this as the basic cause 'of the ongoing violence does not – and I say this as a South African of Jewish descent – constitute anti-Semitism nor does it amount to a denial of Israel's right to exist'.

Explaining that the Holocaust had informed his moral outlook, Kasrils drew a parallel between 'the ruthless security methods employed by the Israeli government against Palestinians' and 'the way fascism in Europe dealt with people that they considered to be non-people'. Kasrils insisted that if Israel wished to become a 're-spected society' it would have to 'grant full, equal rights to all who dwell within its borders'. He called on South Africans of Jewish descent to support justice for Palestine and peace and security for all in the 'Holy Land'.

The speech elicited a vigorous response. Russell Gaddin, national chairman of the Board of Deputies, claimed that Kasrils was uninformed about the Israeli-Palestinian conflict and that he had exploited his Jewish origins to lend credibility to the ANC's pro-Palestinian stance. The *South African Jewish Report* was struck by Kasrils's timing: 'Coming a few months after the UN conference against racism in Durban, where the Arab and Muslim bloc was

so successful in convincing South Africans that Israel is an apartheid-like state, Kasrils's statement pours salt into a wound an anxious Jewish community is already feeling.' Some critics even challenged his right to comment as a 'non-practising' Jew.

Kasrils and Ozinsky issued a 'Declaration of Conscience on the Israeli-Palestinian Conflict by South Africans of Jewish Descent' which attracted 284 signatories, including a number of veteran anti-apartheid activists, among them the Nobel Laureate Nadine Gordimer and the Rivonia Trialists, Arthur Goldreich and Dennis Goldberg. Helen Suzman, human-rights doyenne, and other well-known Jewish liberals refused to sign.

The subsequent 'Not in My Name' campaign generated furious argument both in the media and in Jewish homes. 'There's never been a debate in the South African Jewish community quite like this,' commented Steven Friedman, a prominent political analyst. 'This is raw stuff.' The spiritual leadership of South African Jewry – Chief Rabbi Harris, the *Beth Din* and the Southern African Rabbinical Association – 'utterly' repudiated the declaration. Kasrils responded in kind: he was 'surprised that the ecclesiastical court had seen fit to make comments about issues outside its mandate. I don't believe that priests or rabbis should get involved in matters outside their purview – history has shown the folly of that.' 'It's quite ridiculous,' Chief Rabbi Harris maintained. 'Kasrils doesn't know what he's talking about ... Israel is a democracy. It has tried to broker peace, and it has been rejected by a population that is determined to see Israel destroyed. Apartheid was an evil all to itself.'

Internally, an ageing Jewish community faced stringent budget cuts, especially in Johannesburg, as emigration sapped communal resources. In response the community rationalised and centralised its major administrative structures, creating in 2000 an overarching body in Johannesburg known as Beyachad. Rationalisation and central-

isation took place at lower levels as well. After 52 years of autonomy, Jewish Communal Services in Johannesburg merged with the Johannesburg Jewish Helping Hand and Burial Society (*Chevra Kadisha*).

The restructured organisation took responsibility for Our Parents' Home and Sandringham

Gardens Jewish Aged Home. Caring for the old had become a major problem, especially as emigration had broken up families, in some cases leaving the elderly behind to survive on their own meagre resources. To an increasing extent, Johannesburg pensioners found it difficult to obtain affordable accommodation in inner-city flatlands, as residential hotels closed and street crime became rampant.

The chronic problem of funding the Jewish day schools became more acute when, in April 1999, the government effectively cut off state funding for private schools, limited as it had been. The King David Schools in Johannesburg were particularly poorly prepared for the cutbacks. For the first time in 50 years, children whose parents could not afford tuition were turned away at the start of 2001. 'We have always lived up to our credo that no Jewish child will be deprived of a Jewish education through inability to pay fees – but we no longer have money for the provision of subsidies,' said a distraught Glynn Ismay, chairman of the South African Board of Jewish Education. Ismay called on the community 'to save the situation' as enrolments dropped from 3 850 to 3 600. In February 2001 a Pretoria-based Jewish trust responded generously to the financial crisis and, by June, an innovative plan to solve the King David Schools' financial crisis had been put into place.

While Jewish schools and communal institutions struggled to balance their budgets, Jewish leaders also had to address an emerging 'Israel Question', sometimes infused with antisemitism. 'Jew hatred' in the seventies and eighties had been largely confined to the fringe 'white' radical right. SED Brown's *South African Observer* propagated Holocaust denial and conspiratorial views of Jewish wealth, power and influence.

Eugene Terre'Blanche, leader of the AWB (Afrikaner Resistance Movement), had made it clear that Jews would not have full rights in a Christian country under his leadership. Though the far right had appeared threatening in the early years of the nineties, by the end of the decade it had withered and had become an endangered species.

While 'Jew hatred' from the right faded, South African Jews were increasingly disturbed by a burgeoning anti-Zionist public discourse. This was driven largely by South African Muslims – numbering about 650 000 or 1.3 per cent of the total population in the mid-nineties – who identified strongly with the Palestinian cause and drew analogies between Israel and an apartheid South Africa in which they had been second-class citizens. Tempers fluctuated as the political temperature rose and fell in the Middle East. Al-Quds (Jerusalem) Day, was regularly commemorated, usually with incendiary rhetoric, while radical protestors repeatedly marched on the Israeli and American embassies and consulates, burning flags and chanting 'Death to Israel' and 'One Zionist, One Bullet'.

Anti-Zionism reached its apogee during the World Conference Against Racism in Durban in 2001, which coincided with the second Intifada. A week before the opening of the conference, 15 000 Muslims marched through Cape Town to parliament, protesting what they termed the atrocities that Israel was committing against the Palestinians. The marchers carried banners branding Zionism a form of racism, condemning Ariel Sharon as a war criminal, and lauding Hamas.

Sheik Achmat Sedick, secretary general of the Muslim Judicial Council (MJC), appealed to the government to 'take immediate action against

Shtetl to Stockholm

Between 1979 and 2003 five South Africans won Nobel prizes in literature, chemistry and medicine; three of these – Nadine Gordimer (literature), Sydney Brenner (medicine) and Aaron Klug (chemistry) – were the children of Jewish immigrants from Lithuania and Latvia.

Nadine Gordimer was born in 1923 in Springs, a gold-mining town east of Johannesburg. Her father, Isidore Gordimer, had come to South Africa from Riga at the age of 13. He had left school two years earlier and had learned the trade of watch-making. On arrival in South Africa he made his living travelling to gold mines where he repaired watches. Later he opened a jewellery store. Nadine Gordimer's mother, Nan Myers, was born in England to an established English Jewish family and had come to South Africa with her parents as a young child.

Sydney Brenner was born in Germiston, a short distance from Gordimer's home town, four years later in 1927. His immigrant parents were much less comfortable than Gordimer's. 'My father was a shoe repairer,' he recalled in his autobiography, 'and our first home was in some rooms at the back of his shop. He never learnt to read or write but, in addition to English, Yiddish and Russian, he learned to speak Afrikaans and Zulu.'

Aaron Klug was born in Lithuania in 1926, but came to South Africa at the age of two. His father had trained as a saddler in *der heim* and had worked there in the cattle trade. Though 'not a conventionally well-educated man,' Klug recalled of his father, 'he had some gift for writing, and had a number of articles published in the newspapers of the capital, for which he acted as what would now be called a stringer.'

Gordimer had an unusual childhood. At the age of

Aaron Klug.

Nadine Gordimer.

Sydney Brenner.

eleven she was removed from her school, the Convent of Our Lady of Mercy, by her mother because of a supposed heart ailment, and spent the next five years largely isolated from her peers. In her solitude she became deeply involved in reading and writing and at the age of 13 had a story published in the children's section of a Johannesburg weekly newspaper. Two years later her first 'adult' story was published in *Forum*, a liberal South African magazine. She spent a year at the University of the Witwatersrand. Her exposure to life in Johannesburg and in particular to the life of Sophiatown, one of the city's black townships, was to affect her profoundly.

Brenner was similarly precocious. 'I learned to read at an early age,' he recalled. 'I completed the first three years of primary school in one year and was admitted to the local school at the age of six directly into the fourth year, some two years younger than all my contemporaries. After four years in primary school, I went to Germiston High School where I matriculated … just before turning 15.' While at school Brenner discovered the town's Carnegie-endowed Public Library where he 'found a source

of knowledge and the means to acquire it by reading'. The Town Council of Germiston awarded him a bursary that enabled the 15-year-old Brenner to go to the University of the Witwatersrand to study medicine.

Like Sydney Brenner, the young Aaron Klug 'read voraciously and widely'. He was the star pupil at Durban High School, which also produced the renowned palaeontologist Phillip Tobias who, like Klug and Brenner, proceeded to the University of the Witwatersrand during the Second World War to study medicine. Klug soon shifted to science, and like Brenner left South Africa as a young man to continue his studies and research abroad.

Gordimer remained in South Africa where she sustained a lifelong engagement through literature with the dilemmas and moral challenges of life in a racist and segregated society. For Gordimer, as for many Jews on the left, her primary loyalties were universalist rather than Jewish. As an interview recorded in 2005, 'she is first and foremost a South African' though she fully acknowledged her Jewish identity. Being Jewish, she told the interviewer, is like being black. 'It's something inside you, in your blood and in your bones.'

Israel by breaking off all diplomatic and trade relations.'

In Durban, the Non-Governmental Organisation Forum of the conference lambasted Israel as an apartheid state, drowning out attempts to present a positive view of Zionism by Jewish delegates and activists, both local and from abroad. Accompanying this were antisemitic verbal outbursts and sloganeering of a virulence seldom seen in South Africa since the 1930s. This was 'antisemitism in the guise of anti-Zionism', exclaimed Marlene Bethlehem, national president of the South African Jewish Board of Deputies. Durban was deeply disquieting for many South African Jews. Rabbi Ben Isaacson, a progressive voice during the 'struggle years' against apartheid, drew an ominous lesson, warning that there was 'no long-term future for Jewry in the country we have contributed so much to and the country that we love'.

The Durban conference raised serious questions for South African Jewish leaders who increasingly questioned the government's self-declared policy of even-handedness in the Middle East. Towards the end of the year a delegation of the South African Zionist Federation met Deputy Foreign Minister Aziz Pahad to express concern at what they held to be the blatantly pro-Palestinian stance of the ANC government. Pahad assured the delegation that the government strongly supported the existence and security of Israel, and stressed the urgent need for dialogue between Jews and Muslims in South Africa.

Despite the concern surrounding the 'Israel Question', Jews experienced little discomfort in their daily life. Since the 'normalisation' of South African politics in 1994, antisemitic incidents had been few and far between. The most flagrant of these were linked with PAGAD – People against Gangsterism and Drugs – a Muslim vigilante group based in the Western Cape: the firebombing in 1997 of the Jewish Book Centre, housed in a private residence in Cape Town, and the explosion of a pipe-bomb, late at night, at the door of the Wynberg Synagogue a year later.

Besides these, antisemitic acts were largely confined to sporadic vandalism at cemeteries, to occasional graffiti and hate mail to Jewish institutions, and to the odd appearance on Muslim community radio of Holocaust deniers. As in earlier years, the Board of Deputies monitored these closely and responded where it felt necessary, while its affiliate, the Community Security Organisa-

Brian Joffe of Bidvest, international service and trading company.

tion (CSO), provided protection for Jewish institutions and functions.

But for all the challenges they faced in the 'new South Africa', Jews continued to flourish. A pragmatic ANC-led government had abandoned the movement's historic commitment to nationalisation and had instead adopted market-friendly policies. It had displayed fiscal discipline, resisted populist pressures, and won the confidence of the business sector. In spite of affirmative action and 'Black Economic Empowerment', there were ample opportunities for entrepreneurship in an economy with growing connections to Africa and to the world. While Brian Joffe's Bidvest, an international service, trading and distribution company, expanded exponentially on three continents, other Jewish entrepreneurs also seized, if on a lesser scale, the newfound possibilities.

Generally Jews were well-equipped to succeed in the 'new South Africa'. As a group, they were highly educated, well beyond the average of a society with a burdensome legacy of educational disadvantage. According to a 1998 national Jewish survey, only seven per cent of respondents had failed to complete high school, while one in three held a university degree. Forty-one per cent of males and twenty-nine per cent of females were university graduates. By this time, one in three of the economically active were professionals, while one in five were in managerial occupations. Forty-two per cent of those in paid employment were self-employed.

And yet, for all their success and comparative advantage, Jews harboured serious reservations about the new order and the future. Of those surveyed in 1998 two-fifths believed that there was 'more racial prejudice in South Africa … than there was five years ago'. One in two felt that the 'people of South Africa as a whole' had not profited from the changes since 1994, while a mere one in six acknowledged that they had benefited personally. Two-thirds expected that their 'quality of life' would deteriorate over the next half-decade. Only one in five respondents anticipated that there would 'still be a substantial Jewish community in SA in 20 years'.

Jews also retained a strong sense of distinctiveness. The 1998 survey revealed that only 7 per cent of respondents felt 'more South African than Jewish', 47 per cent 'equally South African and Jewish' and 45 per cent 'more Jewish than South African'. Predominantly, Jews still mixed with and married other Jews. Whereas in an equivalent national Jewish survey in the United Kingdom, 17 per cent of respondents indicated that they had no or very few Jewish friends, the South African figure was a negligible 2 per cent.

In the United Kingdom too, 23 per cent of respondents had married 'out', in sharp contrast to only 7 per cent in South Africa.

Women and men dancing separately at a Jewish wedding in Johannesburg.

If anything, Jewish identity had strengthened in the 'new South Africa'. Close to half of those surveyed felt their Jewishness had become stronger, and only a small proportion felt that it had weakened. The remainder said that their sense of Jewishness had remained unchanged. For the majority of South African Jews, participation in some form of Jewish religious life was important, though of those, only a minority, albeit growing, were 'strictly' observant. Only 14 per cent of respondents in the 1998 survey were *shomrei Shabbat* (Sabbath observant). For the rest, 'non-observant Orthodoxy' remained the norm, with 61 per cent of respondents defining themselves as 'traditional' or 'not strictly Orthodox'. Seven per cent were Reform. Twelve per cent were 'just Jewish' and six per cent 'non-practising' (i.e. secular), in striking contrast with the United Kingdom where 43 per cent belonged to these two categories.

Though only a minority, the 'strictly Orthodox' had gained

President Thabo Mbeki and Chief Rabbi Harris at the centenary celebrations of the South African Jewish Board of Deputies, 2003.

in influence, visibility and assurance, especially in Johannesburg. Through the nineties that city had seen an impressive growth in the *ba'alei teshuvah* (returnees to Judaism) movement. *Ohr Somay-ach* – an outreach movement founded in 1987 by Rabbis Larry Shain and Shmuel Mofson – developed a large following. The movement held educational retreats and ran the Shaarei Torah Primary School. By 2000 it had established an outpost in Cape Town, which lagged behind Johannesburg in the religious revival.

In Johannesburg *shtieblach* continued to mushroom, posing a problem for the Union of Orthodox Synagogues (UOS), the co-ordinating body of the established congregations. 'We are in a threatening situation,' warned Chief Rabbi Harris at the biennial conference of the UOS in 1997. The city was becoming full of 'mini-shuls' to the detriment of the community at large. 'Our community is far too fragmented and, in these difficult times, we must consolidate as much as possible.'

Three years later Harris again expressed concern about the growing *shtiebelizasation*. (There were now about 20 *shtieblach* in

Debating 'the creeping politics of influence': the Board of Deputies in the 'new South Africa'

In December 2004 Tony Leon, leader of the Democratic Alliance, the official opposition in the South African parliament, addressed the Cape Council of the Board of Deputies, about his concerns regarding 'the creeping politics of influence' practised by the Board. He spoke, he said, both as a leading politician and 'as a proud South African Jew, a member of this community with a keen interest in its affairs and a sincere concern for its welfare'.

Leon acknowledged the Board's efforts 'to ensure that each and every Jewish family feels it has a secure future in South Africa', but was concerned about 'the growing reluctance of the community's leaders to speak out openly and publicly on matters of concern to its members … In the past few years, the … Board … seems to have made a strategic shift away from defending the views and interests of the Jewish community in public and towards a more quiet approach. It is willing to take on smaller fry in public … but it becomes quite timid when dealing with the government.'

Leon was critical of a recent statement by Michael Bagraim, national chairman of the Board, that 'in order to fulfil our mandate of protecting South African Jewry, we need to influence those who are in a position to assist us. It is unrealistic for us to publicly attack someone one week and then ask him for favours the next.' To Leon, it seemed 'unclear why the leaders of the Jewish community should feel they have to "ask favours" from anyone at all. The security of the Jewish community and its members is not a privilege granted by the government, the ruling party or the police services; it is a constitutional right … In general, the Board's recent statements and its approach towards government seem to indicate a movement away from open debate and towards the politics of "influence" … The Board's hope appears to be that the Jewish community can better "influence" the ruling party if its leaders voice their concerns in private while praising the government in public.'

Leon contended that he was 'not suggesting that the Board … must necessarily practise an "in-your-face" style of politics … What I am suggesting is that the Board should not shy away from criticism of the government where it is warranted – and not just on Jewish issues, but other issues as well.' Leon noted that it 'is widely accepted within the … Jewish community today that the great error of the community and its leaders in the past was to maintain an official, communal silence about the injustices of apartheid for so long … Though the Board's policy could never be construed as support for the apartheid regime … the Board often deferred to the government in cases where stronger opposition may have been a reasonable and practicable course of action. Now, after ten years of democracy, the Board appears to be slipping back toward a pattern of deferential behaviour.'

'Neither the Jewish community nor any other,' he concluded, 'need ask the government for favours. We are not here on sufferance.'

Leon's critique provoked a response from Bagraim who stressed that the Board was 'not a political party. Its primary mandate is to safeguard the Jewish way of life in South Africa … This aim we pursue through networking and building relationships with the government of the day … Any attempt to politicise the Board of Deputies … is something we will strongly resist … The Board will not, and indeed cannot, take a stand on specific political issues … There have been occasions … where it has been appropriate for the Board to publicly speak out against the government, and in recent years it has not shied away from doing so, particularly with regard to the Middle East issue … I must strongly disagree with your inference that the Board's present-day interaction with government is reminiscent of its dealings with the ruling National Party during the apartheid era.'

Bagraim went on to assert that the 'politics of influence' was effective and had 'resulted in numerous immediate benefits for the Jewish community … Publicly criticising the government may provide a degree of satisfaction in the short term, but it would undermine the level of mutual trust necessary if we are to succeed in our goal of influencing the government in the long term.'

Johannesburg with an estimated 1 300 families affiliated.) While conceding that the growth demonstrated a religious vitality among the younger generation, Harris regretted their desire to maintain their independence and not be affiliated to larger synagogues.

The following year Russell Gaddin, national chairman of the Board of Deputies, identified the changing nature of religious life as the prime reason for Johannesburg Jewry's financial difficulties, rather than emigration, excessive financial contribution to Israel, or the impoverishment of the community. In Gaddin's view, the rise of insular, 'right-wing' Orthodoxy had led to unnecessary duplication. 'Can Johannesburg afford 50 synagogues and temples? And can the northern suburbs afford 17 *shtieblach*?' asked Gaddin. There were 12 Jewish day schools in Johannesburg. These included four new 'Torah' schools whose combined pupil enrolment was less than 80 pupils. There were three systems of *kashrut* in operation. 'The end result,' complained Gaddin, 'is that every one of these little groups is funding its own and not contributing to the mainstream organisations of the community.'

Even with this threatening fragmentation, the UOS had become a major institutional force, drawing strength from the growing intensity of religious life, and taking its place alongside the Board of Deputies and the Zionist Federation as a key institution of South African Jewry. It confidently asserted its authority, sometimes with polarising effect. In 1999 Rabbi Dr EJ 'Jack' Steinhorn, spiritual leader of the Green and Sea Point Hebrew Congregation in Cape Town, was declared *persona non grata* by Chief Rabbi Harris, Rabbi Moshe Kurtstag, the *Rosh Beth Din* (head of the rabbinical court), and his fellow *dayanim* (judges), supported by the Orthodox rabbis of Cape Town. This action was taken on the grounds of his controversial conduct and interpretation of *Halacha* (Jewish religious law).

The declaration almost led to a breakaway from the UOS by the Green and Sea Point Hebrew Congregation, one of its largest members. A motion to this effect was proposed at a general meeting, contending that the relationship between the congregation and the UOS had deteriorated because the UOS and the *Beth Din* had 'moved considerably to the right and had become more hardline'. The motion was not carried.

One year after the Steinhorn affair, it was ru-moured that the local Orthodox rabbis had boy-cotted the annual *Yom Hashoa* commemoration in Cape Town because Rabbi David Hoffman of the Cape Town Progressive Jewish Congre-gation was the guest speaker. This was denied by the Board of Deputies and the UOS, although it appears that Orthodox rabbis had been told not to sit on the platform. An irate Cape Council of the Board issued a statement deploring 'the non-attendance by certain members of the Jew-ish community … which [had] left many in the Cape Town Jewish community feeling deep-ly alienated, hurt and angered. While the Cape Council respects the religious beliefs of those concerned, we call on religious streams to deal with disagreements in a constructive communal manner so as not to harm and divide the Jewish community …'

There was a rerun of this episode in late 2005 when the new Chief Rabbi, the youthful South African-born Dr Warren Goldstein, refused to share a platform with the Reform leader, Rabbi Charles Wallach, at a memorial service in Jo-hannesburg for the assassinated Yitzchak Rabin, former premier of Israel. Once again this set off a furious debate within the Jewish community. Answering his critics, Goldstein explained that as 'chief rabbi of every single Jew in this coun-try, I preach Torah Judaism in its authentic form. I can't with a clear conscience call something Judaism if it is not. Politically it would have been much easier for me to go (to the memorial serv-ice) – I so badly wanted to – but I was torn be-tween the traditions of our community.'

The religious turn, with its inwardness and fo-cus on spiritual fulfilment and rigorous observ-ance, threatened to detract from the communi-ty's traditional Zionist-centredness. Rabbi Ben

Isaacson, a committed Zionist and former anti-apartheid activist, expressed concern that the Zionist Federation was playing second-fiddle in communal affairs, and pointed to the apparent paradox of a huge increase in *Torah* observance among South African Jews at the same time that identification with Israel was decreasing.

Despite these concerns Israel continued to be a centrepoint of Jewish communal consen-sus, a focus of fundraising activity and a force for cohesion, though South African Zionism had long since lost its sparkle. 'Anyone who re-members the powerful role that Zionism played in this community 30 years ago, and the enor-mous influence of Zionist youth movements like *Habonim* and *Betar* on young people's lives,' lamented the *South African Jewish Report* in May 2001, 'can hardly fail to be saddened at how things have changed.' Nevertheless, Israeli Inde-pendence Day events continued to attract large numbers of Jews, and Zionist youth summer camps – particularly that of the religious Zionist *Bnei Akiva* – remained popular.

This continued attachment to Israel was con-firmed in a national survey conducted in 2005, a follow-up to the 1998 survey. The results indi-cated an unwavering consistency of allegiance, with 86 per cent of respondents indicating ei-ther 'strong' or 'moderate' attachment and only 1 per cent expressing 'negative feelings'. Seeming-ly few shared the antipathy towards Israel articu-lated by some 'progressive' South African Jews.

The 2005 survey revealed that a majority of Jews felt that anti-Zionism had increased in South Africa during the preceding half-decade, a period coinciding with the second Intifada which received extensive and sympathetic cov-erage in the South African media. Despite this perception of increasing anti-Zionism, Jews did

Chief Rabbi Goldstein and President Mbeki at the former's installation, Johannesburg, 2005.

not feel targeted as Jews in South Africa. Only 16 per cent of respondents felt that antisemitism was a major problem in South Africa compared with 73 per cent who felt it was a major problem 'in the world'. This was consistent with data gathered by the Board of Deputies to the effect that South Africa had not experienced the upsurge of antisemitism so evident elsewhere. 'South Africa has consistently recorded fewer than 40 antisemitic incidents a year for at least two decades now,' explained David Saks, senior researcher at the Board. When there were incidents, they were not violent in character, and usually involved simply verbal abuse and hate mail.

Alongside their discounting of antisemitism, Jews felt more comfortable now in the 'new South Africa' than they had soon after the advent of democracy. The 2005 survey revealed that Jews, though still very anxious about crime and personal safety, were more positive about the present and more optimistic about the future than they had been seven years previously. The widespread belief recorded in 1998 that young Jews saw little future for themselves in South Africa had dissipated by 2005. The community was now less restless: 79 per cent indicated that they were 'very likely to continue living in South Africa' in the next five years compared to only 44 per cent in 1998.

Nonetheless emigration continued – particularly among young adults – albeit on a lesser scale. Years of attrition had reduced the Jewish population by the beginning of the new millennium to somewhere between 72 000 and 85 000 (a statistical uncertainty resulting from problematic census data), far short of the high-water mark of close to 120 000 thirty years earlier. Two-thirds of Jews were now living in greater Johannesburg and a quarter in Cape Town and its environs. There were still pockets in the larger regional centres: Durban, Port Elizabeth and Bloemfontein. Small-town communities had all but disappeared, although there were some striking exceptions: Plettenberg Bay on the southern Cape coast – the latter-day counterpart to Muizenberg generations before – has a thriving new Jewish community.

Although numbering less than one-quarter of a per cent of the total population, Jews were acknowledged as an integral and valued component of the 'rainbow nation'. Speaking in 2003 at the commemoration of the centenary of the Board of Deputies, South African President Thabo Mbeki expressed appreciation for the historic role of the Jewish community and confirmed its respected place in the 'new South Africa'. For Mbeki the occasion went beyond the celebration of the creation of the Board a century before; it was also an opportunity 'to celebrate the fact that history gave South Africa the Jew-

ish community which has played and is playing … important roles … and which is an integral and inalienable part of all the people we speak of as South Africans. Our Constitution,' continued Mbeki, 'proudly proclaims that South Africa belongs to all who live in it, black and white. It belongs to the Jewish South Africans as much as it belongs to any other South African.'

Mbeki's appreciative sentiments distantly echo those of Sir Harry Smith over a century and half earlier. Like the mid-Victorian British governor of the Cape Colony, Mbeki affirmed that Jews were firmly and fully integrated into the wider society. Integration, however, did not mean, either in the mid-nineteenth century or in the early twenty-first, assimilation. From the first *minyan* in 1841 to the present day, Jews have embraced a distinctive communal identity while at the same time energetically and enthusiastically pursuing full engagement with the dominant culture. In this they have been aided and abetted by circumstances specific to South Africa.

The absence till the doorstep of the present of a commanding common identity – of a powerful 'South Africanism' – provided a comfortable space for Jews and for the expression of their identity. There was no assimilationist imperative, no need to shed ethnic particularism in a South African melting pot, no insistence on cultural conformity. In a society deeply riven by race and ethnicity, where a gulf separated white and black, and where whites were bitterly divided for many years, Jews could readily maintain ethnic cohesion.

Beyond these advantageous external circumstances, there were powerful forces within the community ensuring coherence and continuity. While the founding Anglo-German Jewish fathers created a frail structure which might well have disappeared with the passage of time, the entry of the Litvaks secured a vital and robust Jewish presence and posterity. A potent blending of the Eastern European and the English evolved which ensured long-term endurance.

This abiding vigour, and the confidence that accompanied it, owed much to the absence of any inhibiting memory of historical marginality. Other than for a brief moment in Kruger's Republic, Jews in South Africa had never struggled for emancipation. From their first arrival in the nineteenth century they had enjoyed, as whites, full equality. Their collective confidence was further enhanced by their sharing in the pioneering of the Witwatersrand, the hub of both modern South Africa and of South African Jewry. This sense of assurance underpinned the community's extraordinary success in a wide range of spheres.

While not assimilating, the immigrants and their descendants rapidly acculturated. Though remaining distinctively Jewish, they took on the cultural coloration of their locale. In a segregated society, this meant typically that of their white English-speaking neighbours, though in the countryside some became *Boerejode*. In time a South African Jewishness emerged, characterised by a muted religiosity – a non-observant orthodoxy – at ease with Jewish pluralism, and by a fervent commitment to Zionism, and later to Holocaust memorialisation, which together served as their civil religion.

More recently, South African Jewishness has shown signs of taking a new turn. Old-style pluralism is being challenged as the community moves in a more Orthodox direction. This has placed the community's traditional solidarity under strain. Exemplifying the growing divide is the rivalry between Limmud and the Sinai Indaba, both flourishing adult education initiatives. Founded in 2007, Limmud South Africa, modelled on its British counterpart, has become a self-proclaimed 'free market of ideas', an inclusive forum for a range of views across the South African Jewish spectrum. As such it has failed to draw the support of the Orthodox rabbinate. We 'cannot share a platform on *halacha* with teachers of a dissident Judaism,' said Pinchas Zeckry, Rabbi of the Durban United Hebrew Congregation. In 2012 the Orthodox leadership, inspired by Chief Rabbi Goldstein, countered with the Sinai Indaba, its own well-resourced and highly successful adult education programme. This assertiveness was also evident in other communal spheres, with the leaders of orthodoxy increasingly seeking to set the community's agenda and tone, to the disquiet of the more secularly inclined. But despite these apparent polarities the community maintained its essential and longstanding cohesion. As with its differences in the past – Yiddishists and Hebraists, Zionists and anti-Zionists – the divide was not unbridgeable.

Weighing against any potential rupture is a shared concern about a public discourse increasingly hostile to Israel, with South African Jewry's core Zionist identity under growing challenge, sometimes from within. Operation Cast Lead, Israel's incursion into the Gaza Strip in early January 2009 in response to the rocketing of nearby Israeli population centres, prompted a fierce exchange within the Jewish community about the merits of Israel's action. While the greater part of the community stood solidly in support, with thousands gathering for prayers for Israel, a small but vocal minority – including some who had led *Habonim* – questioned the proportionality of the Israeli response. In a letter to the *South African Jewish Report*, 136 self-described 'members of the South African Jewish community' expressed dismay at 'the disproportionate use of force by the Israeli military in Gaza'. This set off a flood of condemnation from the readership, one of whom spoke of placing the names of the signatories on a communal 'wall of shame'. Shortly afterwards, fourteen Jewish luminaries, including Justice Arthur Chaskalson, Nadine Gordimer and William Kentridge, wrote in support of the embattled 136. Israel's use of 'excessive force' might, they feared, 'imperil relations between

sectors of South African society'.

Their fears were not unfounded. At a mass rally in support of the Palestinian cause in Lenasia, a Johannesburg suburb with a large Muslim population, South Africa's then Deputy Foreign Minister, Fatima Hajaig told a 'wildly cheering' audience that the United States and the West were controlled by 'Jewish money power'. A fellow speaker said that 'the Zionists in South Africa must be kicked out of the shores of South Africa'. Shortly before, Hajaig had summoned the Israeli ambassador to her office where in his own words he was 'bashed very, very badly'. Hajaig's outburst at the rally was condemned by the government and she received a 'dressing down' from Kgalema Motlanthe, Thabo Mbeki's successor as president. Hajaig apologised for 'any hurt' she might have caused the Jewish community. Her hostility to Israel was shared by the ANC members of parliament's Foreign Affairs committee. In a three-hour appearance before a largely hostile committee Israel's unfortunate ambassador experienced 'the same tongue lashing' that he had in his earlier meeting with the deputy minister.

Cast Lead continued to reverberate long after the cessation of hostilities. Judge Goldstone's controversial report on the Gaza conflict to the United Nations' Human Rights Council later in the year undermined the distinguished jurist's personal standing within the Jewish community and led to calls for his ostracism. Separately, an invitation to participate in the Limmud South Africa conference to Lieutenant-Colonel David Benjamin, an ex-South African who had served as legal adviser to the Israel Defence Force during the Gaza operation, caused a minor storm. Pro-Palestinian activists urged the organisers to withdraw the invitation, and, when they refused

The Goldstone Affair

The prospect of Justice Richard Goldstone's presence at the bar mitzvah of his grandson in May 2010 led to unprecedented threats of a public protest outside the synagogue in Sandton. Formerly the object of communal pride as the head of an eponymous commission which had investigated political violence in the run-up to South Africa's first democratic election, as the chief prosecutor of the United Nations International Criminal Tribunal for the former Yugoslavia and for Rwanda, and as a Constitutional Court judge appointed by Nelson Mandela, Goldstone had become the target of fierce criticism following the publication of the Goldstone Report which indicted Israel for its actions in the Gaza war. Faced with the likelihood of protest outside the synagogue, Goldstone announced that he would not attend his grandson's bar mitzvah. The unfolding saga attracted both national and international attention and caused public embarrassment to the community. The impasse was resolved by behind-the-scenes mediation through which the threat of public protest was withdrawn and a meeting arranged between Goldstone and the communal leadership to exchange views about the Report. Goldstone duly attended the bar mitzvah of his grandson. A year later in an op-ed piece in the *Washington Post*, Judge Goldstone expressed grave reservation about his own report: 'If I had known then what I know now, the Goldstone Report would have been a different document.'

to do so, sought unsuccessfully to have him arrested for 'war crimes' in Gaza.

The pressure persisted well after the Gaza incursion, with Archbishop Emeritus Desmond Tutu, a Nobel peace laureate, and other prominent figures regularly castigating Israel's actions. In 2010 the University of Johannesburg severed ties with Ben Gurion University of the Negev

and in 2012 Deputy Foreign Minister Ebrahim Ebrahim called on South Africans not to visit Israel. During 'Israel Apartheid Week' in 2013 protestors led by the South African chapter of the international Boycott, Divestment and Sanctions Movement, disrupted a concert at the University of the Witwatersrand, Johannesburg, by a visiting Israeli musician. Later in the year demonstrators chanted '*Dubula e Juda*' ('Shoot the Jews' in Zulu) outside a concert intended to compensate for the earlier disruption.

Despite mounting anti-Zionism without and tensions within, South African Jewry remains cohesive and vital two decades into the 'new South Africa'. For all the fissures, and notwithstanding the long-term haemorrhaging through emigration, the community continues to thrive and to retain the allegiance of the overwhelming majority. Jewish businessmen, like the former trade unionist Jonny Copelyn, the financier Sean Melnick and the property developer Marc Wainer, have identified new opportunities. In the public realm Max Price at the University of Cape Town is the first Jewish vice-chancellor of a South African university, while Gill Marcus is the Governor of the Reserve Bank of South Africa. Beyond the establishment a new generation of Jewish activists, among them Nathan Geffen of the Treatment Action Campaign and Doron Isaacs of Equal Education, have held the ANC-led government to account over its failures past and present to tackle the Aids epidemic and the schooling crisis – much as their predecessors, including Jewish journalists such as Benjamin Pogrund and Anton Harber, had confronted the apartheid state. Most South African Jews, however, continue to focus inwardly on the

Out of Riteve

Mendel Kaplan (1936–2009) and David Susman (1925–2010), two giants of South African Jewry, who passed away within six months of each other, could both trace their family origins to the modest *shtetl* of Riteve in Lithuania. Susman's family came to South Africa via Northern Rhodesia (Zambia). Here his father Elie joined his friend, Max Sonnenberg, at Woolworths. Educated at the University of the Witwatersrand, David served in the South African forces in the Second World War and in *Machal* during Israel's War of Independence where he was wounded in action. Two years later he went to work at Marks and Spencers in London, and after serving a business 'apprenticeship' with this innovative chain store, returned in 1952 to South Africa where he played a key role in transforming Woolworths into a South African version of the famed British firm. Mendel Kaplan was born in Parow outside Cape Town in 1936, where his family had established Cape Gate, a wrought iron manufacturing company. After studying law at the University of Cape Town and business at Columbia he returned to the family business which he too transformed over time, into an international steel manufacturer.

Both Kaplan and Susman were devoted to Zionist and other Jewish causes. Susman was a key figure in a range of communal bodies, most notably ORT, an organisation devoted to promoting vocational and technical education. While Kaplan too immersed himself in communal affairs, he also played a leading part in the international Jewish arena as chairman of the World Jewish Congress and of the Board of Governors of the Jewish Agency in Israel. He played a significant role in the exodus of Jews from the Soviet Union. Both men were renowned philanthropists, whose generosity benefited the Jewish and wider community. Both personified the abiding Litvak values that had shaped South African Jewry.

wellbeing of their own community. Through their collective efforts, supplemented by the generosity of philanthropists such as Eric Samson and Bertie Lubner, its institutions remain vibrant.

While there are concerns about the present direction of the new South Africa and the capacity of the state to navigate the myriad challenges it faces, the Jewish community remains wedded to its birthplace. A democratic South Africa's celebration of cultural diversity and its deep commitment to religious pluralism promises the continued wellbeing of South African Jewry.

GLOSSARY

aliyah	immigration to the Land of Israel
Av Beth Din	honorific title for the presiding rabbi of a rabbinical court
ba'alei teshuvah	returnees to Judaism
balabatim	communal worthies
bar mitzvah	the traditional coming of age at 13 for the Jewish male
batmitzvah	the female coming of age
beth din	religious court
beth midrash	house of study
bimah	platform in synagogue
bittereinders	Boers who refused to surrender during the Anglo-Boer War
boerejood	Jew acculturated into Afrikaner culture
bris milah	circumcision
Chanukah	Festival of Lights
chazan	cantor
cheder	elementary school
chevra kadisha	burial society
chumash	Pentateuch
daven	pray
dayan	judge in the *beth din*
der heim	the Old Country
dorp	small town

get	religious divorce	*Rosh Beth Din*	head of the rabbinical court
griener	greenhorn	*Rosh Hashana*	Jewish New Year
hachsharah	training	*shechita*	ritual slaughtering
Halacha	Jewish religious law	*Sefer Torah*	Torah scroll
kaddish	mourner's prayer	*Shiur*	religious study class
kaffireatnik	shop assistant in concession store	*Shmoneh Esrei*	Silent Prayer
kashrut	dietary law	*shochtim*	ritual slaughterers
kolboinik	rabbinic Jack-of-all-trades	*shofar*	horn
kollel	intensive Torah study centre	*shomrei Shabbat*	Sabbath observant
kugel	South African Jewish 'princess'	*shtadlan*	intercessor
landsman	compatriot	*shtetl*	small town
landsmannschaften	immigrant fraternal societies	*shtieblech*	small and intimate places of worship
Litvaks	Jews of historic Lithuania	*shul*	house of prayer
loshen kodesh	holy language of prayer	*siddur*	prayer book
Maariv	evening prayer service	*smous*	itinerant pedlar
macher	important person	*Sukkoth*	Festival of Tabernacles
mame loshen	mother tongue	*talmidei chachamim*	Torah scholars
maskilim	followers of the *Haskalah*, the Jewish Enlightenment	*Talmud*	collection of ancient rabbinic writings on law and tradition
matzos	unleavened bread for Passover	*Talmud Torah*	afternoon Hebrew school
mikvah	ritual bath	*Torah*	scroll of the law
Minchah	afternoon prayer service	*treyf medina*	impure and unclean land
minyan	religious quorum of 10 males	*treyf*	non-kosher
mohel	ritual circumciser	*tsdokeh*	charity
nusach	style of service	*yekke*	jovial term for German Jew
olim	immigrants to Israel	*yeshiva*	Talmudic academy
Peruvian	term of opprobrium for Eastern European Jew	*yeshiva bochers*	students of *yeshiva*
Pesach seder	ritual Passover meal	*Yom Kippur*	Day of Atonement

SELECT BIBLIOGRAPHY

This is not intended to be an exhaustive bibliography but instead identifies works that have informed specific sections of the text. It is also meant to serve as a guide to recent scholarly work on South African Jewry.

GENERAL

Arkin, Marcus (ed), *South African Jewry. A Contemporary Survey*, Oxford University Press, Cape Town, 1984.

Herrman, Louis, *A History of the Jews in South Africa from earliest times to 1895*, Victor Gollancz, London, 1930.

Saron, Gustav and Hotz, Louis (eds), *The Jews in South Africa: A History*, Oxford University Press, Cape Town, 1955.

Saron, Gustav (edited by Naomi Musiker), *The Jews of South Africa. An Illustrated History to 1953*, Scarecrow Books, Johannesburg, 2001.

Shain, Milton and Mendelsohn, Richard (eds), *Memories, Realities and Dreams: Aspects of the South African Jewish Experience*, Jonathan Ball Publishers, Johannesburg, 2002.

Shain, Milton, *The Roots of Antisemitism in South Africa*, University Press of Virginia and Witwatersrand University Press, Charlottesville, London and Johannesburg, 1994.

Shimoni, Gideon, *Jews and Zionism: The South African Experience (1910-1967)*, Oxford University Press, 1980.

Shimoni, Gideon, *Community and Conscience. The Jews in Apartheid South Africa*, University Press of New England for Brandeis University Press and David Philip, Hanover, New Hampshire and Cape Town, 2003.

CHAPTER 1: PIONEERS

For the early origins and foundation of the community, see Saron and Hotz (1955); Herrman (1930); Israel Abrahams, *The Birth of a Community: A History of Western Province Jewry from earliest times to the end of the South African War, 1902* (Cape Town: Cape Town Hebrew Congregation, 1955); Milton Shain, *Jewry and Cape Society. The Origins and Activities of the Jewish Board of Deputies for the Cape Colony*, Historical Publication Society, Cape Town, 1983; Clara Friedman-Spitz, *The Fraenkel Saga*, The South African Medical Association, Cape Town, 1998; Howard Phillips, 'The Oldest Jewish Document in South Africa?', *Jewish Affairs*, 59, 1, 2004; John Simon, 'A Study of the Nature and Development of Orthodox Judaism in South Africa to c1935', unpublished MA thesis, UCT, 1996.

For **Nathaniel Isaacs**, see Carolyn Hamilton, *Terrific Majesty. The Powers of Shaka Zulu and the Limits of Historical Invention*, David Philip, Cape Town, 1998; and Nathaniel Isaacs (edited by L Herrman), *Travels and adventures in Eastern Africa*, Van Riebeeck Society, Cape Town, 1937.

For **Jews in the mid-nineteenth century South African economy,** see Mendel Kaplan, *Jewish Roots in the South African Economy*, Struik Publishers, Cape Town, 1986; D Fleischer and A Caccia, *Merchant Pioneers: the House of Mosenthal*, Jonathan Ball Publishers, Johannesburg, 1983.

For **Jews on the diamond fields,** see Eric Rosenthal, 'On the Diamond Fields' in Saron and Hotz (1955); Louis Cohen, *Reminiscences of Kimberley*, Bennet, London, 1911; David Harris, *Pioneer, Soldier and Politician*, Sampson Low, Marston, London, 1931; and Stanley Jackson, *The Great Barnato*, Heinemann, London, 1970.

For **Bloemfontein**, see Richard Mendelsohn, 'Friends of the Free State: the Baumanns of Bloemfontein in the Anglo-Boer War', *Jewish Affairs*, 56, 3, Spring, 2001; Sheila Aronstam, 'A historical and socio-cultural survey of the Bloemfontein Jewish community with special reference to the conceptions of Jewish welfare work', unpublished DSocSc thesis, University of the Orange Free State, 1974.

Chapter 2: Litvaks

For **the Jewish experience in Eastern Europe**, see David Vital, *A People Apart. A Political History of the Jews in Europe 1789-1939*, Oxford University Press, Oxford, 1999; Howard Sachar, *A History of the Jews in the Modern World*, Alfred A Knopf, New York, 2005; Yisra'el Bartal, *The Jews of Eastern Europe, 1772-1881*, University of Pennsylvania Press, Philadelphia, 2005; John D Klier, 'Christians and Jews and the "Dialogue of Violence" in Late Imperial Russia' in Anna Sapir Abulafia (ed), *Religious Violence between Christians and Jews*, Palgrave, Houndmills and New York, 2002; Antony Polonsky, *The Jews in Poland and Russia*, vols 1-3, Littman Library of Jewish Civilization, Oxford, 2010-12.

For **Lithuanian Jewry,** see Dovid Katz, *Lithuanian Jewish culture*, Baltos Lankos, Vilnius, 2004; Masha Greenbaum, *The Jews of Lithuania: a history of a remarkable community, 1316-1945*, Gefen, Jerusalem, 1995; Dov Levin, *The Litvaks: a short history of the Jews in Lithuania*, Yad Vashem, Jerusalem, 2000.

For **emigration from the Pale and migration to South Africa,** see Gur Alroey, 'Bureaucracy, Agents, and Swindlers: The Hardships of Jewish Emigration from the Pale of Settlement in the Early 20th Century' in Ezra Mendelsohn (ed), *Studies in Contemporary Jewry. An Annual XIX, 2003*, Oxford University Press, New York, 2003; Aubrey Newman, 'Why did our Lithuanian Grandparents come to South Africa?', *Jewish Affairs*, 49, 2, 1994; Aubrey Newman, Nicholas Evans, Graham Smith and Saul Issroff (eds), *Jewish Migration to South Africa. The Records of the Poor Jews' Temporary Shelter, 1885-1914*, Jewish Publications – South Africa, Kaplan Centre for Jewish Studies, Cape Town, 2007; Gwynne Schrire, 'In the Belly of the Whale. The Journey to South Africa 1880-1910', *Jewish Affairs*, 49, 2, 1994; Caroline Louise Barker, 'Jewish Migration to South Africa and the Poor Jews' Temporary Shelter, London, 1880-1914', unpublished MPhil thesis, University of Leicester, 1998.

For **immigrant life and the building of the Jewish community**, see Saron and Hotz (1955); Shain (1983); Morris de Saxe (ed), *The South African Jewish Year Book. Directory of Jewish Organisations and Who's Who in South African Jewry 1929, 5689-90*, South African Jewish Historical Society, Johannesburg, 1929; Nehemiah Dov Hoffmann (translated from the Yiddish by Lilian Dubb and Sheila Barkusky), *Book of Memoirs*, Jewish Publications – South Africa, Cape Town, 1996; Michael Pesach Grosman, 'A study of the trends and tendencies of Hebrew and Yiddish writings in South Africa, since the beginning of the early nineties of the last century to 1930', unpublished DPhil thesis, University of the Witwatersrand, 1973. For women's experience, see Riva Krut, 'Building a Home and a Community – Jews in Johannesburg, 1886-1914', unpublished PhD thesis, University of London, 1985; special issue of *Jewish Affairs*, 48, 2, 1993; Veronica Belling, 'Recovering the lives of South African Jewish women during the migration years c1880-1939', unpublished PhD thesis, University of Cape Town, 2013.

For the Witwatersrand and Pretoria, see Mendel Kaplan and Marion Robertson (eds), *Founders and Followers. Johannesburg Jewry 1887-1915*, Vlaeberg, Cape Town, 1991; Morris Abrahams (edited by Naomi Musiker), *The Jews of Johannesburg 1886-1901*, Scarecrow Books, Johannesburg, 2001; Leibl Feldman (translated from the Yiddish by Veronica Belling), *The Jews of Johannesburg: until Union, 31 May 1910*, Jewish Publications – South Africa, Kaplan Centre for Jewish Studies, Cape Town, 2007; Riva Krut, 'The Making of a South African Jewish Community in Johannesburg, 1886-1914' in Belinda Bozzoli (ed), *Class, Community and Conflict. South African Perspectives*, Ravan Press, Johannesburg, 1987; Riva Krut (1985); Rose Norwich, 'Synagogues on the Witwatersrand and in Pretoria before 1932 – Their Origin, Form and Function', unpublished Masters in Architecture thesis, University of the Witwatersrand, 1988; Margot Rubin, The Jewish Community of Johannesburg, 1886-1939: Landscapes of Reality and Imagination', unpublished MA thesis, University of Pretoria, 2004; Anna Catharina van Wyk, 'Jode in Transvaal tot 1910. 'n Kultuurhistoriese Oorsig', unpublished PhD thesis, University of Pretoria 2003; Joshua I Levy (ed), *The Writings of Meyer Dovid Hersch (1858-1933). Rand Pioneer and Historian of Jewish Life in Early Johannesburg*, Ammatt Press, Johannesburg, 2005; Jill Katz (ed), *The Story of the Pretoria Jewish Community up to 1930*, Pretoria Council of the SA Jewish Board of Deputies, Pretoria, 1988.

For Cape Town, see Abrahams (1955); Solly Berger, Howard Phillips and Charles Melzer (eds), *The Centenary of the Great Synagogue, Gardens 1905-2005*, Cape Town Hebrew Congregation, Cape Town, 2005; Howard Phillips, '"A move for the better": Changing health status among Jewish immigrants in Cape Town, 1881-1931', *Journal of Ethnic and Migration Studies*, 32, 4, May 2006; Edna Bradlow, 'The anatomy of an immigrant community: Cape Town Jewry from the turn of the century to the passing of the Quota Act', *South African Historical Journal*, 31, 1994; Gwynne Schrire, 'How Cape Town Jewry cared for its sick poor a century ago', *Jewish Affairs*, 56, 2, 2001; Bonny Feldman, 'Social life of Cape Town Jewry, 1904-1914, with

special reference to the eastern European immigrant community', unpublished BA (Hons) thesis, UCT, 1984; Lauren Brenner, 'Moving Up: Adaptation and Change amongst the Cape Town Jewish Community 1920-1939', unpublished BA (Hons) thesis, UCT, 1990; Jonathan Boiskin, 'The Ochberg Orphans. An Episode in the History of the Cape Jewish Orphanage', *Jewish Affairs*, 49, 2, 1994; Esther Wilkin, 'Jewish Life in the 1920s: District Six', unpublished manuscript, Jewish Studies Library, UCT; Baruch Hirson, *The Cape Town Intellectuals. Ruth Schechter and her Circle, 1907-1934*, Witwatersrand University Press, Johannesburg, 2001.

For Durban, see Stephen Gary Cohen, 'A History of the Jews of Durban 1825-1918', unpublished MA thesis, University of Natal, 1977; Stephen Gary Cohen, 'A History of the Jews of Durban 1919-1961', unpublished PhD thesis, University of Natal, 1982.

For Oudtshoorn, see Daniel Coetzee, 'Immigrants to Citizens: Civil Integration and Acculturation of Jews into Oudtshoorn Society, 1874-1999', unpublished MA thesis, University of Cape Town, 2000; Daniel Coetzee, 'Fires and feathers: Acculturation, arson and the Jewish community in Oudtshoorn, South Africa, 1914-1948', *Jewish History*, 19, 2005; Leibl Feldman (edited by Joseph Sherman; translated by Lilian Dubb and Sheila Barkusky; historical notes by John Simon), *Oudtshoorn: Jerusalem of Africa*, Friends of the Library, University of the Witwatersrand, Johannesburg, 1989; David Scher, '"Yerushalayim B'Dorem Afrika": A Historical Survey of the Oudtshoorn Jewish Community', *Jewish Affairs*, 61, 1, 2006.

For the *smous* and rural life, see Albert Jackson (as told to Eric Rosenthal), *Trader on the Veld*, Balkema, Cape Town, 1958; Milton Shain, '"Vant to puy a vaatch": the smous and pioneer trader in South African Jewish historiography', *Jewish Affairs*, 42, 9, 1987; Phyllis Jowell and Adrienne Folb, *Into Kokerboom Country: Namaqualand's Jewish Pioneers*, Fernwood Press, 2004, Cape Town; *Jewish Life in the South African Country Communities*, vols 1 and 2, South African Friends of Beth Hatefutsoth, Johannesburg, 2002 and 2004.

For the Jewish underworld, see Edward J Bristow, *Prostitution and Prejudice. The Jewish Fight against*

White Slavery 1870-1939, Clarendon Press, Oxford, 1982; Charles van Onselen, 'Jewish marginality in the Atlantic world: organised crime in the era of the great migrations, 1880-1914', *South African Historical Journal*, 43, 2000; Charles van Onselen, *Studies in the Social and Economic History of the Witwatersrand 1886-1914, vol I New Babylon*, Ravan Press, Johannesburg, 1982; Robin Hallett, 'Policemen, pimps and prostitutes – public morality and police corruption, Cape Town, 1902-1904', paper presented to the History Workshop Conference, University of the Witwatersrand, 1978. For the notorious Joe Silver, see Charles van Onselen, *The Fox & the Flies: The World of Joseph Silver, Racketeer and Psychopath*, Jonathan Cape, London, 2007.

For Jews in the Anglo-Boer War, see the special issue of *Jewish Affairs*, 54, 3, 1999. See also Richard Mendelsohn, 'A Jewish Family at War: the Segalls of Vlakfontein', *Jewish Affairs*, 55, 3, 2000; 'Friends of the Free State: the Baumanns of Bloemfontein in the Anglo-Boer War', *Jewish Affairs*, 56, 3, Spring, 2001; Richard Mendelsohn, 'The Jewish War: Anglo-Jewry and the South African War' in Greg Cuthbertson, Albert Grundlingh, and Mary-Lynn Suttie, *Writing a Wider War: Rethinking Gender, Race, and Identity in the South African War, 1899-1902*, Ohio University Press, Athens, Ohio, 2002.

For Jews and the Left in the early twentieth century, see Evangelos Mantzaris, 'Jewish Trade Unions in Cape Town 1903-1907: A Socio-Historical Study' in Mantzaris, *Labour Struggles in South Africa: The Forgotten Pages 1903-1921*, Collective Resources Publications, Windhoek, 1995; Evangelos Mantzaris, 'Radical Community: The Yiddish-speaking Branch of the International Socialist League, 1918-1920' in Belinda Bozzoli (ed), *Class, Community and Conflict. South African Perspectives*, Ravan Press, Johannesburg, 1987.

For education, see Myer Katz, 'Jewish Education at the Cape, 1841 to the present day', unpublished MA thesis, University of Cape Town, 1973; 'The History of Jewish education in South Africa, 1841-1980', unpublished PhD thesis, University of Cape Town 1980; Howard Phillips, *The University of Cape Town 1918-1948. The Formative Years*, University of Cape Town Press, Cape Town, 1993.

For Yiddish language and culture, see Joseph Sherman (ed), *From a Land Far Off. South African Yiddish stories in English translation*, Jewish Publications – South Africa, Kaplan Centre for Jewish Studies, Cape Town, 1987; Joseph Sherman, 'Serving the Natives: Whiteness as the Price of Hospitality in South African Yiddish Literature', *Journal of Southern African Studies*, 26, 3, September 2000; Joseph Sherman, 'Between Ideology and Indifference: The Destruction of Yiddish in South Africa' in Shain and Mendelsohn, 2002; Kay McCormick, 'Yiddish in District Six', *Jewish Affairs*, 48, 3, 1993; Veronica-Sue Belling, 'The History of Yiddish Theatre in South Africa from the late Nineteenth Century to 1960', unpublished MA thesis, University of Cape Town, 2003.

For Jews in economic life, see Richard Mendelsohn, *Sammy Marks. 'The Uncrowned King of the Transvaal'*, David Philip and Ohio University Press, Cape Town and Athens, Ohio, 1991; Kaplan (1986); Georgina Jaffee, *Joffe Marks. A family memoir*, Sharp Sharp Media, Johannesburg, 2001; Rudy Frankel, *Tiger Tapestry*, Struik Publishers, Cape Town, 1988; Phyllis Jowell (assisted by Adrienne Folb), *Joe Jowell of Namaqualand: The Story of a Modern-Day Pioneer*, Fernwood Press, Cape Town, 1994.

For Zionism, see Shimoni (1980); Marcia Gitlin, *The Vision Amazing: The Story of South African Zionism*, Menorah Book Club, Johannesburg, 1950; John Simon, 'The Roots of South African Zionism', *Jewish Affairs*, 53, 2, 1998.

For Gandhi's Jewish associates, see Margaret Chatterjee, *Gandhi and his Jewish Friends*, Macmillan, Basingstoke, 1992; Isa Sarid and Christian Bartolf, *Hermann Kallenbach. Mahatma Gandhi's Friend in South Africa*, Gandhi-Informations-Zentrum, Berlin, 1997; Enid Alexander, *Morris Alexander. A Biography*, Juta, Cape Town and Johannesburg, 1953; George Paxton, *Sonja Schlesin, Gandhi's South African Secretary*, Paxton, Glasgow, 2006; Shimon Lev, *Soulmates: the story of Mahatma Gandhi and Hermann Kallenbach*, Orient Blackswan, New Delhi, 2012.

For Sarah Gertrude Millin, see Marcia Leveson, *People of the Book. Images of the Jew in South African English Fiction 1880-1992*, Witwatersrand University Press,

Johannesburg, 2001; Claudia Braude (ed), *Contemporary Jewish writing in South Africa: an anthology*, University of Nebraska Press, Lincoln, 2001; JM Coetzee, 'Blood, Taint, Flaw, Degeneration: The Novels of Sarah Gertude Millin', *English Studies in Africa*, 23, 1, 1980; Lavinia Braun, 'Not Gobineau but Heine – Not Racial Theory but Biblical Theme: The Case of Sarah Gertrude Millin', *English Studies in Africa*, 34, 1, 1991.

CHAPTER 3: SOUTH AFRICAN JEWS

For antisemitism and the Greyshirts Trial, see Shain (1994); Shimoni (1980); Hadassa Ben-Itto, *The Lie That Wouldn't Die. The Protocols of the Elders of Zion*, Vallentine Mitchell, London, 2005; Patrick Furlong, *Between Crown and Swastika. The Impact of the Radical Right on the Afrikaner Nationalist Movement in the Fascist Era*, University of Witwatersrand Press, Johannesburg, 1991; Hermann Giliomee, *The Afrikaners. Biography of a People*, Tafelberg, Cape Town, 2003; Michael Cohen, 'Anti-Jewish Manifestations in the Union of South Africa during the Nineteen Thirties', unpublished BA (Hons) thesis, UCT, 1968; Shain, '"If it was so good, why was it so bad?" The memories and realities of anti-semitism in South Africa, past and present', in Shain and Mendelsohn (2002); Shain, *Humpty Dumpty was pushed: anti-Jewish conspiracies and the South African experience*, Jacob Gitlin Library, Western Province Zionist Council, Cape Town, 2005.

For German Jewish immigration, see Linda Coetzee, Myra Osrin and Millie Pimstone, *Seeking Refuge: German Jewish immigration to the Cape in the 1930s including aspects of Germany confronting its past*, Cape Town Holocaust Centre, Cape Town, 2003; Frieda Sichel, *From Refugee to Citizen. A Sociological Study of the Immigrants from Hitler-Europe who Settled in Southern Africa*, AA Balkema, Cape Town and Amsterdam, 1966; Franz Auerbach, *No Single Loyalty. Many Strands, One Design: A South African Teacher's Life*, Waxmann Münster, New York and Munich, Berlin, 2002; Franz Auerbach, 'German Jews and their Baggage', *Jewish Affairs*, 60, 4, 2005.

For the wartime surveys of gentile and Jewish opinion, see Albrecht Hagemann, 'Anti-Semitism in South Africa during World War II: A Documentation' in *Simon Wiesenthal Center Annual*, 4, 1987; Simon Herman, *The Reaction of Jews to Anti-Semitism. A Social Psychological Study based upon the Attitudes of a Group of South African Jewish Students*, Witwatersrand University Press, Johannesburg, 1945. For a wartime Jewish childhood, see Dan Jacobson, 'Growing up Jewish' in Shain and Mendelsohn (2002).

For South African Jewry and the Holocaust, see Michael Green, 'South African Jewish Responses to the Holocaust, 1941-1948, unpublished MA thesis, University of South Africa, 1987; Milton Shain, 'South Africa' in David S Wyman (ed), *The World Reacts to the Holocaust*, The Johns Hopkins University Press, Baltimore and London 1998; Sharon Friedman, 'Jews, Germans, and Afrikaners – Nationalist Press Reactions to the Final Solution', unpublished BA (Hons) thesis, University of Cape Town, 1982; Shirli Gilbert, 'Jews and the Racial State: Legacies of the Holocaust in Apartheid South Africa, 1945-60', *Jewish Social Studies*, 16, 3, 2010.

For Jews and the Left, see Shimoni, *Community and Conscience. The Jews in Apartheid South Africa*, University Press of New England for Brandeis University Press and David Philip, Hanover, New Hampshire and Cape Town, 2003; Taffy Adler, 'Lithuania's Diaspora: the Johannesburg Jewish Workers' Club, 1928-1948', *Journal of Southern African Studies*, 6, 1, 1979; Mark Israel and Simon Adams, '"That Spells Trouble": Jews and the Communist Party of South Africa', *Journal of Southern African Studies*, 26, 1, 2000; David Saks, 'The Jewish Accused in the South African Treason Trial', *Jewish Affairs*, 52, 1, Autumn 1997; Glenn Frankel, *Rivonia's Children. Three Families and the Cost of Conscience in White South Africa*, Jonathan Ball Publishers, Johannesburg, 1999; James Campbell, 'Beyond the Pale: Jewish Immigration and the South African Left' in Shain and Mendelsohn (2002); Gideon Shimoni, 'Accounting for Jewish Radicals in Apartheid South Africa' in Shain and Mendelsohn (2002); Glenn Frankel, 'The Road to Rivonia: Jewish Radicals and the Cost of Conscience in White South Africa' in Shain and Mendelsohn (2002); Shula Marks, 'Apartheid and the Jewish Question', *Journal of Southern African Studies*,

30, 4, 2004; Joshua Lazerson, *Against the tide: Whites in the struggle against Apartheid*, Westview and Mayibuye, Boulder, Colo. and Bellville, 1994.

For memoirs and voices from the Jewish left, see Immanuel Suttner (ed), *Cutting through the Mountain. Interviews with South African Jewish Activists*, Viking, Johannesburg, 1997; Joe Slovo, *Slovo. The Unfinished Autobiography*, Ravan Press, Randburg, 1995; Rusty Bernstein, *Memory against Forgetting: Memoirs from a life in South African politics, 1934-1964*, Viking, London, 1999; Baruch Hirson, *Revolutions in my Life*, University of the Witwatersrand Press, Johannesburg, 1995; Miriam Basner, *Am I an African? The Political Memoirs of HM Basner*, Witwatersrand University Press, Johannesburg, 1993; Pauline Podbrey, *White girl in search of the Party*, Hadeda Books, Pietermaritzburg, 1993; Albie Sachs, *The soft vengeance of a freedom fighter*, David Philip, Cape Town, 2000; Ronald Kasrils, *Armed and dangerous: from undercover struggle to freedom*, Jonathan Ball Publishers, Johannesburg, 2004; AnnMarie Wolpe, *The long way home*, David Philip, Cape Town, 1994; Ben Turok, *Nothing but the truth: behind the ANC's struggle politics*, Jonathan Ball Publishers, Johannesburg, 2003; Norman Levy, *The final prize: my life in the anti-apartheid struggle*, South African History Online, Cape Town, 2011.

For Solly Sachs and Ray Alexander, see Leslie Witz, 'Servant of the Workers: Solly Sachs and the Garment Workers' Union, 1928-1952', unpublished MA thesis, University of the Witwatersrand, 1984; Bernard Sachs, *South African Personalities and Places*, Kayor Publishers, Johannesburg, 1959; Emil Solomon (Solly) Sachs, *Rebels Daughters*, MacGibbon & Kee, Manchester, 1957; Ray Alexander Simons (edited by Raymond Suttner), *All my life and all my strength*, STE Publishers, Johannesburg, 2004; Immanuel Suttner (1997).

For South African participation in Machal, see Henry Katzew, *South Africa's 800. The Story of South African Volunteers in Israel's War of Birth*, unpublished, 2003; Shimoni (1980); Cecil Margo, *Final postponement: reminiscences of a crowded life*, Jonathan Ball Publishers, Johannesburg, 1998. For the Six Day War, see Milton Shain, 'Consolidating the Consolidated: the Impact of the Six Day War on South African Jewry' in Eli Lederhendler (ed), *The Six-Day War and World Jewry*,

University Press of Maryland, Bethesda, 2001.

For Jews, the Rabbinate and apartheid, see Shimoni (2003); Gideon Shimoni, 'South African Jews and the Apartheid Crisis', *American Jewish Year Book*, 1988; Solly Kessler, 'The South African Rabbinate in the Apartheid Era', *Jewish Affairs*, 50, 1, Autumn 1995; 'Jews and Apartheid', special issue of *Jewish Affairs*, 52, 1, 1997; Adam Mendelsohn, 'Two Far South: The Responses of South African and Southern Jews to Apartheid and Segregation in the 1950s and 1960s', unpublished MA thesis, University of Cape Town, 2003; Adam Mendelsohn, 'Two Far South: Rabbinical Responses to Apartheid and Segregation in South Africa and the American South', *Southern Jewish History*, 6, 2003; Gerald Mazabow, *To Reach for the Moon. The South African Rabbinate of Rabbi Dr LI Rabinowitz as reflected in his Public Addresses, Sermons and Writings*, Union of Orthodox Synagogues of South Africa, Johannesburg, 1999; Claudia Braude, 'From the Brotherhood of Man to the World to Come: The Denial of the Political in Rabbinic Writing under Apartheid' in Sander Gilman and Milton Shain, *Jewries at the Frontier. Accommodation, Identity, Conflict*, University of Illinois Press, Urbana and Chicago, 1999; Bernard Casper, *A decade with South African Jewry*, Howard Timmins, Cape Town, 1972.

For Chief Rabbis Abrahams and Rabinowitz, see Gerald Mazabow, *To Reach for the Moon. The South African Rabbinate of Rabbi Dr LI Rabinowitz as reflected in his Public Addresses, Sermons and Writings*, Union of Orthodox Synagogues of South Africa, Johannesburg, 1999; John Simon, 'The Ministries of Bender and Abrahams' in Solly Berger et al (2005).

For world Jewry's engagement with South African Jewry during the apartheid era, see Adam Mendelsohn, 'The Board Abroad: The World Jewish Congress' Response to Apartheid in the 1950s and 1960s', *Jewish Affairs*, 59, 3, 2003; '"South African Jews Also Face Racial Crisis": American Jewish Newspapers on Apartheid South Africa during the Civil Rights Era', *Jewish Affairs*, 56, 3, 2001.

For the building of modern synagogues, see Esther Surdut (ed), *The First 100 Years. The Story of the Claremont Hebrew Congregation*, Claremont Hebrew Congregation, Cape Town, 2004; Stephen Gary Cohen, 'A History of the Jews of Durban 1919-1961', unpublished PhD thesis, University of Natal, 1982.

For Jewish economic participation in the post-war decades, see Antony Arkin, 'Economic Activities' in Marcus Arkin (ed), *South African Jewry. A Contemporary Survey*, Oxford University Press, Cape Town, 1984; Mendel Kaplan, *Jewish Roots in the South African Economy*, C Struik Publishers, Cape Town, 1986; Raymond Ackerman, *Hearing grasshoppers jump: the story of Raymond Ackerman*, David Philip, Cape Town, 2001; Ken Romain, *Larger than life: Donald Gordon and the Liberty Life story*, Jonathan Ball Publishers, Johannesburg, 1989; David Susman, *An African shopkeeper: memoirs of David Susman*, Fernwood Press, Cape Town, 2004.

For Zionism, see Gideon Shimoni, 'Zionism in South Africa: An Historical Perspective', *Forum*, 37, 1980; Milton Shain and Richard Mendelsohn, 'Israel, World Jewry and Identity' in Danny Ben-Moshe and Zohar Segev (eds), *Israel, the Diaspora and Jewish Identity*, Sussex Brighton and Portland, 2007.

For Reform Judaism in South Africa, see Edgar Bernstein, 'Reform Comes of Age', *Jewish Affairs*, 9, 19, 1954; David Sherman, *Pioneering for Reform Judaism in South Africa*, Cape Town, 1983; David Sherman, 'Reform Judaism in South Africa. Its Origins, Growth and Principles', *Jewish Affairs*, 48, 1, 1993.

For Jewish education, see Myer Katz, 'The History of Jewish education in South Africa, 1841-1980', unpublished PhD thesis, University of Cape Town, 1980; Isaac Goss, 'An Educational Survey of the Past Year' in Leon Feldberg (ed), *The South African Jewish Year Book 1959*, Fieldhill Publishing, Johannesburg, nd.; Isaac Goss, 'Then and Now in Jewish Education', *Jewish Affairs*, 15, 5, 1960; Louis Rabinowitz, 'Jewish Day Schools are Glory of South African Jewry', *Jewish Affairs*, 19, 2, 1964; Ronnie Mink, 'Education' in Marcus Arkin (ed), *South African Jewry. A Contemporary Survey*, Oxford University Press, Cape Town, 1984; Ronnie Gotkin and Judith Cohen (eds), *Im Tirtzu: If you will it, it is no fable*, United Herzlia Schools, Cape Town, 1990.

For Bertha Solomon, Ellen Hellmann, Helen Suzman and Ruth First, see Bertha Solomon, *Time Remembered: The Story of a Fight*, Timmins, Cape Town, 1968; Elaine Katz, 'Bertha Solomon: A Feminist for her Time', *Jewish Affairs* 48, 2, 1993; Helen Suzman, *In No Uncertain Terms: Memoirs*, Jonathan Ball Publishers, Pretoria, 1993; Millie Pimstone, *Helen Suzman, Fighter for Human Rights*, Kaplan Centre for Jewish Studies and Research, University of Cape Town, Cape Town, 2005; Shula Marks, 'Ruth First: A Tribute', *Journal of Southern African Studies*, 10, 1, October 1983; Gillian Slovo, *Every Secret Thing: My Family, My Country*, Little, Brown, London, 1997; EJ Verwey (ed), *New Dictionary of South African Biography*, HSRC, Pretoria, 1995.

For Irma Stern, see Neville Dubow, *Irma Stern*, Struik, Cape Town, 1974; Mona Berman, *Remembering Irma: Irma Stern, a memoir with letters*, Double Storey, Cape Town, 2003.

CHAPTER 4: JEWISH SOUTH AFRICANS

For Jewish political behaviour, see Henry Lever, 'The Jewish voter in South Africa', *Ethnic and Racial Studies*, 2, 4, 1979; Shimoni (2003); Gideon Shimoni, 'South African Jews and the Apartheid Crisis' in David Singer (ed), *American Jewish Year Book 1988*, The American Jewish Committee, New York, 1988; Mathilda Michele Joffe, 'Major Issues and Dilemmas among Jewish Students at the University of Cape Town as reflected in *Strike*, 1973-1994', unpublished BA (Hons) thesis, University of Cape Town, 2004.

For the Pretoria-Jerusalem axis, see James Adams, *The Unnatural Alliance*, Quartet Books, London, 1984; Shimoni (2003); Naomi Chazan, 'The Fallacies of Pragmatism: Israeli Foreign Policy towards South Africa', *African Affairs*, 82, 327, 1983; Sasha Polakow-Suransky, *The unspoken alliance: Israel's secret relationship with apartheid South Africa*, Jacana, Johannesburg, 2010.

For Sephardi and Israeli Jews in South Africa, see Mathy Joffe, 'From Rhodes to Cape Town: South Africa's Sephardi Jews and their heritage', unpublished research paper, University of Cape Town, 1992; Renée Hirschon, 'Jews from Rhodes in Central and Southern Africa' in C Ember, M Ember, & I Skoggard (eds), *Encyclopedia of Diasporas. Immigrant and Refugee Cultures Around the World*, vol II, Springer, 2007; Sally Frankental, 'A Frontier Experience: Israeli Jews Encounter Diaspora in Cape Town, South Africa' in Sander

Gilman and Milton Shain (eds), *Jewries at the Frontier. Accommodation, Identity, Conflict*, University of Illinois Press, Urbana and Chicago, 1999; Sally Frankental, 'Constructing Identity in Diaspora: Jewish Israeli Migrants in Cape Town, South Africa', unpublished PhD thesis, University of Cape Town, 1998.

For the religious revival within South African Jewry, see Jocelyn Hellig, 'Religious Expression' in Marcus Arkin (ed), *South African Jewry. A Contemporary Survey*, Oxford University Press, Cape Town, 1984; Shimoni (2003); Jeremy Hayman, 'A Case Study of the Modern Orthodox and Ultra-Orthodox Sectors of Johannesburg Jewry with Special Reference to the Educational Institutions', unpublished MEd thesis, University of Cape Town, 1998.

For the Kugel, see Illana Hitner Klevansky and Alan H Levine, *The Kugel Book*, Jonathan Ball Publishers, Johannesburg, 1982.

For demography and attitudinal surveys, see Stuart Buxbaum, 'The Demographic Structure of the Jewish Community in South Africa', *Jewish Affairs*, 34, 7-9, 1979; Stuart Buxbaum, 'Synagogue Marriages in South Africa, 1935-1966: An Analysis of Official Statistics' in UO Schmelz, P Glikson and S DellaPergola (eds), *Papers in Jewish Demography 1973*, Institute of Contemporary Jewry, Hebrew University of Jerusalem, Jerusalem, 1977; Sergio DellaPergola and Allie Dubb, 'South African Jewry: A Sociodemographic Profile' in David Singer (ed), *American Jewish Year Book 1988*, The American Jewish Committee, New York, 1988; S DellaPergola and Allie Dubb, *The Jewish Population of South Africa. The 1991 Sociodemographic Survey*, Jewish Publications – South Africa, Kaplan Centre, University of Cape Town, 1994; Barry Kosmin, Jacqueline Goldberg, Milton Shain and Shirley Bruk, *Jews of the 'new South Africa': highlights of the 1998 national survey of South African Jews*, Institute for Jewish Policy Research, London, in association with the Kaplan Centre, UCT, 1999; Shirley Bruk, *The Jews of South Africa 2005: report on a research study*, Kaplan Centre, University of Cape Town, 2006.

For Jewish education, see Bernard Steinberg, 'South Africa: Jewish Education in a Divided Society', in Harold S Himmelfarb and Sergio DellaPergola (eds),

Jewish Education Worldwide. Cross-Cultural Perspectives, University Press of America, Lanham, 1989; Ronnie Mink, 'Education' in Marcus Arkin (ed), *South African Jewry. A Contemporary Survey*, Oxford University Press, Cape Town, 1984; Chaya Herman, *Prophets and profits: managerialism and the restructuring of Jewish schools in South Africa*, HSRC Press, Cape Town, 2006.

For South Africa's Jewish Nobel laureates, see Kader Asmal, David Chidester and Wilmot James (eds), *South Africa's Nobel Laureates. Peace, Literature and Science*, Jonathan Ball Publishers, Johannesburg and Cape Town, 2004, and the Nobel Prize website. For Gordimer, see Ronald Suresh Roberts, *No Cold Kitchen. A Biography of Nadine Gordimer*, STE Publishers, Johannesburg, 2005. For a critical appraisal of Gordimer's treatment of Jewish characters in her fiction, see Marcia Leveson, *People of the Book. Images of the Jew in South African English Fiction 1880-1992*, Witwatersrand University Press, Johannesburg, 2001.

For antisemitism and anti-Zionism, see Milton Shain and Margo Bastos, 'Muslim Antisemitism and Anti-Zionism in South Africa since 1945' in *Antisemitism International*, 3-4, 2006; Margo Bastos, 'Muslim anti-Zionism and antisemitism in South Africa since the Second World War, with special reference to Muslim news/views', unpublished MA thesis, University of Cape Town, 2002; Shain (2005); online database of the Stephen Roth Institute for the Study of Contemporary Antisemitism and Racism, Tel Aviv University; Milton Shain, 'Antisemitism and Anti-Zionism in the "new South Africa": Observations and Reflections' in Charles A Small (ed), *Global Antisemitism: A Crisis of Modernity*, Martinus Nijhoff Publishers, Leiden and Boston, 2013.

For African views of the Jews, see Melville Edelstein, *What Do Young Africans Think?*, South African Institute of Race Relations, Johannesburg, 1972; Melville Edelstein, 'The Urban African Image of the Jew', *Jewish Affairs*, 27, 2, 1972; Shimoni (2003); Part Mgadla and Stephen Volz (eds), *Words of Batswana. Letters to Mahoko A Becwana, 1883-1896*, Van Riebeeck Society, Cape Town, 2006.

For Jews in the 'New South Africa', see Milton Shain, 'South African Jewry: Emigrating? At Risk? Or

Reconstructing the Future?' in Leslie Stein and Sol
Encel (eds), *Continuity, Commitment, and Survival: Jewish
Communities in the Diaspora*, Greenwood Press, Westport,
2003; Shimoni (2003); Cyril Harris, *For Heaven's Sake:
The Chief Rabbi's Diary*, Cape Town, 2000; Joel Pollak,
'The Kasrils Affair: Jews and Minority Politics in the
New South Africa', unpublished MA thesis, University
of Cape Town, 2006; Kosmin et al (1999); Bruk (2006).

FURTHER USEFUL SOURCES

Leon Feldberg (ed), *The South African Jewish Year Book*,
1959, 1965, 1967-68; *Jewish Life in the South African
Country Communities*, vols 1-5, South African Friends of
Beth Hatefutsoth, Johannesburg, 2002-12; 'South Africa'
in *American Jewish Year Book*, 1988, 1992-2012.

For a comprehensive guide to further reading, see Veronica
Belling, *Bibliography of South African Jewry*, Jewish
Publications – South Africa, Kaplan Centre for Jewish
Studies, Cape Town, 1997.

INDEX